PASSENGERS
ARE NOT ALLOWED
CROSS THE RAILW
EXCEPT BY THE BRID

AN ILLUSTRATED ENCYCLOPEDIA OF

LOCOMOTIVES

NR

AN ILLUSTRATED ENCYCLOPEDIA OF LOCOMOTIVES

A GUIDE TO THE GOLDEN AGE OF TRAIN ENGINES FROM 1830 TO 2000

COLIN GARRATT

LORENZ BOOKS

Contents

The 1950s to 2000 128

The Birth of the Railway

The following section looks at the development of the railway, from its very beginnings up to 1900, touching on both the technical changes it underwent and the role it played in societies and industries around the world. The text and photographs provide a comprehensive account of the railway pioneers and the machines and lines they created, while the technical boxes give an at-a-glance record of some of the most influential and innovative locomotives.

● OPPOSITE
Locomotion No. 1 – a working replica built in 1975. The first locomotive built at the Stephensons' Forth Street works, Newcastle upon Tyne, in 1825, it also established the advent of mechanical traction for public railways. The original locomotive survives in Darlington Railway Museum, County Durham, north-east England.

● ABOVE
A Puffing Billy-type engine built by William Hedley of Wylam Colliery, Northumberland, in 1813. From a painting by David Weston (born 1936).

From Tramways to Steam

● BELOW
Before railways, canals were the main means of moving heavy goods such as coal. With the coming of the railways, waterways fast fell into disuse. Today, they are basically used for pleasure.

In Britain, one of the first tramways was built about 1630 to serve collieries near Newcastle upon Tyne. The Tanfield Waggonway in County Durham was begun about 1725, and by 1727 included the Causey Arch, the world's first railway viaduct, built by Ralph Wood. At first, the rails were made of wood but these wore quickly, and in 1767 iron plates were affixed to them for durability. The first cast-iron plates were made by the Coalbrookdale Ironworks in Shropshire. Plate rails, that is iron-flanged rails, were introduced underground at Sheffield Park Colliery in 1787 and on the surface at Ketley Incline in 1788.

● STAGECOACH IMPROVES ROADS

Transportation in the 17th and 18th centuries was either by stagecoach or water. In 1658, the state of the roads was so bad that the stagecoach took two weeks to travel from London to Edinburgh. Even by the end of the 1700s, with responsibility for the maintenance of main roads handed from parishes to turnpike trusts, the state of the roads was not much better. In winter, they were blocked by snow or floods; in summer, hard-baked ruts made journeys uncomfortable. This was acceptable while most travel was on horseback. With the ever-increasing use of coaches for public transport, however, the roads improved. By the 1750s the stagecoach had come into its own.

● RAILWAYS REPLACE WATERWAYS

With industrialization, however, the need for transportation of heavy goods remained. By about the mid-18th century, artificial canals came into being as arteries for goods making their way to the larger rivers and to the sea for export to various parts of Britain. The waterways' half-century of posterity and public service ended, however, with the coming of the railways. Many became ruins or were bought by local railway companies. Turnpike roads ceased to be the chief arteries of the nation's lifeblood. Posting-inns were replaced by hotels springing up at railway termini. The Railway Era saw the demise of the public mailcoach and heavy family coach. In some instances, however, when such conservative-minded gentry as the Duke of Wellington travelled by rail, they sat in their coaches, which were placed on flat trucks. By 1840, with railways halving the cost of travel, canal and stagecoach were doomed.

● THE FIRST RAILWAYS

In 1804, the world's first public railway company, the Surrey Iron Railway Company, opened a horse-drawn line from Wandsworth Wharf, on the River Thames in south London, to Croydon in Surrey. The line was extended to Merstham, Surrey, but

● **RIGHT**
The Rocket – a working replica built in 1980. This represents the appearance of the locomotive as it competed in the Rainhill Trials.

● **FAR RIGHT**
Richard Trevithick (1771–1833): the great pioneer. The Cornish inventor and engineer graduated from building mines' pumping-engines in 1803–4 to construct the first steam locomotive to haul a load on iron rails.

● **OPPOSITE BELOW**
The packhorse bridge was a means of crossing rivers. Cutaways provided passing-points for approaching animals and people.

never reached its intended destination, Portsmouth in Hampshire.

● RICHARD TREVITHICK

Another landmark in the history of railways also occurred in 1804 when British engineer Richard Trevithick (1771–1833) tested his newly invented steam locomotive. This drew five wagons and a coach with 70 passengers along the ten miles of track from the Pen-y-Darren Ironworks to the Glamorganshire Canal. This historic event saw the world's first steam locomotive to run on rails hauling a train carrying fare-paying passengers.

Trevithick continued his experiments and in 1808 erected a circular track in Euston Square, London, on which he ran his latest production "Catch Me Who Can". The public was invited to pay a shilling, almost a day's wages for the average working man, to ride on this novel method of transportation, but the venture failed financially and in a few weeks Trevithick had to close it.

● GEORGE STEPHENSON

Between 1814–21 Northumbrian engineer George Stephenson (1781–1848), born in Wylam, a village near Newcastle upon Tyne, built 17 experimental locomotives. Although he was not the first to produce a steam locomotive, he was the prime mover in introducing them on a wide scale. His turning-point came in 1821 when he was appointed engineer-in-charge of what became the 42 km (26 mile) long Stockton & Darlington Railway, between the County Durham towns of Stockton-on-Tees, a seaport, and Darlington, an industrial centre. It was opened in September 1825. Stephenson's Locomotion No. 1 drew the first train.

This historic event saw the world's first public railway regularly to use steam locomotives to haul wagons of goods (the main traffic was coal) and carriages of passengers. Passengers were carried in horse-drawn coaches until 1833.

In 1829, Lancashire's Liverpool & Manchester Railway, built mainly to carry cotton, offered a £500 prize to the winner of a competition for the best steam-locomotive design to work the line. The trials were held at Rainhill, near Liverpool. Of the three locomotives entered, George Stephenson's Rocket, gaily painted yellow, black and white, won at a speed of about 26 mph (42 kph).

ROCKET

Date	1829
Builder	George Stephenson
Client	Liverpool & Manchester Railway (L&MR)
Gauge	4 ft 8$^1/_2$ in
Type	0-2-2
Capacity	2 cylinders outside 8 x 17 in inclined
Pressure	50 lb
Weight	4 tons 5 cwt

British Locomotives of the 1830s

By 1830 almost 100 locomotives had been built in Britain. These early experimental engines were of two main types: those with inclined cylinders and those with vertical cylinders. Then, in 1830 George Stephenson introduced the 2-2-0 Planet type. This was a radical step forward from the Rocket and its derivatives and established the general form that all future steam locomotives were to take. Planet combined the multi-tubular boiler with a fully water-jacketed firebox and a separate smokebox. The cylinders were now inside and horizontally mounted, while the engine's boiler and motion were carried on a sturdy outside frame of oak beams sandwiched by iron plates. The first Planet was a passenger-engine with 5 ft driving wheels and 3 ft carrying wheels, but Stephenson was quick to see that the frame arrangement would allow him to substitute two pairs of coupled 4 ft 6 in wheels to create a heavy-goods locomotive. The resulting engines, Samson and Goliath, were supplied to the Liverpool & Manchester Railway (L&MR) in 1831.

● **ABOVE**
Robert Stephenson (1803–59): at the age of 20 he was put in charge of his father's locomotive works in Newcastle upon Tyne. He became the leading locomotive engineer of his day. He built railway bridges and viaducts, notably the tubular bridge over the Menai Strait between Anglesey and mainland Wales.

● **BELOW**
Lion, built in the same year as Samson, shows how far heavy-goods engine design had really progressed. The first engine built by Todd, Kitson & Laird, this 0-4-2 had 5 ft driving wheels and is still in working order.

PATENTEE

Date	1833
Builder	Robert Stephenson
Client	Liverpool & Manchester Railway (L&MR)
Gauge	4 ft 8½ in
Type	2-2-2
Driving wheels	5 ft
Capacity	2 cylinders 12 x 18 in
Pressure	50 lb

Hackworth, meanwhile, was still firmly wedded to the archaic vertical cylinder arrangement. In 1831 he built six engines of the Majestic class for heavy-coal haulage on the Stockton & Darlington Railway (S&DR). Their cylinders were carried on an overhanging platform at the back of the boiler and drove a crankshaft carried on a bracket below. The crankshaft in turn drove the nearest pair of the six coupled wheels, allowing all axles to be sprung. The boilers combined Hackworth's longitudinal flue with a return multi-tubular arrangement intended to provide the best features of both layouts. In the event, the small grate area possible in the single flue severely limited the engines' steaming power. Also, they were heavy on fuel as well as being cumbersome in appearance with a tender at each end of the locomotive. Their ponderous performance in traffic was such that the line's rigid speed limit of 6 mph (9.7 kph) did not trouble them.

Edward Bury had intended his first locomotive, Liverpool, to take part in the Rainhill Trials but it was not ready in time. Noting Rocket's superior features,

● **FAR LEFT**
George Stephenson (1781–1848): the world's most well-known locomotive engineer. He worked as an engineer for several railway companies and built the first railway line to carry passengers (1825).

● **ABOVE LEFT**
Comet was the first locomotive put into service on the Leicester & Swannington Railway (L&SR). On the inaugural run, in May 1832, the 13 ft high chimney was knocked down in the Glenfield Tunnel, near Leicester, covering the travelling dignitaries in soot. Swannington, in Leicestershire, is 19 km (12 miles) north-west of the county town.

● **BELOW LEFT**
Atlas was the first 0-6-0 goods engine built by Robert Stephenson. It was delivered to the L&SR in 1834. At the time, this was the largest, heaviest and most powerful locomotive running on any railway.

he was able to modify his design and deliver the engine to the L&MR in 1830. In its rebuilt form, it was bristling with innovations and became an international prototype. Most striking were the 6 ft coupled wheels, bigger than any previously made, but equally notable were the multi-tubular boiler, inside bar-frames and raised-dome firebox-casing. The cylinders, too, were inside, inclined slightly upwards to allow the piston rods to pass beneath the leading axle. On the line, Liverpool proved capable of hauling an 18-wagon train at an average of 12½ mph (19 kph). In short, she was a stunning little creation, topped off by a small chimney with a procession of cutout brass liver birds around its crown. (The liver is a fanciful bird on the arms of the city of Liverpool.)

With progress came the need for more powerful locomotives, and it had to be admitted that Planets were unsteady at any speed and their firebox capacity was limited. Robert Stephenson rectified this by extending the frames rearwards, adding a trailing axle behind a much-enlarged firebox. Thus was born the Patentee 2-2-2 Type, which became the standard British express-engine for the next four decades and was exported widely to inaugurate railway services across Europe. Stephenson's Patentees also incorporated great improvements in boiler construction and valve gear. All had flangeless driving wheels.

The design could be varied to incorporate coupled driving wheels, as other manufacturers were quick to see. Perhaps the best known front-coupled Patentee is the 0-4-2 Lion, built for the L&MR in 1838 by Todd, Kitson & Laird of Leeds, Yorkshire.

● **BELOW**
Samson, built by Timothy Hackworth in 1838 for heavy-goods work on the Stockton & Darlington Railway (S&DR), already looked outdated by the standards of the time. Note the fireman feeding the single-flue boiler from the front end.

THE BATTLE OF THE GAUGES

• LEFT
A classic GWR broad-gauge single powers an express-train westwards through the Sonning Cutting, near Reading, Berkshire. It is late in the broad-gauge era for a third rail has been laid on each track to allow rolling stock of both gauges to operate.

Isambard Kingdom Brunel (1806–59) conceived railways on a grand scale. For his Great Western Railway (GWR), authorized in 1835, he dismissed the well-established 4 ft 8½ in gauge as inadequate to cope with the greater speeds, safety and smoother travel he planned for his relatively straight and level main line from London to Bristol. So he fixed his gauge at a spacious 7 ft. The main drawbacks were that this set the GWR apart from all other railways and meant that all goods and passengers had to change trains when travelling to or from areas not served by GWR trains.

The first GWR train steamed out of Paddington Station, west London, on 4 June 1838 behind the Stephenson 2-2-2 North Star, a large example of the Patentee type, which was originally built for the 5 ft 6 in gauge New Orleans Railway in the USA. A broken contract caused her to be altered to 7 ft gauge and to go to the GWR instead. A sister engine, Morning Star, entered service at the same time. North Star had 7 ft driving wheels and the inside-cylinders were 16 x 16 in. Obsolescence was rapid in those days, but North Star was rebuilt with a large boiler and new cylinders in 1854, lasting in service for 33 years. When finally withdrawn, she was preserved at Swindon, Wiltshire, until, in an act of official vandalism, she was scrapped in 1906. In something of an atonement, GWR built a full-sized replica incorporating original parts in 1925. This is displayed at Swindon Railway Museum.

For the most part, the other original GWR broad-gauge locomotives were a collection of mechanical freaks, the best of a poor lot being six 2-2-2s with 8 ft driving wheels from Tayleur's Vulcan Foundry, which were Patentee copies but

IRON DUKE

Date	1847
Builder	Daniel Gooch, Swindon, Wiltshire, England
Client	Great Western Railway (GWR)
Gauge	7 ft
Type	4-2-2
Driving wheels	8 ft
Capacity	2 cylinders 18 x 24 in
Pressure	100 lb later 120 lb
Weight	35 tons

● **ABOVE LEFT**
The importance of the broad gauge and its hitherto unimagined speeds caught the imagination of the populace. People flocked to experience this revolutionary form of travel in which speeds of 90 mph (145 kph) had been reported.

● **ABOVE RIGHT**
Tiny: built by Sara & Co., of Plymouth, Devon, in 1868, this broad-gauge locomotive went into service on England's South Devon Railway (SDR).

● **OPPOSITE MIDDLE**
Isambard Kingdom Brunel (1806–59), the 19th-century English engineer who pioneered the broad gauge of the Great Western Railways, between London and Exeter in Devon. His father was a French engineer in England, Sir Marc Isambard Brunel (1769–1849).

● **OPPOSITE BOTTOM**
Iron Duke (replica): built by Gooch, this 4-2-2 of the Duke Class was named after Arthur Wellesley, the first Duke of Wellington (1769–1852), on whose birthday – 1 May – it first ran.

with small low-pressure boilers. They were delivered from Manchester, Lancashire, to London by sea and then on to West Drayton, Middlesex, by canal. Among their more bizarre stablemates were two 2-2-2s from Mather & Dixon with 10 ft driving wheels fabricated from riveted iron plates.

There was much opposition to the broad gauge, and in July 1845 the Gauge Commission sat to choose between the rival claims of both gauges. High-speed trial runs were organized, the honours going to Daniel Gooch's 7 ft GWR single "Ixion", which achieved 60 mph (96.6 kph) hauling an 80 ton (81,284 kg) train. The best standard-gauge performance was 53 mph (85.1 kph) behind a brand new Stephenson 4-2-0 with 6 ft 6 in driving wheels. Although the Commission considered the 7 ft gauge in every way superior, the standard gauge was selected on the basis of the greater mileage already in use. In 1848, Parliament decided there should in future be only one gauge, the narrow, and eventually the GWR had to bow to the inevitable, laying a third rail to give 4 ft 8½ in throughout its system and abolishing the broad gauge altogether in May 1892.

● **RIGHT**
Rain, Steam and Speed **(National Gallery, London): Turner (1775–1851), the English landscape painter, welcomed the Industrial Revolution of the 18th and 19th centuries and painted this picture of one of Gooch's singles crossing the Maidenhead Viaduct, Berkshire, during a squally storm in the Thames valley.**

British Locomotives – 1840–60

• BELOW
Derwent: built by W.A. Kitching in 1845, this 0-6-0 went into service on the Stockton & Darlington Railway (S&DR) between Stockton-on-Tees port and Darlington, County Durham, the first passenger-carrying railway in the world (1825). This railway largely developed the industrial town.

In 1841, Robert Stephenson introduced the first of his "long-boilered" locomotives. In these, he sought to obtain greater boiler power by grouping all the axles in front of the firebox and having a much longer boiler barrel than usual. The necessarily short wheelbase was dictated by the small turntables of the period. "Long-boiler" engines also featured inside frames of iron-plate and the inside-cylinders shared a common steam-chest placed between them. The design could be built in almost any form: a 2-2-2 or 2-4-0 for passenger work and an 0-6-0 for goods-trains were the commonest configurations. But as line speeds rose, the passenger types were found to oscillate dangerously on their short wheelbase chassis and soon fell out of favour. For goods work, however, the design was an undoubted success and these were most numerous on Stephenson's home turf. The North Eastern Railway (NER), a successor to the Stockton & Darlington Railway (S&DR), had no fewer than 125 long-boiler 0-6-0s of the 1001 class built between 1852 and 1875. Fittingly, No. 1275 is preserved in the National Railway Museum at York.

Thomas Russell Crampton (1816–88) was an ambitious young engineer working at Swindon, Wiltshire, under Daniel Gooch. He began to develop his own ideas for an express-locomotive with a large boiler and driving wheels but low centre of gravity and took out his first patent in 1842. In his design, the driving axle was placed right at the base of the frame, behind the firebox. To keep the connecting-rods as short as possible, the cylinders were displaced rearwards outside the frames and fed from the smokebox by prominent outside steam-pipes. The motion and valve gear was all placed outside, allowing the boiler to

LARGE BLOOMER

Date	1852
Builder	W. Fairbairn/ E.B. Wilson
Client	London & North Western Railway (LNWR)
Gauge	4 ft 8 1/2 in
Type	2-2-2
Driving wheels	7 ft 6 in
Capacity	2 cylinders 18 x 24 in
Pressure	150 lb
Weight	31 tons 4 cwt

● **BELOW MIDDLE**
A 2-2-2 Single of 1851 built by Robert Stephenson for LNWR.

● **BELOW**
The classic outline of E.B. Wilson's Jenny Lind as painted by architect and Royal Academy summer exhibitor Ernest W. Twining.

be sunk down in the frames but making the engine very wide. Crampton left the GWR to promote his design to a wider market. His first two engines were built by Tulk & Ley for the Liège & Namur Railway, Belgium, in 1846.

One of the Cramptons destined for Belgium was tested on the Grand Junction Railway (GJR), leading the London and North Western Railway (LNWR) to build one for themselves at Crewe, Cheshire, in 1847. This was the 4-2-0 Courier with 7 in driving wheels, inside-frames and a boiler of oval cross-section. At the same time, larger versions with 8 in driving wheels, the 4-2-0 London by Tulk & Ley and the 6-2-0 Liverpool by Bury, Curtis & Kennedy, were tried out by the LNWR, the latter with great destructive effect on the track. Cramptons could run at speeds approaching 90 mph (145 kph), but they never achieved great popularity in Britain because of their rough riding caused by the position of the driving axle. On the Continent, it was a different matter and the French Northern Railway in particular gained its reputation for lightweight fast expresses by the use of Crampton locomotives. "Prendre le Crampton" even entered the French language as slang for "a quick getaway". These French Cramptons had very strong outside-frames, because the continental loading-gauge left room for the resulting enormous width over cylinders and cranks. A British example built the same way by J.E. McConnell of LNWR earned the nickname "Mac's Mangle" following the trail of broken platforms and lineside structures left in its wake.

In 1847, from E.B. Wilson's Railway Foundry in Leeds, Yorkshire, emerged the first engine built to their most famous design, the Jenny Lind class. This 2-2-2 passenger-engine was the brainchild of the young chief draughtsman, David Joy. Built at a cost of about £2,500 each, the basic model had 6 in driving wheels powered by 15 x 20 in inside-cylinders, making it capable of a mile-a-minute in regular service. For the first time, railways could buy an off-the-peg express locomotive of peerless quality. This most elegant machine, with its polished mahogany boiler lagging and classically fluted bronze dome and safety-valve casings, rapidly became top-link motive power for many of Britain's main lines. The largest Jenny Lind was the Salopian built for Shrewsbury & Birmingham Railway (S&BR) in June 1849. It had a boiler with more than 1,270 sq ft of heating surface and a pressure of 120 lb with $15\frac{1}{2}$ x 22 in cylinders driving 6 ft 6 in wheels.

● **OPPOSITE**
Built by W. Fairbairn and E.B. Wilson for the LNWR, this Large Bloomer is pictured at Milton Keynes Central in 1992. The English new town in Buckinghamshire was founded in 1967.

● **RIGHT**
The inside-framed Crampton Kinnaird, built for Scotland's Dundee & Perth Junction Railway by Tulk & Ley in 1848.

British Locomotives – 1860–75

Patrick Stirling's early locomotives were cabless and had domed boilers. His first 2-2-2 was built for Scotland's Glasgow & South Western Railway (G&SWR) in 1857 and bore many of the design hallmarks that were refined into their finest flowering in his Great Northern 4-2-2 No. 1 of 1870. His crowning achievements were the 8 ft 4-2-2 singles, built at Doncaster, Yorkshire, from 1870 onwards, said to be one of the most handsome locomotives ever made. With modification these were used on all main-line trains for the next 25 years. In 1895, they took part in the railway Races to the North with average speeds of more than 80 mph (129 kph) between King's Cross Station, London, and York.

When William Stroudley became Locomotive Superintendent of the London, Brighton & South Coast Railway (LB&SCR) in 1870, he found a bizarre assortment of locomotives, which were by no means a match for the work they had to do. Over the next two decades, he restocked with a fine series of soundly engineered machines for every purpose from express-passenger to branch-line haulage. His smallest, yet most celebrated class, was the Terrier 0-6-0Ts of 1872. Fifty engines were built, originally for suburban work in south London but later widely dispersed to more rural

ABOVE
William Stroudley's beautiful livery is captured to perfection on Terrier 0-6-0T No. 55 Stepney, built in 1875 and preserved in full working order on England's Bluebell Railway in Sussex.

LEFT
Kirtley's double-framed 2-4-0 No. 158A breathes the spirit of the Midland Railway in the 19th century at the Midland Railway Centre, Butterley, Derbyshire. Butterley was a seat of ironworks and collieries.

● **BELOW**
A 4-2-2 Massey Bromley of 1879. Dübs & Co. built ten for the Great Eastern Railway (GER). Kitsons built ten more in 1881–2.

● **BELOW**
A 2-4-0 of Scotland's Highland Railway in about 1877. Note the louvred chimney, which produced a current of air with the object of lifting the exhaust above the cab.

surroundings. They had 4 ft driving wheels, a 150 lb boiler and 12 x 20 in cylinders. Most were rebuilt with slightly larger boilers without in any way spoiling their appearance. Always useful, they notched up a working life of more than 90 years. Today, nearly a dozen exist in preservation.

Joseph Beattie of the London & South Western Railway (L&SWR) was an ingenious Irishman who sought to increase the steaming power of the locomotive boiler by incorporating elaborate firebox arrangements. A typical Beattie firebox had two compartments, divided by a water-filled partition. Heavy firing took place in the rear portion, the forward fire being kept as far as possible in an incandescent state. Like Kirtley, he made great use of the 2-4-0 type, both in tender form as an express-engine and as a tank-engine for suburban work. He was determined to obtain the maximum steam output from every ounce of coal, and his express 2-4-0s also featured combustion chambers, thermic siphons and auxiliary chimneys. His 2-4-0 tank-engines carried their water supply in a well-tank between the frames. In 1874, 88 entered service.

● **ABOVE**
Joseph Beattie's L&SWR express 2-4-0 Medusa, fitted with double firebox and auxiliary chimney, as captured by artist Cuthbert Hamilton Ellis (born 1909).

STIRLING SINGLE

Date	1870
Builder	Doncaster, Yorkshire, England
Client	Great Northern Railway (GNR)
Gauge	4 ft 8½ in
Type	2-4-0
Driving wheels	8 ft 1 in
Capacity	2 cylinders 18 x 28 in outside
Pressure	140 lb
Weight	38 tons 9 cwt

British Locomotives – 1875–1900

In 1882 Francis William Webb designed a three-cylinder compound express-engine with uncoupled driving wheels – the 2-2-2-0. The engine, LNWR No. 66 Experiment, had two outside high-pressure cylinders driving the rear axle and one huge low-pressure cylinder between the frames driving the leading axle. The absence of coupling-rods meant that one pair of wheels could slip without the other, and it was not unknown for the driving wheels to revolve in opposite directions when attempts were made to start the train. The best of this type were the Teutonics introduced in 1889, with their larger boilers and 7 ft 1 in driving wheels.

The first main-line 0-8-0 tender-engine to run in Britain was introduced on the newly opened Barry Railway in 1889. Built by Sharp, Stewart of Glasgow, they proved ideal for hauling heavy South Wales coal-trains, with their 18 x 26 in outside-cylinders and 4 ft-3 in driving wheels.

● ABOVE
The Jones Goods engines of 1894 were Britain's first 4-6-0s. No. 103 shows off its immaculate Highland Railway livery and Jones's louvred chimney.

● ABOVE
F.W. Webb's LNWR Precedent 2-4-0s were introduced in 1874. By 1882, the Crewe works had built 90 examples. They performed prodigious feats of haulage, culminating in No. 790 Hardwicke's performance in the 1895 Race to the North. Although Webb tried to displace them from top-link work with his compounds, the little 2-4-0s were the most reliable of all 19th-century LNWR passenger types.

● LEFT
A Neilson & Co. 4-2-2 with 7 ft driving wheels. Built in 1886, it is seen here in 1963, before heading the Blue Belle excursion.

● OPPOSITE
This Johnson Single of the former Midland Railway is one of a class known as Spinners, regarded by many as the most beautiful locomotives of all time. With variations, the class totalled 95 engines, all in service by 1900.

● **ABOVE LEFT**
Ivatt's Great Northern No. 990 was the first British Atlantic 4-4-2 and was built at Doncaster Works, Yorkshire, in 1898. Ten more were in service by 1900. In 1902, a larger boiler version appeared, No. 251, which was the first of one of Britain's most successful express-passenger types. Both the original engines are preserved and are shown here running together.

● **ABOVE RIGHT**
Nicknamed Cauliflowers because of the appearance of the LNWR coat of arms on their driving splashers resembling that vegetable, these were F.W. Webb's 18 in express goods-engines, 310 of which were built between 1880 and the turn of the century.

A serious problem on many railways was the blowing back of the exhaust into the crew's faces as they descended gradients. To remedy this, in 1877 David Jones of the Highland Railway introduced locomotives with a louvred chimney. This produced a current of air that lifted the exhaust above the cab. Jones also introduced a counter-pressure brake to assist in controlling trains descending the formidable Highland gradients. His most famous locomotives were his 4-6-0s of 1894, the first engines of this wheel arrangement to work in the British Isles. Sharp, Stewart built 15, which were, at the time, the most powerful main-line engines in Britain.

Few inside-cylinder 4-4-0s surpassed Dugald Drummond's famed T9s of 1899 for the London & South Western Railway (L&SWR). By extending the coupled wheelbase of his earlier designs to 10 ft, he made room in his T9s for a large firebox. The new engines were a success. With their 6 ft 7 in driving wheels, they were fast and able to haul heavy expresses over the difficult South Western main line west of Salisbury, Wiltshire.

CAULIFLOWER

Date	1880
Builder	F.W. Webb, Crewe Works, Cheshire, England
Client	London & North Western Railway (LNWR)
Gauge	4 ft $8^1/_2$ in
Type	0-6-0
Driving wheels	5 ft 2 in
Capacity	Cylinders 18 in x 24 in
Pressure	150 lb
Weight	36 tons

British Builders of the 19th Century

Britain's railways were developed piecemeal by private companies with locomotives coming from outside firms, but once the operating companies joined together to form larger organizations they established their own works for overhauling and building. These company workshops caused places like Crewe (LNWR), Doncaster (GNR), Derby (MR) and Swindon (GWR) to become known as the Railway Towns. Tens of thousands of locomotives were built in these and other towns – over 7,000 in Crewe alone – all for home use rather than export.

The first centre of locomotive building in Britain was established in the mining town of Newcastle in 1821 when George Stephenson and his son Robert opened the world's first workshop dedicated solely to locomotive building. By 1855 the company had built more than 1,000 for Britain and the rest of the world. In 1899 the private company was shut down and a new limited company took its place.

One of the first builders of locomotives in Leeds was Fenton, Murray & Wood. Founded in 1795, their first locomotive, "Prince Regent", was built for Middleton Colliery in 1812. Although the company only built five more

● ABOVE LEFT
Charles Beyer (1813–76) of the locomotive building partnership Beyer Peacock.

● ABOVE RIGHT
Richard Peacock of the locomotive building partnership Beyer Peacock.

● LEFT
Beyer Peacock letterhead.

● ABOVE
Works plate from Kitson & Co., Leeds, one of the Leeds builders who made that city famous across the world.

● ABOVE
Another great Glasgow builder, Sharp, Stewart, who had moved to Springburn from Great Bridgwater Street in Manchester.

● ABOVE
A plate of Falcon Engine and Car Works Company of Loughborough – the forerunner of the famous Brush Works, which continues the tradition of building hi-tech locomotives for today's railway.

● RIGHT
A 4-6-0 locomotive built by Robert Stephenson of Newcastle.

● BELOW LEFT
The Greek god of Fire used as the symbol for Charles Tayleur & Co., whose works became the famous Vulcan Foundry.

● BELOW RIGHT
James Naysmyth, legendary Victorian engineer and founder of Naysmyth Wilson Patricroft Locomotive Works.

locomotives, one of Murray's apprentices, Charles Todd, went on to found his own business, with James Kitson, in 1835. At first they built only parts, but by 1838 they had produced their first complete locomotive. It was so large that they had to pull down one of the workshop walls before it could be delivered.

One of the earliest manufacturers of locomotives in Manchester was William Fairbairn, who had founded an iron foundry in 1816 and who entered into locomotive building in 1839. In 1863, having built about 400 locomotives, the firm was taken over by Sharp, Stewart & Co., a firm which had been established in 1828 by Thomas Sharp and Richard Roberts. By the 1880s Sharp, Stewart had expanded so much that they left their Manchester foundries and relocated in Glasgow. In 1903 the three firms of Sharp, Stewart, Neilson Reid and Henry Dübs merged to become the North British Locomotive Company Ltd. Another of the great Manchester builders was Beyer, Peacock & Co., which, unlike the companies mentioned so far, had been founded, in 1854, purely as a locomotive building works.

One of the earliest building firms founded in Glasgow was that of Walter Neilson and James Mitchell. Although they had commenced the production of stationary engines in 1830, it was not until 1843 that they produced their first locomotives. By 1860 the small works could not keep pace with orders, and a new foundry was built in Finniston. Even this factory soon became too small, and in 1861 work began on new premises in Springburn. The firm's locomotives were exported to many countries, including India, South Africa and Argentina. In 1864 Henry Dübs left the company to establish his own locomotive factory at Polmadie. Within three years the firm had achieved such a reputation that it was exporting to India, Cuba, Spain, Finland and Russia.

The great export trade that developed as Britain took railways to many parts of the world continued to be developed by private builders who in turn made cities like Manchester, Leeds, Newcastle and Glasgow famous throughout the world.

● ABOVE
Dübs works plate from an early Spanish locomotive.

● RIGHT
Henry Dübs, one of the great Glasgow builders, whose works were in Polmadie.

EARLY NORTH AMERICAN LOCOMOTIVES

● LEFT
The York was Phineas Davis's winning entry in the 1831 Baltimore & Ohio locomotive competition. Like many early American designs, it featured a vertical boiler – but this style was called a "cheese".

Horse-drawn railways for hauling coal first appeared in the United States of America from about 1826. Then, having heard of events in England, in 1828 a commission of three American engineers visited the works of Robert Stephenson in Newcastle upon Tyne, the great engineering centre, and those of Foster, Rastrick & Co. in Stourbridge, a market-town and manufacturing centre in Worcestershire, west central England. The result of this visit was that, the next year, four locomotives were ordered, one from Stephenson and three from Foster, Rastrick. Stephenson's was delivered first in January 1829, but, for reasons which are unclear, it was not put into service. Foster, Rastrick's Stourbridge Lion arrived next and was the first steam-driven locomotive put into operation in the USA.

● ABOVE
Ross Winans built vertical-boiler, vertical-cylinder locomotives called "grasshoppers" for the Baltimore & Ohio line, at its Mount Claire Shops, Baltimore, Maryland. In 1927, for its "Fair of the Iron Horse", B&O posed the Andrew Jackson of about 1835 as the Thomas Jefferson.

● MATTHIAS BALDWIN

The second Stephenson locomotive sent to America, a six-wheeler built in 1829, had, like the first, bar-frames. This type of design, soon to be abandoned in Britain, remained the standard in America for many years. Stephenson's third, a Planet-type 2-2-0, was delivered to the Mohawk & Hudson Railway (M&HR) in 1832. This was examined by Matthias Baldwin who went on to build Old Ironside, which on its first run reached 30 mph.

At about the same time, Stephenson sent another locomotive to the Camden & Amboy Railroad & Transportation Co. (C&AR&TC). Camden is a seaport in New Jersey, which became a terminus in 1834, Amboy is in Illinois. The locomotive had a circular boiler and domed "haystack" firebox. A year after its arrival, its front wheels were removed and a four-wheeled bogie with a cowcatcher substituted, to make it suitable for local conditions. It entered service in November 1831 at Bordentown, New Jersey. The oldest complete locomotive in the USA, it was brought out of retirement in 1893 to haul a train of two 1836-type C&A passenger-coaches. The train did the 1,481 km (920 miles) from New York City to Chicago in five days.

● LEFT
The De Witt Clinton was built for the Mohawk & Hudson line by the West Point Foundry, New York, in 1831.

● **PETER COOPER**

In 1830, the Baltimore & Ohio (B&O) line put into service Peter Cooper's Tom Thumb, on the 21 km (13 mile) stretch across Maryland between Baltimore and Ellicott's Mill. This was more of a scientific model than a proper locomotive, but it convinced American business that steam traction was a practical thing. The same year, the West Point Foundry of New York City constructed the first all-American-built locomotive, "The Best Friend of Charleston", for the South Carolina Railroad (SCR). In 1832, the same foundry completed Experiment, later named Brother Jonathan. This, the first locomotive in the USA to incorporate a leading bogie, was also the first to operate on a regular scheduled run. The locomotive came to a premature end when its vertical bottle-like boiler burst.

In 1831, the De Witt Clinton, built by the West Point Foundry, made her first journey on the M&HR line. The locomotive, with cylinders mounted either side of the footplate's rear, reached 15 mph on the Albany-Schenectady line, which had been built across New York state to connect the two eponymous rivers. It could not have been a successful engine, for it was scrapped in 1835.

● **ABOVE AND INSET**

Camden & Amboy's first locomotive, John Bull, was built by Stephenson in England. It was assembled in the USA by Isaac Dripps. He added a pilot, making it the first locomotive in America to employ a cowcatcher pilot.

TOM THUMB

Date	1830
Builder	Peter Cooper, New York, USA
Client	Baltimore & Ohio (B&O)
Gauge	4 ft 8½ in
Driving wheels	2-2-0
Capacity	2 cylinders 3 x 14 in

● **RIGHT**

In 1830, New York businessman Peter Cooper demonstrated the first American-built locomotive on the Baltimore & Ohio railroad. This locomotive was later named Tom Thumb. A 1926 replica poses here.

Early Baldwin Locomotives

In 1834, Baldwin, having already built Old Ironside, produced his second engine, the E.L. Miller. This was for the Charleston and Hamburg Railroad (C&HR). Old Ironside's composite wood-and-iron wheels had proved fragile, so Baldwin fitted his six-wheeled machine with solid bell-metal driving wheels of 4 ft 6 in in diameter. A sister locomotive, Lancaster, appeared in June the same year and promptly set an American record by hauling 19 loaded cars over Pennsylvania's highest gradients between Philadelphia and Columbia. This persuaded the railway's directors to adopt steam power instead of horse traction and they placed an order with Baldwin for five more locomotives. The first Baldwin engine to

● **LEFT**
This Class 152 2-6-0 is typical of early wagontop boilered Moguls from Baldwin. The usual array of fluted and flanged domes, diamond chimney, short smokebox, cross-head-driven boiler-feed pump with back-up injector is completed by a decorated headlight.

have outside-cylinders, the Black Hawk, was delivered to the Philadelphia & Trenton Railroad (P&TR) in 1835.

● POWER DEMANDED

Railways were now demanding more powerful locomotives. Baldwin considered there was no advantage in the eight-wheeled engine, arguing it would not turn a corner without slipping one or more pairs of wheels sideways. None the less, in May 1837, he built his first eight-wheeler. Baldwin's outside-cylindered 0-8-0 Ironton of 1846 had the two leading coupled axles on a flexible beam truck, allowing lateral motion and the relatively long wheelbase to accommodate itself to curves.

● CONCERNS ABOUT ADHESION

As railroads spread, so 1:50 gradients or steeper were met, bringing concerns about adhesion. Baldwin's initial response was to incorporate a supplementary pair of smaller-diameter wheels on an independent axle, driven by cranks from the main driving wheels. The first such engine was sold to the Sugarloaf Coal Co. in August 1841. On a trial run, it hauled 590 tons across Pennsylvania from Reading to Philadelphia, a distance of 87 km (54 miles) in 5 hours 22 minutes, yet another American speed-and-haulage record.

Baldwin's classic locomotive development for heavy freightwork was the 2-6-0- Mogul. In this design, he substituted an extra pair of coupled wheels and single carrying-axle for the leading bogie of the classic American 4-4-0 passenger-engine. The result was a machine that could also be turned to passenger work in mountainous country.

Baldwin's earliest locomotives were built at Matty, his modest assembly-shop in Lodge Alley, Philadelphia. The company he formed became the world's largest locomotive-builder. In the 117-year history of Baldwin Locomotives' work more than 7,000 engines were built.

OLD IRONSIDES

Date	1832
Builder	Baldwin, Philadelphia, Pennsylvania, USA
Client	Camden & Amboy Railroad (C&AR)
Gauge	4 ft 8½ in
Driving wheels	4 ft 6 in
Capacity	2 cylinders 9½ x 18 in

● **OPPOSITE TOP, INSET**
The builder's plate of the Baldwin-built 2-6-0 Mogul No. 20, Tahoe.

● **OPPOSITE TOP**
Matty Baldwin's first locomotive-building shop, in Lodge Alley, Philadelphia.

● **OPPOSITE BOTTOM**
The Tahoe, a Baldwin-built 2-6-0 Mogul-type, once operated by the Virginia & Truckee (V&T) line in Nevada, displayed at the Railroad Museum of Pennsylvania, Stroudsburg, Pennsylvania.

● **RIGHT**
From the early years, Baldwin built many saddle-tanks of distinctive generic appearance. This veteran, working at the E.G. Lavandero Sugar Mill, Cuba, is typical.

American Locomotives – 1840–75

The years between 1840 and the American Civil War (1861–5) saw locomotive production treble. By the end of the 1850s, not only were there 11 main American builders but they had also progressed beyond the experimental stage to bulk production of well-defined standard types suited to local conditions.

With the development of the railroad over the Appalachian Mountains, separating the American East from the West, Richard Norris & Son of Philadelphia, Pennsylvania, extended the classic 4-4-0 by adding an extra coupled axle at the rear to become the 4-6-0 type ("Ten-Wheeler"). This allowed a much larger boiler and the extra pair of drivers gave 50 per cent extra adhesion to cope with steep gradients. The use of bar-frames by American locomotive builders allowed the simple enlargement of existing designs without needing to retool or create more workshop capacity.

● RIGHT
The Pioneer, a 2-2-2 single-driver "bicycle"-type built in 1851 by Seth Wilmarth for the Cumberland Valley Railroad. This was the first locomotive to operate in Chicago.

● LEFT
The railroad depot at Nashville, Tennessee, during the American Civil War.

● BELOW
This replica of the Central Pacific Railway's 4-4-0 Jupiter and Union Pacific Railroad's No. 119 stands at the Golden Spike National Monument, Promontory, Promontory Point, Utah.

● RIGHT
A typical American express train of the 1860s headed by a 4-4-0. This was the most important type of American locomotive providing the flexibility for running at speeds over lightly laid and often rough track beds.

● MOGULS AND CONSOLIDATIONS

Many American engineers became concerned that the increasing length of locomotive boilers interfered with the driver's view. In 1853 Samuel J. Hayes of the Baltimore & Ohio Railroad (B&OR) built a 4-6-0 with the cab perched on top of the boiler, surrounding the steam dome. It looked strange but the mechanical design was sound. The layout was copied by other builders.

In the 1860s, the New Jersey Railroad Co. (NJRC) was an early customer for the Baldwin 2-6-0 Mogul freight locomotives already described. As line speeds rose and trains became heavier still, an even larger freight engine was needed. In 1866, the Lehigh & Mahoning Railroad (L&MR), eponymous with rivers in Pennsylvania and Ohio, added a leading two-wheeled truck to the 0-8-0 design to create the Consolidation, the name by which heavy-freight 2-8-0s were henceforth known.

● ABOVE
The 1855 Brooks-built General, owned by the Western & Atlantic Railroad (W&AR), is famous for its role in the American Civil War. It was stolen from the Confederacy by Union spies and involved in a great chase. This is a typical 4-4-0 American-type of the period.

ATLAS

Date	1846
Builder	Baldwin, Philadelphia, Pennsylvania, USA
Client	Philadelphia & Reading
Wheels	0-8-0
Capacity	Cylinders $16\frac{1}{2}$ x $18\frac{1}{2}$ in
Weight	23.7 tons

Transcontinental links were planned in 1862 as part of President Lincoln's aim to unite the North and preserve the Union. As the 1860s ended, the last rails of the Union Pacific Railroad (UPR) and the Central Pacific Railway (CPR) were joined at Promontory, near Ogden, Utah. CPR President Leland Stanford, who had built eastwards from California, drove in the gold spike to fasten the track when the two lines met to form the first American transcontinental railway on 10 May 1869. The event, commemorated by the Golden Spike Monument, linked the Atlantic and Pacific Oceans by rail and left the way open to the large and powerful locomotives that were to come, serving settlement of the West, which now leapt ahead.

AMERICAN LOCOMOTIVES – 1875–1900

Industrialization and modernization meant free time and more spending money for the American workforce to buy things such as day trips and holidays. To meet this demand, in the late 1870s heavy traffic developed, especially weekend travel between Philadelphia and New Jersey. This called for longer passenger-trains and faster schedules.

● AIR-BRAKES AND ANTHRACITE

Until the 1870s, the 4-4-0 engine proved ideal for American railroads. Then, faster, heavier traffic began to demand something larger. Bigger locomotives led to heavier rails, stronger bridges, bigger turntables, better cars, longer passing-loops and, most important of all, air-brakes. George Westinghouse's

● ABOVE

The 4-4-0 American type was the universal locomotive from about 1850 to 1895. More than 24,000 were built. On this high-drivered Philadelphia & Reading camelback-design 4-4-0, the engineer rides above the boiler, the fireman behind.

● LEFT

The 2-8-0 type was popular with narrow-gauge railroads for high adhesion on mountain rails. This 1881 Baldwin, built for the D&RG, is displayed at the Colorado Railroad Museum, Golden, Colorado.

● LEFT

This 1895 Baldwin-built 36 in gauge 2-8-0 Consolidation-type was typical of locomotives operating in Colorado before the turn of the century. It first operated on the Florence & Cripple Creek Railroad (F&CCR) and later on the Denver & Rio Grande (D&RG). It is displayed at Durango, Colorado.

CHICAGO BURLINGTON & QUINCY 2-4-2

Date	1895
Builder	Baldwin, Philadelphia, Pennsylvania, USA
Client	Chicago Burlington & Quincy (CB&Q)
Gauge	4 ft 8½ in
Driving wheels	7 ft ¼ in
Capacity	Cylinders 19 x 26 in

● LEFT
When built in 1886, this Baldwin 2-10-0 "Decapod" was reported to be the world's largest locomotive. No. 500 and its sister No. 501 beat a temporary track across the mountains while a tunnel was being completed.

● ABOVE
A 4-4-0 on the Pennsylvania Railroad.

compressed air-brake replaced hand-brakes almost immediately after he introduced it in 1868, allowing the high speed of modern trains.

Baldwin's 5,000th production was the 4-2-2 Lovett Eames. Built in 1880, the locomotive was fitted with a wide-grate Wootten firebox for burning anthracite coal, a fuel fast replacing coke and wood. The 6 ft 6 in driving wheels made the locomotive well suited for high-speed passenger service: Baldwin guaranteed it would maintain a 60 mph average speed pulling four cars. It was to have been No. 507 of the Philadelphia & Reading Railroad (P&RR) but only ran trials before the railroad went bankrupt and returned it to her builder.

● "DECAPOD" – WORLD'S LARGEST LOCOMOTIVE

Six years later, Baldwin produced what was reported to be the largest locomotive in the world – a 2-10-0 "Decapod". Its ten 3 ft 9 in driving wheels were intended as much for spreading its great weight over as many axles as possible as they were for gaining adhesion on a temporary track over the mountains while a tunnel was being driven. To facilitate negotiating tight curves, the second and third pairs of drivers were flangeless. A rival claimant for the title of largest engine in the world was the 4-8-0 Mastodon heavyfreight engine of the 1890s.

The American type 4-4-0 was eclipsed on all major railroads by the end of the century. Its final flowering, in 1893, was the L Class of New York Central Railroad (NYCR). That year, No. 999 topped 100 mph at the head of the Empire State Limited between New York City and Buffalo.

● BELOW
A 4-4-0 built in 1881 by Sharp, Stewart, of Glasgow, Scotland, for the St John & Maine Railroad (SJ&MR), linking St John and Maine.

American Locomotive Builders

The first British locomotive was imported into the USA in 1829. Within a year the first American-built machine, "The Best Friend of Charleston", from the West Point Foundry of New York City, was on the rails. By the end of the 1830s, about a dozen workshops had tried their hands at locomotive-building. By 1840, as railways were being built or projected in all parts of the USA, the three main American builders – Baldwin, Norris and Rogers – had made 246 locomotives between them, the first two in Philadelphia, the third in New Jersey.

● **LEFT**
The builder's plate for Florence & Cripple Creek Railroad's No. 20, a Schenectady-built 4-6-0. Schenectady was one of several builders consolidated into the American Locomotive Company (Alco) in 1901.

● **ABOVE**
Baldwin's erecting shop (*The American Railway*, 1892).

● STANDARDIZATION OF COMPONENTS

In the USA, as in Britain, there were operating-company workshops as well as private builders. Generally, company shops concentrated on repair and maintenance, leaving building of complete locomotives to private companies. An exception was the Pennsylvania Railroad's Altoona Works, which began locomotive production in 1866 and quickly standardized components within classes. This was a great improvement because, at this time, locomotives were still mainly handbuilt, meaning it was rarely possible to interchange parts, even on locomotives of the same type from the same builder.

● **BELOW**
The William Crooks was the first locomotive to operate in Minnesota. It was built by the New Jersey Machine Works in Paterson, New Jersey, in 1861 for the St Paul & Pacific Railroad (SP&PR), a predecessor of American railway pioneering entrepreneur James J. Hill's Great Northern Railway (GNR). Hill was nicknamed "the Empire Builder".

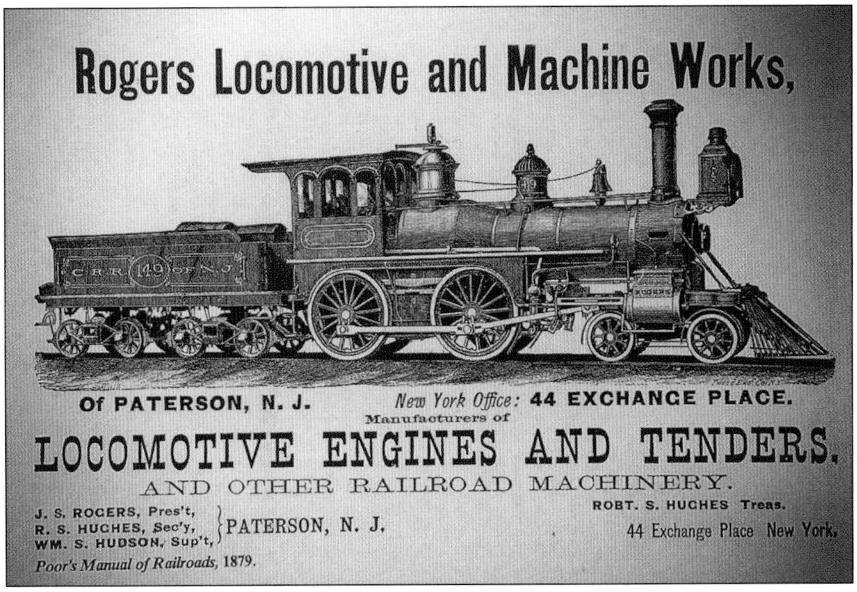

Poor's Manual of Railroads, 1879.

● **LEFT**
Rogers Locomotive and Machine Works, of New Jersey, one of the USA's most important. The works produced 6,200 locomotives in the 76 years 1837–1913.

● **ABOVE RIGHT**
A Baldwin builder's plate dated 1878, found on a locomotive shipped to Cuba.

● **BELOW LEFT**
Manchester Locomotives Works, of Manchester, New Hampshire, built this high-drivered 4-4-0 American type for the Boston & Maine Railroad (B&MR).

● **BELOW**
Florence & Cripple Creek Railroad's No. 20, a 36 in gauge Schenectady-built 4-6-0, later used by the Rio Grande Southern Railroad.

● **BOTTOM**
The numberplate for Duluth & Northern Minnesota's No. 14, a Baldwin 2-8-2 Mikado-type built in 1912.

● SPECIALISTS TAILOR-MADE FOR INDUSTRY

Apart from main-line railroads, rail transport was spreading widely across industry, and specialist locomotive-manufacturers sprang up to tailor-make machines for industry's needs. Doyen of these was Ephraim Shay, a sawmill-owner from Haring, Michigan. He brought timber down from forests on temporary, corkscrew tracks. As these could not stand the weight of a conventional locomotive, he designed his own. In 1880, he mounted a boiler in the centre of a flat bogie-car. This was offset to one side, to allow a pair of vertical cylinders to drive a horizontal shaft turning along the locomotive's right-hand side at wheel-centre level. This engine was nothing like a conventional locomotive, but it was perfect for its job.

● VOLUME OUTPUT FROM FACTORIES

Before 1880, most American locomotives were fairly small machines of weights rarely exceeding 30 tons. This meant they could be built in small workshops without the need for big overhead cranes and their bar-frame components could be made by hand in an ordinary blacksmith's forge. However, by 1890, locomotives had grown so much in size that traditional shops had become useless. The largest builders, such as Baldwin and Cook, set up multi-storied factories with heavy-duty power cranes to build locomotives on a volume-production scale. Smaller firms could no longer compete and collapsed financially.

CANADIAN LOCOMOTIVES

Canada's first railway was a wooden tramway in Quebec extending just more than 27 km (17 miles) between Laprairie and St Johns. The line, opened for traffic in 1832, was for combining rail and water transport via the Hudson and Richelieu rivers. In the first winter of operation, the wooden rails were torn up by adverse weather. The next spring, metal rails replaced them.

● AMERICAN ENGINES

In July 1836, the Champlain & St Lawrence Railroad (C&SLR) was opened. Its first train was pulled by horses because the Canadian engineer could not get the English-built locomotive, Stephenson's 0-4-0 Dorchester, nicknamed "Kitten", to work. An engineer from the USA found that all it needed was "plenty of wood and water", and eventually it built up steam and managed an "extraordinary" 20 mph.

Canadian steam locomotives displayed British and American characteristics and the classic American-outline 4-4-0 was popular. Canadian winter conditions could play havoc with the track, and the American design proved more satisfactory than the British-style 2-4-0 with its relatively rigid wheelbase. American 4-4-0s were supplied in quantities to Canada in the 1870s and were regarded as a general-service type.

● ABOVE
The Samson was built in 1838 by Hackworth, of Wylam, Northumberland, in England for use in Canada. It was the first locomotive to operate in Nova Scotia and one of the earliest used in Canada.

● BELOW
The Countess of Dufferin, a typically Canadian 4-4-0, was the first locomotive put into service on the Canadian Pacific Railway (CPR).

● LEFT
A 4-4-0 built in 1870 by Dübs, of Glasgow, Scotland, for the Canadian ICR. Note the ornate headlamp and wheel bosses.

● RIGHT
In 1868, a 4-4-0 was built by Neilson of Glasgow, Scotland, for the 5 ft 6½ in-gauge Canadian Grand Trunk Railway (CGTR). The massive spark-arrester chimney top was 6 ft wide.

● COUNTESS OF DUFFERIN

The Countess of Dufferin was built by Baldwin in 1872 and used on governmental contracts in Manitoba, Canada's easternmost Prairie Province, before going to the Canadian Pacific Railway (CPR) in 1883 – the same year the CPR built its first locomotive. Designed by the Scottish engineer F.R.F. Brown, it was a typical "American" type 4-4-0 with 5 ft-2 in coupled wheels. Canada followed American locomotive practice very closely, but there were subtle differences. The Countess featured a British-style parallel boiler, not the steeply coned American wagon-top pattern; the spark-arresting stack's shape bespoke Canadian rather than American design.

However, the wagon-top boiler did feature in the early Canadian 4-6-0 and 2-8-0 designs. Its provision for additional steam space over the firebox crown, the hottest part of the boiler, helped avoid priming, particularly when locomotives were tackling the 1:25 gradients of the CPR's Rocky Mountain section. On this section, passenger- and freight-trains were handled by small-wheeled 2-8-0s, loads often limited to no more than two bogie-cars per locomotive. When a long train had to be worked over the mountains, engines were interspersed through the train at two-car intervals. By the end of the 19th century, coal replaced wood as fuel, and the need for hitherto prominent spark-arrester chimneys ceased.

A 4-4-0

Date	1868
Builder	Neilson, Glasgow, Scotland
Client	Canadian Grand Trunk Railway (CGTR)
Gauge	5 ft 6½ in
Driving wheels	4-4-0
Capacity	Cylinders

● LEFT
The Albion, often cited as the third locomotive to operate in Canada, was made by Rayne & Burn at Newcastle upon Tyne, England. This locomotive is often misrepresented as a Hackworth product.

Early European Locomotives

The first locomotive built on mainland Europe was the unsuccessful Berliner Dampfwagen 1, a 0-4-0, constructed in Germany in 1816 for the horse-drawn Köningsgrube Tramway. The first successful steam trials in Europe were on the Saint-Etienne & Lyons Railway in 1828, using a pair of early Stephenson engines. In November 1829, French engineer Marc Séguin put his own engine into service on the line. It had a multi-tubular boiler with huge rotary fans, mounted on the tender and blowing fire through leather pipes. It could pull up to 18 tons but could not exceed 2 mph.

AJAX

Date	1841
Client	Austrian North Railway
Gauge	1,435 mm
Driving wheels	0-6-0

● ALTERNATING SAWS

Séguin produced two more locomotives. They went into service but had problems with belt-driven bellows mounted in the tender. These continually broke down from lack of steam. To allow for this, a wagon with four horses always accompanied the locomotive to provide traction should it be needed. These faults were ironed out, and by 1835 Séguin had completed 12 more locomotives of the same type that, because of the action of the levers, were referred to as *scieurs de long*, "alternating saws".

● BELOW
Der Adler, the first steam locomotive used on the Nuremberg-Fürth Railway, Bavaria, on 7 December 1835.

● ABOVE
A Buddicom 2-2-2 locomotive built for the Paris-Rouen Railway in 1843. It could average 38 mph and is pictured arriving for display at the Festival of Britain in London in 1951.

● BELOW
Ajax, built by Isambard Kingdom Brunel in 1841 for the Austrian North Railway, entered service on the Floridsdorf-Stockerau stretch of the line, north out of Vienna.

● FIRST IN GERMANY AND THE NETHERLANDS

The inaugural locomotive used in 1835 on Germany's first steam railway, in Bavaria, between Nuremberg and Fürth, was Der Adler. This 2-2-2 Patentee-type, built by Stephenson, had outside-frames and an enormously tall chimney of small diameter. It became popular in Europe and was the first locomotive introduced into several countries, including the Netherlands in 1839 when one opened the country's first line, in North Holland province, between Amsterdam, the commercial capital, and Haarlem 19 km (12 miles) west.

● AUSTRIAN EMPIRE'S FIRST

The first steam railway in the Austrian Empire was the Kaiser Ferdinand Nordbahn, which opened in 1837 using two Stephenson Planet-type locomotives, the Austria and the Moravia. Robert Stephenson's assistant John Haswell (1812–97) accompanied the engines to Vienna and stayed on to take charge of the rail workshops there. He was responsible for much early Austrian locomotive development.

● BRITISH INFLUENCE IN RUSSIA

Russia's first public railway was opened in 1837 between the royal centres of St Petersburg, the capital (1712–1914), and Tsarskoye Selo – "The Tsar's Village" summer residence 24 km (15 miles) south. Its first three locomotives were all Patentee 2-2-2s, one each from Timothy Hackworth, Robert Stephenson & Co. and Tayleur & Co. However, the first Russian-built engine was already at work on an industrial line in the Urals. This was a 2-2-0, built in 1833 by M. Cherepanov, a man who had seen early Stephenson locomotives in action in England.

Europe – Mid-19th Century

The Alps are a mountain barrier in south Central Europe extending more than 1,000 km (650 miles) from the Mediterranean coast of France and north-west Italy through Switzerland, northern Italy and Austria to Slovenia. Their highest peak is 4,807 m (15,771 ft) Mont Blanc.

From 1844, the Austrian Government built the main line southwards from Vienna over the Alps via the Semmering Pass, 980 m (3,215 ft) above sea level. Engineer Karl Ghega used heavy gradients and severe curvature to conquer this barrier. The 29 km (18 mile) ascent from Gloggnitz to the summit is graded almost continually at 1:40. No existing locomotive was powerful enough to work trains over the pass, and it was at first thought that trains would have to be cable-hauled or worked by atmospheric power. Finally, a German technical magazine suggested a locomotive competition, on the lines of the Rainhill Trials, to find the best design of engine for mountain haulage. The Government Locomotive Superintendent, Baron Engerth, agreed. The Semmering Trials were held in July 1851.

● ABOVE
Wesel, built in 1851 by Borsig of Berlin, ran on the Cologne-Minden line across what since 1946 has been the Federal German state of North-Rhine Westphalia.

● BELOW LEFT
RENFE locomotive No. 030-2016, built by Kitson, Thomson & Hewitson, of Leeds in 1857, is seen here working as a station-pilot at Valencia, eastern Spain, in 1962.

● BELOW RIGHT
Gmunden was built in 1854 by Gunther, of the Lower Austrian town of Wiener Neustadt, for the narrow-gauge (1.106 metre) Linz-Gmunden line crossing Upper Austria.

● Semmering Trials

Of the four entrants, three became milestone-makers in articulated-locomotive development. All four competitors more than fulfilled the test conditions, climbing the pass with the test-load faster than the required minimum speed. The winner of the first prize of 20,000 gold florins was the German entry Bavaria

LIMMAT	
Date	1846
Builder	Emil Kessler, Karlsruhe, Baden, Germany
Client	Swiss Northern
Gauge	1,435 mm
Driving wheels	4-2-0
Capacity	Cylinders 14.25 x 22 mm

● **BELOW**
Pfalz, a Crampton-type locomotive, was built in 1853 by Maffei of Munich for the Bavarian Palatine Railway. This replica is pictured in front of locomotive sheds at Nuremberg, Bavaria.

built by Maffei of Munich, a 0-4-4-4 tender-locomotive with rod-coupled groups of driving wheels linked by roller chains. The other entries were Vindobona, a rigid-framed 0-8-0 by John Haswell of Vienna; Seraing, a double-boilered articulated machine by John Cockerill of Belgium; and Wiener Neustadt, a double-bogie articulated with a single boiler, built locally by Wilhelm Günther.

The railway bought all the engines, and Bavaria was rebuilt in 1852 by Engerth as an 0-6-0 with its tender-frames extended forward to support the firebox's weight. Thus was created the Engerth-type of semi-articulated locomotive, which became popular in Austria, France, Switzerland and Spain. Seraing was progenitor of the double-boiler Fairlie-type articulated. Wiener Neustadt's design led to the Meyer articulated-locomotive layout. Both types achieved worldwide acceptance.

● ANATOLE MALLET

The first compound engine was built by Swiss-born, French-educated engineer Anatole Mallet (1837–1919) in 1876 for the Bayonne and Biarritz Railway in south-western France. Steam was admitted to a single high-pressure cylinder from where it was exhausted into a larger-diameter low-pressure cylinder, working twice over. The claimed advantage was fuel efficiency. Right to the end of steam operation, French Railways were strongly committed to compounds. Two-cylinder compounding was developed in Germany by von Borries of Hanover State Railways, who introduced his compound 2-4-0s for express work in 1880.

● **RIGHT**
Limmat, a long-boilered engine built by Emil Kessler of Karlsruhe, Baden, in the German state of Württemberg, was the first locomotive to run from Zurich, Switzerland, to Baden, south-western Germany, on 19 August 1847. The line became known as the "Spanische Brötli Bahn" – a popular type of confectionery.

Europe to 1900

● BELOW
This de Glehn compound running on France's Nord railway is typical of the closing years of the 19th century. Similar engines played a prolific part in express service across France and were also exported to many countries by French and other continental builders.

By 1879, the total track length on Russian railroads was 20,125 km (12,500 miles). Between 1860–90 the ever-growing demand for locomotives could not be met by Russian building alone, and many engines were imported from Britain, France, Germany and Austria. Two features of Russian locomotives of this period were the fully enclosed cabs, giving protection from harsh winters, and the promenade-deck effect, produced by handrails extending round the footplating on either side of the boiler to stop the crew slipping off in icy weather. In 1895, the first of 29 0-6-6-0 Mallet articulated-compound tender-engines was put into service, on the 3 ft 6 in gauge Vologda-Archangel railway in north Russia.

● Alfred de Glehn

Alfred de Glehn (1848–1936), an inspired British engineer working in France as technical chief of Société Alsacienne, evolved a system of compounding using two high- and two low-pressure cylinders. His first locomotive was an advanced 4-2-2-0 in which the outside high-pressure cylinders were set well back in Crampton fashion and drove the rear-pair of uncoupled wheels. The low-pressure cylinders, set forward between the frames, drove the leading driving-axle. In partnership with Gaston du Bousquet (1839–1910), chief engineer of the Northern Railway of France, bigger, better and faster derivatives with coupled driving wheels were introduced in the 1890s, placing the Nord at the fore of high-speed locomotive performance. The first four-cylinder de Glehn compound was made in 1886 – the last in 1929.

● Karl Gölsdorf

Compound locomotives were also developed in Austria by Karl Gölsdorf (1861–1916), engineer to Austrian State Railways – Österreichische Bundesbahnen (ÖBB). His earliest two-cylinder engines were freight 0-6-0s introduced

● LEFT
One of Europe's early, huge, heavy-hauling 0-8-0 tender-engines from the German builder Hartmann, exported to Spain in 1879.

● ABOVE
This Czech 0-8-0 was originally built in 1893 for the Austrian State Railways as their locomotive No. 73175, by STEG, of Vienna.

EMMETT 2-6-0T	
Date	1886
Builder	Emil Kessler, Karlsruhe, Baden, Germany
Client	Portuguese CN Railway
Gauge	Metre
Driving wheels	3 ft 3½ in
Capacity	Cylinders 13 x 19 mm

● LEFT
In 1886 these Emmett light 2-6-0Ts were introduced by builder Emil Kessler, of Karlsruhe, capital of the then state of Baden, for Portugal's metre-gauge lines.

● BELOW LEFT
An early Portuguese Railways 5 ft 6 in gauge saddle-tank built by Beyer Peacock, of Manchester, England.

● BELOW RIGHT
This type 0-8-0 of the Volga Dam Railway was imported from Britain's Sharp, Stewart in 1871.

in 1893. Gölsdorf's main concern was to provide both passenger- and freight-engines capable of hauling trains over Alpine passes. His heavyfreight 2-8-0s, designed for the Arlberg Tunnel, and of which more than 900 were built, were so successful they lasted in service until the 1950s.

● CAESAR FRESCOT

In 1884, Caesar Frescot, chief mechanical engineer (CME) of the Upper Italian Railway, gave Europe its first standard-gauge 4-6-0 tender-locomotive, Vittorio Emanuele II. These locomotives, built at Turin's works, were intended for heavy passenger and freightwork over the 8 km (5 mile) long Giovi Pass railway tunnel at an altitude of 329 m (1,080 ft), across the Apennine mountain range of central Italy, linking Genoa, Turin and Milan in northern Italy. They had outside-cylinders and were decorated with much ornamental brasswork, though their appearance was spoilt by the short wheelbase bogie. They were built into the 1890s and lasted well into the 20th century.

European Builders of the 19th Century

One of Europe's first locomotive builders was Matthias von Schönner, the architect of the horse-drawn Budweis & Linz Railway linking the then German-named brewing city of České Budějovice, in southern Bohemia (now Czech Republic) and the Upper Austrian commercial city. Von Schönner visited America in the 1830s and was greatly influenced by the Philadelphian builder William Norris. He returned home to build the Vienna & Raub line which opened in 1842.

The Vienna & Gloggnitz Railway, immediately after opening in 1841,

● ABOVE
European builders, such as Kuntze & Jürdens of Germany, exported their locomotives as far afield as Cuba.

● ABOVE
One of Germany's most prolific locomotive builders was Henschel & Sohn whose works were in Kassel. The company built its first locomotive in 1848. Henschel produced for domestic railways and world export.

● ABOVE
Another prolific world-export market builder was Richard Hartmann, of Chemnitz, a town known as the "Saxon Manchester", standing at the base of the Erzgebirge, the "Ore Mountains" chain.

● ABOVE
The former German builder BMAG of Berlin was initially known as Schwartzkopff, as shown by this ornate maker's plate.

● ABOVE
A lesser-known German builder was Rheinische Metalfrabrik of Düsseldorf, capital of North-Rhine Westphalia and commercial hub of the Rhine-Ruhr industrial area. Its name is pictured on a Class 20 2-6-0, built in 1922, of Yugoslav Railway – Jugoslovenske Železnice (JŽ).

● ABOVE
Borsig of Berlin was a prolific builder for home and export markets.

● ABOVE LEFT TO RIGHT
Orenstein & Koppel builder's plates.

● LEFT
A 700 mm gauge 0-4-4-0T 4 cylinder compound Mallet built by Ducroo & Brauns of Weesp, Holland of 1928 on a sugar plantation in Java.

● BELOW
Borsig of Berlin were a prolific builder for both the home and export market. One of their products is this, the world's last surviving steam tram.

erected its own works to maintain its existing engines and to build new ones. The Scottish engineer John Haswell was in charge and his first locomotive, Wien, was built the same year. In 1842 Wenzel Günther, who worked with Haswell, left to take over as manager of the Wiener Neustadt locomotive works. In 1844, Haswell produced the first 4-4-0 for the Vienna & Gloggnitz. This was followed by his two famous locomotives Grosse Gloggnitzer and Kleine Gloggnitzer. Such was the former's success that it hauled 160 ton passenger-trains and 380 ton freight-trains between Mürzzuschlag, south-west Wiener Neustadt, and Leibach.

● AUGUST BORSIG

August Borsig's first locomotive, built in Berline-Moabit, was completed in July 1841 for use on the Berlin & Anhalt Railway, linking the then Prussian capital with the then duchy Prussia surrounded by Saxony. In this production he sought to improve on the American Norris 4-2-0 design by adding a pair of trailing-wheels behind the firebox. This helped weight distribution but robbed the engine of vital adhesive weight on the driving-axle. In his 2-2-2 locomotive Beuth of 1843, also for the Berlin & Anhalt, Borsig embodied the best of English locomotive practice of the time, owing much to Edward Bury but with Stephenson's inclined outside-cylinders. Borsig went on to become one of Germany's most prolific locomotive factories, supplying a worldwide market.

The firm of Henschel & Sohn, founded in 1817 and based in Kassel, then the capital of Westphalia before becoming part of the Prussian province of Hesse-Nassau, built its first locomotive, Drache (Dragon), in 1848. It was a 4-4-0 of hybrid appearance, combining the Stephenson long-boiler and haystack-firebox with the short-wheelbase Norris leading-bogie. Henschel's output was quite modest – no more than eight engines a year up to 1860 when its 50th locomotive emerged. After the works was extended in 1865, production soared.

● BELOW
Arthur Koppel set up his foundry to produce large railway equipment in 1885, leading to creation of Orenstein & Koppel, Germany's principal builder of narrow-gauge industrial locomotives. This is an original Arthur Koppel engine of 1898. She is the 0-4-0 well-tank Laurita and bears a plate stating "Primera Locomatora Chacao Paraguayo", that is "first locomotive on the Paraguayan Chaco" – the Gran Chaco being the south-central South American plain of huge swamps and scrub forest covering 780,000 sq km (300,000 sq miles).

Indian Locomotives

India's first stretch of railway was part of the Great Indian Peninsular Railway (GIPR) between Bombay City and Thana, Maharashtra, 34 km (21 miles) away. It opened in April 1853. For the opening, Tayleur's Vulcan factory at Newton-le-Willows supplied eight inside-cylindered 2-4-0s with domeless boilers, haystack-fireboxes and 5 ft driving wheels.

Just as the GIPR originated in Bombay, so the East Indian Railway (EIR) began in Calcutta. In 1862, ten 2-2-2 express-locomotives with outside-cylinders were built for EIR priority train services. Large canopies over the cabs protected crews from the sun's heat and glare. Their 6 ft 6 in driving wheels equipped them for high-speed running, and they had surprisingly large tenders. The firebox was also relatively large for the period, having an 18 sq ft grate area.

● LEFT
The Indian metre-gauge Class E was an 0-4-2 mixed-traffic version of the D Class. Between 1874–91, 147 examples of a standard design entered service.

● WESTERN GHATS OBSTACLE

From its start, the GIPR had problems operating trains over the 900-1,500 m (3,000-5,000 ft) high Western Ghat range. Banking over the mountains' zigzag inclines with heavy tank-engines was common practice. In 1862, Sharp, Stewart & Co., of Glasgow, Scotland, built a tough-looking outside-framed 4-6-0 saddle-tank to the requirements of GIPR engineer J. Kershaw. The first engine of this wheel arrangement to be built in a British works, it was fitted with sledge-brakes. These were applied to the rails during descent of the western escarpments of the hills where gradients reached 1:37. It was superseded in 1891 by a massive 59 ton 0-8-0ST from the Vulcan Foundry and Neilson of Glasgow.

Webb's three-cylinder compounds were much admired in some quarters, despite precocious behaviour on Britain's LNWR. It may have been that, seen from India, distance lent enchantment to their engineering peculiarities. So it was that the Oudh & Rohilkhand Railway (ORR),

● LEFT
The metre-gauge F Class 0-6-0 dominated Indian railways and is one of the most celebrated locomotive types in world history. The engines worked on many railways. More than 1,000 examples were constructed with little more than detailed variations, between 1884–1922 by 12 different builders.

● RIGHT
The Indian metre-gauge Class D 0-4-0 was a standard design comprising ten engines built at Sharp, Stewart's Great Bridgewater Street Foundry, Manchester, England, in 1873.

in what today is the state of Uttar Pradesh, ordered a 5 ft 6 in gauge version from Dübs of Glasgow in 1883. Despite different cab and valve arrangements, it closely resembled the Crewe original, right down to the uncoupled driving wheels.

● BENGAL-NAGPUR LEADS DEVELOPMENT

In the late 19th century, Indian broad-gauge locomotive practice often mirrored that on British main lines with 4-4-0s for passenger work and 0-6-0s for goods. Increasing train weights, however, pressed for the development of the small-wheeled six-coupled engine into something rather bigger for Indian conditions. Hence, the Bengal-Nagpur Railway, which linked Calcutta and the capital of the Central Provinces (later Madhya Pradesh) and was always at the fore of technical development, commissioned a class of mixed-traffic 4-6-0s, delivered between 1888–91. Aside from their headlamps and cowcatchers, they were of typical British appearance with straight running-plates, outside-cylinders and inside valve-gear.

F CLASS 0-6-0	
Date	1874
Builder	Various: Britain, Germany, India
Client	Various: Indian State Railways
Gauge	Metre
Driving wheels	3 ft 6 in
Capacity	Cylinders 13 x 20 in
Weight in full working order	20 tons

● LEFT
The coat of arms of India's Bengal-Nagpur Railway (BNR).

● LEFT
The most celebrated of all Indian 2 ft gauge designs are the 0-4-0 saddle-tanks built for the Darjeeling Railway from 1889. The line took Bengal government officials to their hot-weather headquarters.

● BELOW
The metre-gauge O Class 4-4-0 was an outside-cylinder version of the early M Class. It was the standard passenger-engine on most lines. Some were superheated. The class totalled 297 examples, from six different builders between 1883–1912.

Chinese Locomotives

China's first railway was opened in 1876 in the eastern province of Kiangsu. It was an 8 km (5 mile) long stretch of 2 ft 6 in gauge between Shanghai and Wusung, Shanghai's outport, that is a subsidiary port built in deeper water than the original port. The first locomotive on the line was the Pioneer, built by Ransomes & Rapier of Ipswich, Suffolk, England. Used by the railway's builders, this 1½ ton engine with 1 ft 6 in driving wheels had a service-truck attached on which the driver sat. The line had a short history. After it had operated for only a month, a local man was fatally injured. Riots ensued and the line was closed. A few months later, it was reopened with two 9 ton 0-4-2STs, Celestial Empire and Flowery Land, both with outside-cylinders and 2 ft 3 in wheels. On these locomotives the water-tanks, a combination of side and saddle, completely enveloped the boiler but left the smokebox clear. However, by the end of 1877, the Chinese authorities ordered line and engines dismantled.

● LEFT
Built by Dübs of Glasgow, Scotland, in 1886, this 0-4-0 saddle-tank, Speedy Peace, Works No. 2254, was scrapped when more than 20 bound Chinese were thrown in the approaching engine's path as part of the uprising against railways. Note Dübs's ornately enhanced diamond worksplate.

ROCKET OF CHINA

Date	1881
Builder	C.W. Kinder
Client	Kaiping Tramway
Gauge	Narrow gauge
Driving wheels	0-6-0
Capacity	Cylinders 14.25 x 22 mm

● Kaiping Tramway

The next attempt to provide a railway in China was in 1881 in the northern province of Hopeh. A mining company built the narrow-gauge Kaiping Tramway as an 8 km (5 mile) link between the Kaiping coalfield near Tangshan, north of Tientsin, and the canal that connected with the Pehtang River. At first, because of Chinese prejudices against steam locomotion, mule traction was used. C.W. Kinder, the company's resident engineer, decided nonetheless to build a steam locomotive. Using odds and ends recovered from various scrap-heaps, he secretly built a small 2-4-0 locomotive, which he named Rocket of China. When the Chinese authorities heard about the locomotive, they sent a commission to investigate. Forewarned of their imminent arrival, Kinder dug a pit and buried his engine.

● ABOVE
The Kaiping Tramway in Hopeh Province was China's first permanent railway. The 2-4-0 Rocket of China pictured here was built in China by British engineer C.W. Kinder and was the tramway's first locomotive.

● The Chinese Imperial Railway

In 1886 Dübs & Co. of Glasgow, Scotland, built two 0-4-0STs for a 2 ft gauge section of the Imperial Chinese Railway (ICR). Named Speedy Peace and Flying Victory, they were instantly opposed by the Chinese, who were convinced that the

● **RIGHT**
Sung Wu Railway 2-4-2T No. 2 was built by Brooks Locomotive Works, Dunkirk, New York, USA. This celebrated American builder produced more than 4,000 locomotives until it combined with seven others in 1901 to form the American Locomotive Company (Alco).

● **RIGHT**
A 2-6-2 saddle-tank built by Dübs in 1887 entered service on the Tientsin Railway in Hopeh Province.

"devil's machines" would desecrate ancestral graves. To prevent this, many trains were halted by Chinese being thrown in front of the locomotives. Many were run over and killed. After about 20 of these deaths, the line was eventually closed and the locomotives scrapped.

● **BELOW**
This engine is an example of how American locomotives exported to China exerted permanent influence on developments. It was built by Baldwin in 1899 and was No. 230 on the Chinese Eastern Railway (CER). Although the CER was operated by Russians, most of its motive power was of American origin. No. 230 was one of 121 Vauclain compound 2-8-0s built for the line by Baldwin in 1899. Samuel Vauclain (1856–1940) worked for Baldwin for 51 years, becoming chairman in 1929. He invented his compounding system in 1899.

East Asian Railways

In Malaya, the first train service started in 1885 in Perak State, between Taiping and Port Weld. Then, in 1886, the first section of the metre-gauge Perak Government Railway (PGR), the 11 km (7 mile) stretch between Kelung and Kuala Lumpur, Perak's capital, was opened. The railway came when the country was covered in dense jungle and transport was entirely by river. The first locomotive was a little 0-6-0 tank by Ransomes & Rapier, of Ipswich, Suffolk, England, similar to the Pioneer and one of the few built by the firm. Small tank-engines were the most suitable for the infant railway system, with the Class A 4-4-0Ts favoured. The larger B Class engines of 1890 were later developed into a tender-engine version. Malayan locomotives were distinguished by their huge headlight – a necessary item on line in dark jungle. Nonetheless, one of these locomotives was charged and derailed by a bull elephant, which lifted the tender clear off the track.

● RIGHT
Indonesian State Railways (ISR) C12 Class 2-6-0 Tank No. C1206 was a two-cylinder compound built for the Staats Spoorwegen by Hartmann of Chemnitz, Germany, in 1895.

● **SINGAPORE-PENANG**

By 1909 passengers could travel by train between Singapore and Penang. Completion of the Johore Causeway in 1923 brought the line into Singapore. Singapore had had a railway from Tank Road to Bukit Timah since 1903. In eastern Malaya, goods and passengers could go by train from Gemas to Kota Bharu from 1931.

● **BRITISH INFLUENCE IN JAPAN**

Japan's first line was built by British engineers in 1872. The first locomotive, a 14¾ ton 2-4-0T with 4 ft 3 in driving wheels, to run on the 3 ft 6 in gauge line was built in 1871 by the Vulcan Foundry of Newton-le-Willows, England. The early equipment on Japanese railways was almost entirely British and included some outside-cylinder 4-4-0s supplied by Dübs & Co. of Glasgow. Other British locomotives to run in Japan were made

● LEFT
One of Java's Staats Spoorwegen B50 Class 2-4-0s, No. B5012, built by Sharp, Stewart of Great Bridgewater Street, Manchester, England, in 1884. When built, these were main-line passenger-engines for Java's 3 ft 6 in gauge lines.

● RIGHT
A 3 ft 6 in-gauge 4-4-0 engine with inside-cylinders, built in 1899 for the Imperial Government Railways of Japan, by Neilson, of Glasgow, Scotland.

● OPPOSITE CENTRE
Another Indonesian State Railways B5014, also from Sharp, Stewart's foundry in 1884, wheezes along the Madian Slahung line. Burning both coal and wood the engine issues shrouds of fire from its chimney.

by Sharp, Stewart of Manchester and by Kitson of Leeds.

One of Kitson's creations was a 0-6-0 goods-engine built in 1873, which three years later was rebuilt in the shops at Kobe, Honshu, as a 4-4-0, a type which became the standard Japanese passenger-locomotive. In 1876 Kitson built another 4-4-0, of typical British appearance, its only oriental feature being the small louvred shutter in the cab side. Class 1800s were introduced in 1881. These engines were fitted with smart copper-capped chimneys bearing the number in brass.

● AMERICAN INFLUENCE IN JAPAN

In 1897, Baldwin exported to Japan the Mikado-type. These were the first locomotives built with a 2-8-2 wheel arrangement with a tender. Named in honour of the Japanese head of state, these locomotives were designed to burn an inferior quality of coal, requiring a large grate area and a deep, large firebox.

One of Japan's steepest railways, up to 1:40 gradient, was the Hakone line serving the eponymous mountain resort near Mount Fuji, on Honshu. For this, Moguls were bought from Rogers in 1897. Japanese railways were Americanized even more in 1900 by the introduction of Schenectady-built 4-4-0s.

● JAVA

Perhaps East Asia's most remarkable railway system was on Java whose network serving the islands was developed during the Dutch East Indies period. The main lines were developed in the last 20 years of the 19th century. Innumerable feeder lines, known as steam tramways, joined them. A gauges battle occurred between the 3 ft 6 in gauge and the standard. For a while, a third rail was laid over the 4 ft $8\frac{1}{2}$ in gauge to enable through 3 ft 6 in gauge trains to operate. The gauge was finally standardized at 3 ft 6 in.

The multiplicity of state and private enterprises that built Java's railways produced a wide diversity of motive power primarily of Dutch, German and British origin.

INDONESIAN STATE RAILWAYS (ISR) B50 CLASS 2-4-0

Date	1880
Builder	Sharp, Stewart, Manchester, England
Client	Staats Spoorwegen
Gauge	3 ft 6 in
Driving wheels	1,413 mm
Capacity	Cylinders 381 x 457 mm

● LEFT
A rare example of Java's standard-gauge network of the NISM, that is Nederlandse Indische Spoorwegen Maatschappij. These 0-6-0 goods-engines, from Beyer Peacock, of England, resemble that company's Ilfracombe goods class. This rare veteran was pictured at Indonesia's southern Javan city of Yogyakarta.

● BELOW
The standard O Class outside-cylinder 4-4-0 of the metre-gauge lines of the Indian subcontinent heading the Royal Train on the Burma State Railway.

AUSTRALASIAN RAILWAYS

In the 19th century, Australia consisted of a series of separate colonies, all with administrations operating independently of each other. This, added to personalities and poor communications, led to the mess of gauge problems from which the country has suffered ever since.

The first steam locomotive to run in Australia was locally built by Robertson, Martin, Smith & Co. It entered service on the Colony of Victoria's Melbourne and Hobsons Bay Railway on 12 September 1854. New South Wales (NSW) followed by opening a 21 km (13½ mile) line from Sydney to Parramatta on 26 September 1855.

● DIFFICULT TERRAIN

Australian locomotive design was much governed by the difficult country to be traversed with mountainous country close to coast. The standard gauge in NSW had many 1:30 gradients with curves as tight as 8-chains radius on the main lines. Branch and narrow-gauge states' lines were even worse.

Early locomotives that became standards were generally of the 4-4-0 or 0-6-0 wheel arrangements and of British design or styling. Australia's most significant development was probably the

● BELOW

Baldwin supplied ten K(294) Class goods engines in 1885. They were put on lesser duties, including working water-trains between Lake Menindee and Broken Hill mining-town in NSW's dry west. The large wagon behind the locomotive is a 32,000 litre (7,000 gallon) water "gin" to augment the tender's supply.

● ABOVE

One of South Australia's Y Class "Colonial Moguls" introduced in 1886. This class originally totalled 134 examples, 58 of which were converted to YX Class with higher-pressure boilers from 1907.

CLASS K TANK	
Date	1892
Builder	Neilson Reid
Client	Western Australian Government Railways (WAGR)
Gauge	3 ft 6 in
Driving wheels	2-8-4
Capacity	Cylinders 19 x 24 in

● LEFT
One of six D(55) Class 4-4-0s with 6 ft ½ in driving wheels supplied to NSW Railways by Beyer, Peacock in 1882. Able to achieve 70 mph, they were soon dubbed the "Peacock High-fliers". Ten similar locomotives were supplied to Victorian Railways as their old A Class.

● OPPOSITE TOP
"Number 10" was the first locomotive built in NSW. She was a 2-4-0 designed on the Stephenson long-boiler principle. Completed in 1870, she was used as an express passenger-locomotive. She is pictured at Picton Station, south-west of Sydney, soon after entering service.

4-6-0 type, well before Jones introduced it to the Highland Railway in Britain. The 30 R Class was introduced from 1886 in South Australia. The P6 Class introduced in NSW in 1892 eventually numbered 191 units.

On the narrow gauge, Beyer, Peacock's development of the "Colonial Mogul" had the most impact, with 134 Y Class in South Australia, 47 G Class in Western Australia and 28 C Class in Tasmania.

● NEW ZEALAND'S GAUGES

New Zealand also started with a mess of gauges. South Island had a 3 ft gauge horse-drawn railway from Nelson, in 1862; a 5 ft 3in gauge steam railway from Christchurch in 1863; a wooden-railed line, worked unsuccessfully on the Davies or Prosser principle, from Invercargill in 1864; and a 4 ft 8½ in gauge steam-line from Invercargill in 1866. Finally, the 3 ft 6 in gauge was selected as standard and introduced, with double Fairlie locomotives, at Dunedin in September 1872.

New Zealand had, as well as regular designs, a great variety of types: vertical-boilered locomotives, single- and double-Fairlies, flangeless Prosser-types, Fell locomotives and locally made curiosities. Mainly, short lines radiated from coastal ports, so the most significant design would have been the 88-strong F Class 0-6-0T saddle-tanks.

American locomotives were more successful in New Zealand, starting with eight K Class supplied by Rogers Locomotive works in 1878.

● ABOVE
A New Zealand Government Railways (NZGR) 1873-built A Class 0-4-0 tank by Dübs. These little engines, nicknamed "Dodos", worked well and lasted into the 1920s.

● RIGHT
One of 77 members of the New South Wales (NSW) A(93) Class 0-6-0s, shunting at Sydney's Darling Harbour goods yard.

Southern African Railways

South Africa's first public railway was a 3 km (2 mile) stretch in Natal between Durban and The Point, opened in June 1860. The locomotive was the "Natal". It was built by Carrett Marshall & Co., of Leeds, England, stripped down, crated and sent to Durban, where it was rebuilt by Henry Jacobs. The engine had a large dome cover and its chimney, of typical American design, incorporated a wire-mesh spark-arrester. This locomotive, however, was not the first to run in South Africa, for in September 1859, E. & J. Pickering had imported a 0-4-2 built by Hawthorn & Co. of Leith, Scotland.

● **LEFT** South Africa's first steam locomotive, which operated in Cape Province, was a contractor's engine for building the Cape Town – Wellington Railway in 1859. She was built by Hawthorn & Co.'s works in Leith, Scotland, as a 4 ft 8 in gauge 0-4-2. Here is the preserved veteran, proclaimed a national monument in 1936.

● **LEFT** The first locomotive to serve the Ugandan Railway was this Dübs 2-4-0T, one of two locomotives bought secondhand from Indian State Railway (ISR). Dübs of Glasgow built 25 of these engines in 1871–2.

CLASS 6	
Date	1893
Builder	Dübs, of Glasgow, Scotland
Client	Cape Government Railway (CGR)
Gauge	3 ft 6 in
Driving wheels	4 ft 6 in
Capacity	Cylinders 17 x 26 in
Weight in full working order	80 tons

● KITSON VERSUS FAIRLIE

In 1875, the Cape Government Railway (CGR) introduced a back-to-back from Kitson & Co. of Leeds, Yorkshire, and a 0-6-0+0-6-0 Fairlie-type from Avonside Engine Co. of Bristol. In 1864, Robert Fairlie introduced his double-ender. This could be driven in either direction and was adopted in hilly countries where curves and gradients challenged ordinary locomotives. When the two machines were tested against each other, the Fairlie worked around curves with facility, up

● **RIGHT** The Class 6s were one of the most important types in South African locomotive history. Between 1893–1904, almost all the 268 engines being built to a basic design came from Glasgow. They operated express passenger-trains across the entire republic, with the exception of Natal.

and down gradients, and the Kitson lurched badly descending a decline and was much heavier on fuel.

In 1887, Black Hawthorn, of Gateshead, County Durham, England, built a woodburning 0-4-2ST for the Cape of Good Hope & Port Elizabeth 3 ft 6 in gauge line. It had spark-arrester rails above the tank for wood storage, single slide-bars and Ramsbottom safety-valves with single exhaust.

● EAST AFRICAN LINES

The two pioneer public railways in East Africa were Kenya's Mombasa & Nairobi laid in 1896 and the Usambara Railway through the eponymous highlands of Tanga Province of German East Africa (later Tanganyika) on which work began in 1893 but was not completed until 1911. A private railway was built from Tanga to Sigi, to serve the logging interests of the Deutsche Holtzegesellschaft für Ostafrika. The first engine used on this line, naturally a woodburner, was a 0-4-2 tank built in 1893 by Vulcan of Stettin, then capital of Pomerania, a province of Prussia.

In May 1896 the first locomotives were delivered to the Ugandan Railway. They were secondhand 2-4-0Ts, bought from Indian State Railways (ISR), built in 1871 by Dübs of Glasgow, Scotland.

● ABOVE
The Cape Government Railway (CGR) Class 7 was a small-wheeled freight version of the Class 6 passenger-locomotive. It was introduced in 1892. More than 100 were built, all by the three Glasgow builders Dübs, Neilson and Sharp, Stewart.

● BELOW
These locomotives began as main-line 4-10-2Ts on the Natal Government Railway (NGR). They were among more than 100 engines built by Dübs in Polemadie, Glasgow. Replaced by tender-engines, they were converted to 4-8-2Ts for further use as shunting- and trip-engines.

Northern African Railways

Although the first steam tramway in North Africa was built at Egypt's El Dikheila quarries near Alexandria as early as 1838, the first public railway in the region was the British-built Cairo-Alexandria line opened in 1854. By 1870, Egyptian State Railway (ESR) took delivery of a mixed collection of 241 locomotives of over 50 classes supplied by 16 builders from five countries. Besides the usual types, there were a few exotic 2-2-4T saloon locomotives to carry visiting royalty.

MOGUL	2-6-0
Date	1891
Builder	Baldwin, Philadelphia, Pennsylvania, USA
Client	Bône-Guelma Railway, Algeria
Gauge	3 ft 6 in
Driving wheels	4 ft
Capacity	Cylinders 18 x 22 in

● F.H. TREVITHICK'S IN THE NILE VALLEY

British occupation of the Nile Valley in 1882 put railways under the direction of F. H. Trevithick, grandson of the Cornish pioneer. The first new locomotives he introduced were Great Western in concept, with inside-cylinders and strong double-frames. These frames were essential to negotiate Egypt's rough tracks. For the lightest and fastest duties, he ordered 25 2-2-2s from Kitson and the Franco-Belge Company of La Coyère. These sturdy locomotives were the last singles to work in Africa. Some were still in use in World War II.

● **ABOVE**
A type 0-6-0 tender built by North British, of Glasgow, Scotland, for ESR. The driving wheels are 5 ft 1/4 in diameter, the cylinders of 18 x 24 in capacity.

● **BELOW**
Built by Neilson, of Glasgow, Scotland, this design was on display at the Great Exhibition of 1862, where it was seen by Said Pasha, Viceroy of Egypt, who later ordered one for Egyptian State Railways (ESR).

● **FRENCH DESIGN FOR ALGERIA**

Algeria's railway development was put in the hands of the French Paris, Lyons & Mediterranean Company in 1863. Secondhand PLM 0-6-0s of characteristic French design were shipped to get services started. Some of these redoubtable 0-6-0 designs, as SNCFA classes 3B, 3E and 3F, were destined to last almost until the end of steam on the Algerian standard gauge. The Algiers-Oran main line opened in 1871 when more 0-6-0s were supplied, with the first of the successful 0-8-0 goods-engines of classes 4A and 4C for the 1:80 gradients up from Philippeville. Operations between Algeria and Tunisia were begun with 0-6-0s built by Batignolles. By 1883, 39 of these, assisted by 18 0-6-0Ts built by the same firm for shunting and banking, were in operation. On the 300 km (184 mile) of the Algerian Western, the sparse service was operated by 26 0-6-0s that were built by Fives Lille and SACM. These ultimately became SNCFA classes 3L and 3M. In 1899 the Bône-Guelma Railway in eastern Algeria turned to Baldwin for ten of its ready-made American-style Moguls. These performed well but were rebuilt as tank-engines in the early 20th century.

● **BRITISH PRESENCE IN TUNISIA**

Tunisia's first railway was built with British capital and equipment, as part of a move to extend British influence in the region. The standard-gauge line was opened from Tunis to La Marsa in 1874 using four little Sharp, Stewart 2-4-0 tanks. The Italians took over the line in 1876 and ran it until it was acquired by Algeria's Bône-Guelma Co. in 1898. In 1895, under Bône-Guelma's auspices, an extensive metre-gauge network was inaugurated along the coastal region south of Tunis. As motive power, a fleet of no fewer than 135 Mallet articulated engines was built – the largest concentration of these tank-engines in Africa. The first batch of eight 0-4-4-0s came from Batignolles to start services, and larger machines were delivered early in the new century.

LATIN AMERICAN RAILWAYS

In 1836, three Baldwin locomotives were exported to Cuba, then a Spanish territory. These would have been for the line between the capital, Havana and the small town of Bejueal in La Habana Province. It opened in July 1837.

● LEFT
The 4-4-0 was the classic locomotive type in the first few decades of railroading in America, because it provided a good turn of speed and stability over inevitably roughly laid tracks. This example, from the 1840s-50s, was exported to Chile and is pictured in Santiago.

● ARGENTINE CAUTION

Railways came to Argentina in 1857 when a line opened between the towns of Parque and Floresta. The line manager had so little faith in his own product that he rode on horseback to the opening rather than trust himself to his own railway. The four-wheeled engine used on this occasion was La Portena, a locomotive which had been used in the Crimea, Ukraine.

B CLASS

Date	1906
Builder	Beyer, Peacock, Manchester, England
Client	Buenos Aires and Great Southern (BAGS)
Gauge	5 ft 6 in
Driving wheels	6 ft
Capacity	Cylinders 19 x 26 in (high pressure) $27^1/_2$ x 26 in (low pressure)
Weight in full working order	115 tons

● AMERICAN INFLUENCE IN BRAZIL

The first railway in Brazil, a short 5 ft 3 in gauge line in the neighbourhood of Rio de Janeiro, the then capital, opened in 1854. The inaugural train was hauled by the 2-2-2 Baroneza. The bulk of Brazil's railway track was laid to metre gauge, though in 1889 the Huain railway was built to the peculiar gauge of 3 ft $1^1/_4$ in. Most Brazilian woodburning locomotives of the 19th century were supplied by American builders. Typical was a series of relatively small 2-8-0s from Baldwin with driving wheels of only 3 ft 1 in diameter.

● BELOW
This classic 4-6-0 two-cylinder compound was built by Beyer, Peacock for the British-owned 5 ft 6 in gauge Buenos Aires and Great Southern Railway (BAGS). These locomotives were a principal express-passenger type for many years.

● LEFT
Another early 4-4-0, almost certainly of European origin and sporting a cowl, is pictured heading a tourist-train in the desert border region between Tacna in Peru and Arica in Chile, disputed territory until 1930.

● **LEFT**
Superficially American in style, this British engine has no running-plate but plate-frames, splashers and a brass dome. It was built by Sharp, Stewart at Springburn Works, Glasgow, Scotland, in 1892 for Brazil's metre-gauge Mogiana Railway. It hauled trains of varnished teak coaches through the Atlantic seaboard's lush tropical scenery.

● MEXICAN CHOICES

In Mexico, a 424 km (265 mile) line opened in 1873 between the capital Mexico City and the seaport Veracruz. The railway was an early user of double-boilered Fairlie 0-6-6-0 tanks. These were successful, unlike the totally impractical American-built Johnstone articulateds of 1888. These were so large they had to be partly dismantled to pass through the 2,608 m (8,560 ft) high Raton Tunnel, Colorado, during delivery. The Mexicans, ever willing to try another form of flexible wheelbase engine, in 1890 bought two Baldwin Mason-Fairlie articulated 2-6-6 tanks. This engine was essentially an American interpretation of the single Fairlie principle, with a power-bogie and a trailing-truck supporting a large boiler with deep firebox.

● **ABOVE**
Numberplate and worksplate of the Leopoldina Railway.

● **RIGHT**
This metre-gauge 2-6-0 was one of a class of 15 engines built by Beyer, Peacock of Manchester, England, at the end of the 19th century for Brazil's Leopoldina Railway. The Leopoldina system, all on the metre gauge, has approximately 3,200 km (2,000 miles) of track and was owned by the British-controlled Leopoldina Railway Co.

The Golden Age 1900–50

The first half of the 20th century may truly be called the Golden Age of railways. The railway was the primary form of transport for moving people and freight. The railway was perceived as being the heartbeat of society. Furthermore, throughout the period the vast majority of the world's railways were powered by steam. The period began with a legacy of modest 19th century locomotive designs, which rapidly gave way to 20th century concepts – larger, heavier and more powerful engines, which by the advent of World War II had evolved almost to the ultimate potential within the existing loading gauges. One of the many precepts that accelerated the world change from steam to modern forms of traction was that the necessary power and speeds demanded by railway administrations were outstripping the capacity of steam within the physical restrictions imposed on it.

● **ABOVE**
In the late 19th century the principle of compounding was adopted by many railways throughout the world. Shortly after the turn of the century, Britain's Midland Railway produced a set of 4-4-0s in which two high-pressure cylinders exhausted into a larger low-pressure one. Building continued after the grouping under the London, Midland & Scottish (LMS) Railway and the Midland. Compounds have gone down in locomotive history as one of the most successful classes and remained in Britain until their demise in the 1950s.

● **OPPOSITE**
One of Germany's magnificent unrebuilt Reichbahn Standard 01-class Pacifics seen in the soft countryside north of Dresden, Saxony, with an express from Berlin. The Pacific is pictured in charge of a 450-ton train. Coal-fired, these engines operated on timings faster than a mile a minute and were Europe's last high-speed steam expresses.

BRITISH MAIN-LINE LOCOMOTIVES – PASSENGER

• **BELOW**
The 4-6-0 manifested in both inside- and outside-cylinder form. The former type shown here is one of Holden's Great Eastern engines introduced in 1911 with 6 ft 6 in-diameter wheels, which gave them speed over the flat lands of eastern England.

The turn of the century saw the elegance of the Atlantic-type locomotive established on the main lines of Britain. The type soon led to the Pacific, which in essence was an Atlantic with an extra pair of driving wheels. When Gresley introduced his A1 Pacifics to the Great Northern Railways (GNR) in 1922, they represented in terms of size and power as large an increase over the GN's biggest Atlantic as the first Atlantics of 1898 exerted over the earlier 4-4-2 singles. The Pacific represented the end of the evolutionary line. Nothing bigger ever appeared in Britain, apart from Gresley's incursions into huge 2-8-2 Mikados and his solitary 4-6-4.

The Pacific captured the popular imagination, especially during the competition for Scottish traffic over Britain's East and West Coast routes in the early 1930s. Worldwide, the streamlined Pacifics of this decade generated much publicity. Gresley's A4s proved to be the "Concordes" of their day and have become the most celebrated British locomotive type. No. 4468 Mallard achieved the world speed record for steam traction of 126 mph in 1938.

The Pacific as an express passenger locomotive was backed up by the 4-6-0, which began to become profuse after the turn of the century. By 1923, the 4-6-0 in both two- and four-cylinder form was

● **RIGHT**
In the 1920s, need arose for an extra passenger locomotive on Britain's Southern Railway, one able to work a 500-ton train at an average speed of almost one mile a minute. So, four-cylinder Lord Nelsons were introduced. They totalled a class of 16 engines named after famous British Sea Lords. These engines worked the Continental Expresses between Victoria Station, London, and the English channel port of Dover, and served the south-western sections of Britain's Southern network.

widespread, largely replacing the Atlantic. Not until 1933 did the first Stanier Pacific take the title of the most powerful express-passenger-locomotive type away from the 4-6-0. In 1930, the 4-4-0 made its last flourish with Britain's Southern Railway's three-cylinder Schools engine, the most powerful of this wheel arrangement ever to run in the country.

From the mid-1930s, the 4-6-0 became increasingly used as the basis for powerful mixed-traffic types. In this guise, it continued to play an important role in main-line passenger duties. With Britain's policy of frequent and relatively light trains, the 4-6-0, despite its restrictive firebox capacity, was sufficient, with the quality of coal available, to provide the necessary power and adhesion for most express duties until the end of steam. The next logical step, to the 4-8-0, although proposed, was never taken.

● **BELOW**
Britain's Great Western Railway experimented with compounding in 1903 when Churchward introduced several engines on the De Glehn system. The first engine was built at Belfort, France, and named Le France. These compound Atlantics did not convince the Great Western to adopt the principle and they progressed to ultimate success with conventional 4-6-0s of two- and four-cylinder varieties.

PRINCESS CORONATION CLASS

Date	1937
Builder	Crewe Works, Cheshire, England
Client	London, Midland & Scottish Railway
Gauge	Standard
Driving wheels	6 ft 9 in
Capacity	4 cylinders 16 x 28 in
Total weight in full working order	165 tons

● **OPPOSITE**
William Stanier followed up his Princess Royal Pacifics with the Princess Coronations introduced in 1937. They hauled many of the heaviest trains on Britain's West Coast route until the end of steam.

● **ABOVE**
One of W.P. Read's Atlantics. These were the largest engines built for the North British Railway. They were introduced in 1906 and given Scottish names such as Aberdonian, Waverley and Highland Chief. They worked on the North British main lines, especially on the heavily graded Waverley route between Edinburgh and Carlisle in Cumbria.

British Main-line Locomotives – Freight

The freight locomotive's evolution was less dramatic than that of its express passenger-hauling counterpart. The inside-cylinder 0-6-0s and 0-8-0s so prolific in the late-19th century continued to be built into the 20th century, although a major advance occurred in 1903 when Churchward introduced his 2800 class 2-8-0s. The 2-8-0 was pre-eminent until the end of steam. Churchward's engines were followed by Robinson's 04s for the Great Central Railway in 1911. Two years later, the 2-8-0 was taken up by Gresley on the Great Northern Railway. The London, Midland and Scottish (LMS) built most 2-8-0s: Stanier's 8Fs for LMS totalled 772 locomotives.

The modest size of British freight engines was given a massive boost in 1927 when the LMS introduced its 2-6-6-2T Garratts. These were built by Beyer Peacock of Manchester, northern England, to alleviate the double-heading of inside-cylinder 0-6-0s on Britain's Midland main line. Of these four-cylinder giants, 33 went into operation and demonstrated a potency hitherto unknown on Britain's railways. Gresley turned to the 2-8-2 with his P1s of 1925. Two of these giants were built and hauled coal-trains weighing upwards of 2,000 tons.

The 2-8-2 was the next logical phase of development; as compared with the 2-10-1, it readily provided for a deep firebox with adequate space for the ashpan. Sadly, however, no further heavyfreight hauling 2-8-2s were ever built for use on the home railway, and the ultimate in British freight locomotives

● BELOW
Stanier's class 8F 2-8-0s were freight engines and provided Britain's LMS with a robust heavyfreight locomotive. They were a huge advance on the 0-6-0 and 0-8-0 types.

● BELOW LEFT
Britain's first 2-10-0s were built for the Ministry of Supply in World War II by the North British works in Glasgow. With their more numerous 2-8-0 counterparts, they served in many countries during the war. The example shown here was taken into the stock of Greek State Railways.

● BELOW RIGHT
Gresley's V2 2-6-2 Green Arrow was one of the most successful classes in British locomotive history. They were true mixed-traffic engines capable of enormous haulage. They did monumental service in World War II and were popularly known in Britain as "the engines which won the war". Here, one is seen on the rollers of the British locomotive-testing plant at Swindon, Wiltshire.

was the 2-10-0. This was not truly established until the 1950s, under the British Railways (BR) standard locomotive scheme. The 2-10-0s had first appeared as an Austerity version of the World War II 2-8-0s used for military operations, but these were primarily for light-axle loadings rather than sustained heavy haulage. The BR 9Fs were mineral haulers in their own right and building continued until 1960. An engine of this design became the last main-line locomotive built for Britain. It was named Evening Star. The 9Fs had a very short life for by 1968 steam operation in Britain ceased. They went to the scrapyard with all earlier forms of British freight locomotives – inside-cylinder 0-6-0s and 0-8-0s and the main 2-8-0 types.

LMS GARRATT

Date	1927
Builder	Beyer Peacock, Manchester, England
Client	London, Midland & Scottish Railway
Gauge	Standard
Driving wheels	5 ft 3 in
Capacity	4 cylinders 18 x 26 in
Steam pressure	190 lb sq in
Total weight in full working order	156 tons
Tractive effort	45,620 lbs

● **ABOVE LEFT**
The inside-cylinder 4-6-0 appeared on Scotland's Caledonian Railway in 1902. Over the next 12 years, the company's chief mechanical engineer (CME) J. F. McIntosh produced six different designs totalling 42 locomotives.

● **ABOVE RIGHT**
One of Churchward's 2800-class 2-8-0s introduced in 1903. The design caused his successor, Collett, to produce more between 1938-42 with only slight variations. Very few classes in British locomotive history have been built over a period as long as 40 years.

● **BELOW**
The LMS Garratt was a most exciting development in British freight-locomotive history. The engines were built for the LMS by Beyer Peacock. The class totalled 33 engines and hauled coal-trains over the Midland main line between Toton (Nottingham) and Cricklewood (north London). They took the place of two inside-cylinder 0-6-0s.

British Shunters and Industrial Locomotives

The traditional main-line shunting tank has been either an 0-4-0 or, more commonly, an 0-6-0. Numerous designs were created, especially Britain's LMS Jinty 0-6-0, of which more than 500 were built, and the Great Western 5700-class 0-6-0 pannier tanks, totalling 863 examples. Many more classes of 0-6-0 and even 0-8-0 tanks would have been built for shunting had not these forms of locomotives been heavily supplemented by downgraded inside-cylinder 0-6-0s and 0-8-0s. These engines, important main-line freight haulers in the closing years of the 19th century, became ideal heavy shunters and tripping engines in their later years. Wagons had grown bigger, loads much heavier and the abundance of these downgraded freight engines meant the traditional 0-6-0 tank-engine did not evolve to any great size, remaining largely unchanged for almost a century.

Some larger marshalling yards – especially those with humps – needed something bigger than the 0-6-0, so special designs evolved to fill this niche. The first of these giants appeared in 1907 when John George Robinson introduced a three-cylinder 0-8-4T for humping at the Great Central Railway's Wath Yards, in the North Riding of Yorkshire. Two years later, the ever-prolific Wilson Worsdell, CME of the North Eastern Railway, put into traffic some three-cylinder 4-8-0Ts. The LNWR introduced the first 30 0-8-2Ts in 1911, followed by 30 0-8-4Ts. These two classes were, in effect, a heavy tank-engine version of their standard 0-8-0 freight engines.

The definitive industrial locomotive evolved as either a side or saddle tank, four- or six-coupled. Larger industrial locomotives invariably came in the form of former main-line engines, which had been sold out of service. This practice led to tender-engines appearing on industrial lines. These environments often gave a massive extension of life to engines that

GWR 5700 CLASS

Date	1929
Builder	Swindon Works, Wiltshire, England
Client	Great Western Railway
Gauge	Standard
Driving wheels	4 ft 7 in
Capacity	2 cylinders 17 x 24 in
Steam pressure	200 lb sq in
Total weight in full working order	51 tons
Tractive effort	2,255 lbs

● LEFT
Britain's Great Western Railway adopted the pannier tank for shunting operations. GWR's ultimate design was Collett's 5700-class with 4 ft 7 in wheels. Between 1929-49, 863 engines were built. When building ended, they were the largest class in Britain.

● LEFT
Worldwide, anywhere that was anywhere had steam railways. The steam locomotive was the prime source of motive power for all facets of industry. In Britain, typical of the diversity of the locomotive's locations was the railway network at Cadbury's chocolate-factory.

● BELOW LEFT
Andrew Barclay & Son, locomotive builders of Kilmarnock, Strathclyde, south-west Scotland, were famous for a long range of 0-4-0 and 0-6-0 saddle-tanks, which formed a distinctive family of engines built almost unchanged over a 70-year period. Here, one of their 0-4-0s works on the Storefield Ironstone system in Northamptonshire, in the English Midlands, taking iron ore to the connection with British Railways' main line.

had outlived their normal life span on main lines.

The basic industrial engine changed little in its century of pre-eminence. One fascinating variation, however, occurred in the form of the Fireless, of which some 200 worked in Britain. These engines were a low-cost shunting unit for industries with a ready supply of high-pressure steam. They took their steam secondhand from the works' boilers.

Up until World War II, several thousand industrial engines were active the length and breadth of Britain. Many survived in their industrial habitats after main-line steam working ended in 1968. This was historically appropriate. The world's first steam locomotive, created in a South Wales ironworks in 1804, was an industrial.

● BELOW LEFT
Britain's LMS Jinty 0-6-0s represented the ultimate manifestation of a long line of Midland Railway 0-6-0 shunting-tanks. They were found all over the English part of the LMS system in the years before most freight carriage was transferred from rail to road.

● BELOW RIGHT
Andrew Barclay pioneered the Fireless type in Britain and built many examples, both 0-4-0 and 0-6-0, for industrial establishments. The Fireless was arguably the most efficient and economical shunting unit ever devised.

British Main-line Tank Engines

The engines that worked suburban trains around Britain's great cities and conurbations were almost exclusively tank designs. The absence of a tender facilitated ease of running in either direction and cut out cumbersome and time-consuming turning. Also, the water's weight above the coupled wheels provided adhesion useful for rapid starts from stations. For similar reasons, tank-engines were favoured on branch lines across Britain.

In the 19th century, the urban and branch-line tank-engine evolved in many forms: 2-4-0, 4-4-0, 4-4-2, 0-4-2, 0-4-4 and 0-6-0.

The 0-4-4 was particularly favoured. It had flexibility to run in either direction. Its boiler and cylinder blocks were often interchangeable with sister inside-cylinder 0-6-0s and inside-cylinder 4-4-0 express-passenger engines.

As the population of Britain's cities grew, so did the suburban tank's proportions. It graduated to the 4-4-2 and by the turn of the century, with the harmonious 4-4-4, in sheer aesthetic terms, reached its pièce de résistance, the ultimate in balanced proportions.

The most remarkable suburban engine was Holden's Decapod 0-10-0T for the Great Eastern Railway (GER). Advocates of electrification claimed that a 315-ton train could be accelerated to 30 mph in 30 seconds. Holden, in producing his Decapod, proved that this achievement could be bettered with steam. As a result,

• LEFT
Britain's London and North Western Railway used many tank engines on suburban and branch lines, particularly 0-6-2 and 2-4-2 types. For faster intermediate work, Bowen Cooke introduced this class of 4-6-2 superheated tank engine.

• BELOW
An 0-6-0 shunting-tank of Britain's North Eastern Railway, from a class of 120 engines built between 1886–95. The type's suitability is shown by the introduction of a second and similar batch in 1898 of which 85 were built by 1925. Then, 28 more were built between 1949–51, under British Railways. This created the unique situation of a design being built over a 54-year period. Possibly no other class in world locomotive history has achieved this distinction.

● LEFT
The 0-4-4 T's flexibility was shown by this example from England's North Staffordshire Railway. Classified as "M", five examples of the type were built in 1907–8.

● BELOW
Britain's Great Western Railway (GWR) achieved excellent standardization in all categories of motive power. For suburban and branch-line work, Churchward introduced a range of 2-6-2s.

the proposed electrification of GER's suburban services from London's Liverpool Street Station was shelved. Alas, the Decapod was so heavy on the track that it never entered service.

Six-coupled engines in the form of 0-6-2s and 0-6-4s progressed to 2-6-2s and 2-6-4s, the preferred power from the 1930s onwards. Many of these engines were mixed-traffic types, equally suited for cross-country and branch-line work as well.

LNER CLASS J72 0-6-0T	
Date	1898
Builder	Darlington Locomotive Works, Co. Durham, England
Client	North Eastern Railway; London & North Eastern Railway; British Railways
Gauge	4 ft 8 in
Driving wheels	4 ft 1 in
Capacity	2 cylinders 17 x 24 in
Steam pressure	140 lb sq in
Weight	43 tons
Tractive effort	16,760 lbs

Electrification – especially of metropolitan and suburban services – progressively eroded the need for tank engines, particularly on Britain's Southern Railway. A partial erosion of need also occurred on branch lines, where demoted express-passenger designs of earlier years were used, 2-4-0s and 4-4-0s being especially common.

The tank-engine is popularly thought of as something of a plodding machine. In truth, many were extremely fast runners, and speeds of 70 mph were quite normal on many suburban and outer-suburban workings, some of which were very tightly timed and had to be fitted in between the paths of more important, longer-distance trains.

● BELOW
This engine belonged to a class of Ivatt 0-6-2Ts with 5 ft 8 in wheels, built for the Great Northern Railway (GNR) between 1906–12. The class totalled 56 engines. These appeared prolifically on suburban workings out of London's Kings Cross Station. Many had condensing apparatus for working through metropolitan tunnels. In their later years, many were found on suburban workings around Leeds and Bradford, in west Yorkshire.

British Exports

The steam-locomotive was arguably Britain's greatest technological contribution to mankind. Her lead in railways ensured wide opportunities, and she became railway builder to her empire and the world. A vast locomotive industry developed quite separately from that of the famous railway towns, which served Britain's domestic needs. Legendary foundries in Glasgow, Scotland, and in the English provinces at Leeds in Yorkshire, Newcastle upon Tyne in Northumberland (now Tyne and Wear), Darlington in Durham, Manchester and other parts of Lancashire, and in Stafford, west central England, sent locomotives worldwide, often exporting the industrial revolution with them. Lands beyond the British Empire were served, including those having no political affinity with Britain. Exported locomotives reflected the designs of engines running in the mother country, and the types of engines seen rolling through the soft English countryside were soon found crossing barren, rugged and jungle-clad landscapes in many countries of Africa, Australia, South-east Asia and South America.

Britain's role as locomotive-builder to the world remained largely unchallenged throughout the 19th century, but the early 20th saw serious competition for the first time, especially from America and, to a lesser extent, from builders in continental Europe. America's engines were a commercial threat and also challenged conventional British design. These, though produced by skilled craftsmen, nonetheless had deficiencies. These, not apparent in Britain, caused problems in the rough-and-tumble of world railways.

● LEFT
Manning Wardle of Leeds, west Yorkshire, built this Crane Tank locomotive in 1903. It lifted tree trunks at an Indian sawmill, replacing elephants.

● LEFT
The lineage of these British build Pacifics is fully shown in this scene of a South African Railways 3 ft 6 in gauge 16CR heading over flood waters of the tidal Swartkops River in Port Elizabeth, Cape Province, South Africa.

● RIGHT
One of a group of Moguls built in 1899 by Beyer Peacock of Manchester, Lancashire, for Brazil's Leopoldina Railway. This Mogul is an example of exported types being used abroad before coming into service in the country of manufacture.

● **RIGHT**
In East Africa, the scrublands of Tanzania resounded to the wail of British locomotives in the 1920s after the territory was mandated to Britain at the end of World War I, when it was known as Tanganyika. This light-axle 2-8-2 was ideal for riding the lightly laid and rough track beds common in Africa.

BAGNALL 2-8-2	
Date	1947
Builder	Bagnall's of Stafford, Staffordshire, England
Client	Tanganyika Railway, East Africa
Gauge	Metre
Driving wheels	3 ft 7 in
Capacity	Cylinders 17 x 23 in
Steam pressure	180 lb sq in
Total weight full working order	100 tons
Tractive effort	25,050 lb

Most British locomotives had small fireboxes set between the frames, a restriction that caused steaming difficulties when inferior coal was used.

Traditional British plate frames gave problems when engines ran on the developing world's poor quality tracks. American engines had wide fireboxes suitable for inferior fuel. Their bar-frames enjoyed greater tolerance in adverse conditions. Some British locomotives' limited bearing surfaces also gave trouble in rough conditions. American engines' bearing proportions were more generous.

An immediate effect of America's aggressive export drive in the early 20th century was the amalgamation in 1903 of Glasgow's three big builders – Sharp Stewart, Neilson and Dübs – to form the North British Locomotive Company. Although there was a shift towards a more international design of locomotive, created in the light of world experience, British builders retained a significant role right to the end of the steam age.

● **RIGHT**
Britain's private locomotive builders often built for companies in Britain whose works were unable to supply engines quickly enough. Here, at the North British Works in Glasgow, Scotland, an LNER class B1 4-6-0 is in the background, by a light-axle loaded 2-8-2 for East African Railways.

British Record-breakers and Streamliners

The commonly held view that the steam-locomotive was replaced because it was slow is incorrect. Many of today's diesel and even electrically operated services are not appreciably faster than steam was 50 or more years ago.

The magical three-figure speed was reached in 1903 by the Great Western Railway's 4-4-0 City of Truro. This achieved 102.3 mph down Wellington Bank in Somerset, south-west England, with an Ocean Mails train, the first time any form of transport reached 100 mph.

GWR featured in another speed dash, with a Churchward Saint Class 4-6-0, which allegedly reached 120 mph while running light engine on a test trip after an overhaul at Swindon works in Wiltshire. This alleged achievement is not authenticated, but over the years authorities have claimed it to be true.

The 1930s, the "streamlined era", were a time of epic record-breaking runs all over the world. Streamlining was in vogue. It inspired and fascinated the public, but its usefulness in reaching high speeds was soon questioned.

The legendary speed records of the

LNER A4 PACIFIC

Date	1935
Builder	Doncaster Works, south Yorkshire
Client	London & North Eastern Railway
Gauge	Standard
Driving wheels	6 ft 8 in
Capacity	3 cylinders 18 x 26 in
Total weight in full working order	167 tons
Steam pressure	250 lb sq in
Tractive effort	33,455 lb

● **BELOW**
Great Western Railway's Castles were distinguished among British express-passenger designs. They first appeared in 1923. Their exploits on the Cheltenham Flyer were legendary, and for some years the Flyer was the world's fastest train. In 1924 the engine shown, No. 4079 Pendennis Castle, running from Paddington, London, to Plymouth, Devon, averaged 60 mph between Paddington and Westbury, Wiltshire, with a 530-tonne train.

● **LEFT**
The LNER's plaque affixed to the boiler of Mallard to commemorate its world record-breaking run in 1938.

● **BELOW**
The LNER class-A4 No.4468 Mallard, dubbed the world's fastest steam locomotive. Mallard's record may remain unbeaten.

● **BELOW**
The Princess Royals were followed by the Princess Coronations. One of these engines, streamlined, briefly held the world record for steam traction of 114 mph. Over the years after World War II, all streamlined examples lost their casing.

● **ABOVE**
Stanier's record-breaking Princess Royal Pacific No. 6201 Princess Elizabeth, which in 1936 covered the 401 miles between Glasgow, Scotland, and London Euston in 5 hours 44 minutes – an average speed of 70 mph. Almost 60 years later, in November 1996, the *Daily Telegraph* reported that many electrically operated services on the West Coast route were slower than Princess Elizabeth's epic run.

1930s were again the result of competition between the East and West Coast routes linking London and Scotland. Both the LMS and the LNER had brand new designs of Pacific locomotives in service – streamlined Coronations on the former and Gresley A4s on the latter.

In terms of maximum speed, the LMS bid for the world speed record on 29 June 1937 when a special run of the Coronation Scot was made for the press six days before the service's official start. The locomotive, No. 6220 Coronation, reached 114 mph down Madeley Bank on the approaches to Crewe, Cheshire, in northern England. Alas, the bank was not long enough and the train was still doing 60-70 mph when the platform signal came into sight and rapid braking for a standstill in Crewe Station smashed all the crockery in the dining car.

The LNER would not countenance the LMS taking the honour in this way. Almost a year later, on 3 July 1938, the A4 class Pacific Mallard, ostensibly on a special run to test braking, achieved 126 mph on the descent of Stoke Bank, between Grantham in Lincolnshire and Peterborough in Cambridgeshire, eastern England, thus beating the LMS and setting a never-beaten world speed record for the steam locomotive.

Non-streamlined activity in the 1930s was also exciting, not least with the Cheltenham Flyer express, which was booked to run the 77.3 miles from Paddington, London, to Swindon, Wiltshire, in 65 minutes. On one occasion the distance was covered in 56 minutes. This involved a start-to-stop average of 82 mph.

World War II ended any such performances and in the postwar period the railway network's recovery was slow. Not until the 1950s did three-figure speeds with steam reappear.

American Mikados

The 2-8-2 Mikado-type locomotive was developed in 1897 for Japancsc Railways by the Baldwin Locomotive Works, the largest and most prolific locomotive-builder in the United States of America.

● LEFT
Denver & Rio Grande Western used several classes of 36 in gauge Mikados on its narrow-gauge lines in Colorado. A K36 and larger K37 are seen at Chama, New Mexico. The K37s were rebuilt from standard-gauge locomotives.

● AN AMERICAN ENGINE FOR JAPAN

The Mikado-type locomotive derives its name from this first owner, though during World War II, when America was fighting Japan, American nationalists tried to change the name to "MacArthur-type". Many Americans call these locomotives "Mikes".

In 1905, the Northern Pacific Railway was the first railroad to embrace the Mikado in large numbers. The locomotive quickly caught on, and many were produced for many railroads until about 1930. Some 10,000 were built for domestic use, and more than 4,000 were built for export.

● A SOLID DESIGN

The 2-8-2 wheel arrangement was a natural progression from the popular 2-8-0 Consolidation-type and 2-6-2 Prairie-type. The Mikado's overall design was outstanding. It was well balanced, providing excellent tractive effort and a good ride. The trailing truck allowed for a larger firebox, therefore more steam capacity and larger cylinders, giving the engine greater power than earlier designs which it rendered obsolete. When technological advances such as superheating were developed, they were used on the Mikado to great success. The locomotive's primary application was heavy freight service, though many railroads used lighter Mikes on branch lines.

● NARROW-GAUGE APPLICATION

The Mikado type was particularly well adapted to narrow-gauge freight service because of its balanced design and four sets of drivers. These provided the traction needed on heavy mountain grades, while producing only minimum wear and tear on lightweight track and right-of-way. In the West, Denver & Rio Grande Western (D&RGW) operated four classes of Mikado on its rugged mountain grades. Its

● LEFT
Saginaw Timber No. 2 is a light Mikado typically used on short lines for hauling freight and passengers.

● **LEFT**
Pennsylvania Railroad (PRR) No. 1596, a Class-L1s Mikado-type, features a boxy Belpaire-type firebox, standard on most late-era PRR steam locomotives. It is pictured near the end of its active life, at Enola, Pennsylvania.

line over the 3,048 m (10,003 ft) high Cumbres Pass, in the San Juan Mountains of south Colorado, featured gruelling 4 per cent grades, which gave the 3 ft narrow-gauge Mikado a real proving ground. In the East, narrow-gauge coal hauler East Broad Top also preferred the Mikados, owning several from Baldwin. Many of these narrow-gauge locomotives are preserved in working order.

MISSOURI PACIFIC MIKADO TYPE

Date	1923
Builder	American Locomotive Co. (Alco)
Client	Missouri Pacific
Gauge	4 ft $8\frac{1}{2}$ in
Driving wheels	65 in
Capacity	2 cylinders 27 x 32 in
Steam pressure	200 lb
Weight	305,115 lb
Tractive effort	62,950 lb

● **RIGHT**
The Duluth & Northern Minnesota's Mikado No. 14 clips along north of Duluth, Minnesota. This light Mikado was built by Baldwin in 1913.

● **RIGHT**
This 2-8-2 Mikado-type was built by the American Locomotive Company (Alco) at its Brooks Works in 1920. It worked for the Aberdeen & Rockfish Railroad, and serves the Valley Railroad at Essex, Connecticut, New Maryland.

AMERICAN ARTICULATED LOCOMOTIVES

The Mallet-type compound articulated steam locomotive, named after Swiss inventor Anatole Mallet, had been popular in Europe for decades before its eventual introduction in the United States of America.

● OPPOSITE TOP
The Baltimore & Ohio's articulated 2-8-8-2 Class KK1 was an experimental locomotive that featured a water-tube boiler (most American locomotives had fire-tube boilers). It delivered a 90,000 lb tractive effort.

● LEFT
Union Pacific (UP) 4-6-6-4 Challenger-type simple articulated No. 3985 at Portola, California. UP owned more than 100 locomotives of this type for heavy-freight service in western USA.

● B&O EMPLOYS THE MALLET

After the turn of the century, a need for greater tractive effort led American railroads to employ articulated steam locomotives with two sets of driving wheels. The compound articulated engine reused steam from high-pressure cylinders, in low-pressure cylinders, to achieve maximum efficiency. On most Mallets, very large low-pressure cylinders were used at the first set of drivers, while high-pressure cylinders were used at the second.

In 1904, the American Locomotive Company (Alco) built the first American Mallet-type, a 0-6-6-0 compound articulated nicknamed "Old Maud", for the Baltimore & Ohio Railroad (B&O), a coalhauler facing many steep grades. While Mallet-types were effective for slow-speed service, few railroads used them for general service on the main line.

BALTIMORE & OHIO MALLET-TYPE NO. 2400 "OLD MAUD"

Date	1904
Builder	American Locomotive Co. (Alco)
Client	Baltimore & Ohio Railroad
Gauge	4 ft 8½ in
Driving wheels	56 in
Capacity	4 cylinders: 2 (20 x 32 in) and 2 (32 x 32 in)
Steam pressure	235 lb
Weight	334,500 lb
Tractive effort	71,500 lb

● THE SIMPLE ARTICULATED GAINS POPULARITY

The articulated concept achieved greater popularity in a more traditional format. This was the simple articulated engine, which has two sets of cylinders but does not reuse steam. Most articulated engines

● LEFT
The Baltimore & Ohio's No. 2400 was the first American locomotive to use the Mallet design. It was built in 1904 by Alco and widely known as "Old Maud". It weighed 334,500 lb and had a 71,500 lb tractive effort.

built after about 1910 were not compounds and thus not true Mallets. While many railroads preferred simple articulated engines, the Norfolk & Western (N&WR) continued to perfect the Mallet. The N&WR class-Y6b built by the railroad's Roanoke shops in North Carolina for main-line service represented the zenith of the type. N&WR was one of the last American railroads to use Mallets in regular main-line service.

The development of articulated steam locomotives, combined with other improvements such as mechanical stokers and superheaters, eventually led to the building of the world's largest locomotives. Among the largest articulateds were the 2-8-8-4 Yellowstone type used by Northern Pacific and ore-hauler Duluth, Missabi & Iron Range (DM&IR); the 2-6-6-6 Allegheny type built by the Lima Locomotive works for the Chesapeake & Ohio and Virginian Railway, in 1941 and 1945 respectively; and the 4-8-8-4 Big Boy type built for Union Pacific lines between 1941–44.

● SOUTHERN PACIFIC CAB FORWARD

The Southern Pacific (SP) developed a unique variation of the articulated engine. The traditional steam locomotive configuration featuring the cab behind the boiler proved unsatisfactory on the big articulateds when operating in the long tunnels and snowsheds found on the 2,174 metre (7,135 ft) Donner Pass in California's Sierra Nevada. Crews suffered from smoke inhalation. So SP turned the engine around, placing the cab in front of the boiler. The first of SP's 256 cab-forward articulated was a Mallet-type built in 1910. The last were Baldwin-built articulated 2-8-8-4 types, the SP class-AC-12, built in 1944.

● **ABOVE**
Among the heaviest articulated steam locomotives ever built were 2-8-8-4 Yellowstone types made for Northern Pacific (NP) and Duluth, Missabi & Iron Range (DM&IR).

● **RIGHT**
Norfolk & Western continued to perfect the Mallet compound-articulated-locomotive design long after other railroads adopted the simple articulated. An N&WR Y6 Mallet 2-8-8-2 pictured near Blue Ridge Summit, West Virginia, in 1958.

American Pacifics

● **BELOW**
The Baltimore & Ohio's Pacific type, No. 5305.

● **OPPOSITE TOP**
The Louisville & Nashville's Pacific-type No. 152 was built by Alco's Rogers Works in January 1905. This locomotive served the railroad for nearly 50 years.

The 4-6-2 Pacific-type steam locomotive came into favour shortly after the turn of the century and was produced widely for many American railroads until the 1930s.

● PREMIER PASSENGER POWER

This locomotive followed the logical developmental progression from the 4-4-0 American-type, 4-4-2 Atlantic-type and, to a lesser extent, the 2-6-2 Prairie-type. Most Pacifics, designed for high-speed passenger service, had relatively large fireboxes and high drivers. By 1915, this type had supplanted 4-6-0 Ten Wheelers and 4-4-2 Atlantics on crack passenger-trains. All around America, flashy high-drivered Pacifics were hauling name trains. These included Northern Pacific's luxurious North Coast Limited, Southern Pacific's Sunset Limited and the Pennsylvania Railroad's Broadway Limited.

● THE PACIFIC ADAPTS WELL TO NEW TECHNOLOGY AND STYLES

The Pacific-type was well suited to technological improvements. Superheating, mechanical stokers and roller bearings were developed. Superheating recirculated hot steam through the engine's firetubes, allowing for more power and greater efficiency. These developments were applied to both new and existing Pacifics, dramatically improving the performance of the engines. In the 1930s, when streamlined trains became the latest thing in railroad style, some railroads dressed up their Pacifics in snazzy shrouds.

● PENNSYLVANIA RAILROAD K4

The best-known, most loved and perhaps the best-performing Pacific was the Pennsylvania Railroad's Class K4. PPR received its first Pacific-type from Alco in 1907, an experimental locomotive Class K28. This locomotive led to several other

classes of Pacific, with the culmination of design exhibited in the 1914 Class K4. A masterpiece of engineering, the K4 was an outstanding performer. Eventually, Pennsylvania rostered some 425 K4s, an exceptional number for a single class of locomotive. They were the railroad's preferred passenger locomotive for nearly 30 years. Some K4s were built by Baldwin but many were constructed at the railroad's Juniata Shops. Like many PRR steam locomotives, the K4 featured the boxy Belpaire-type firebox. The last K4 was retired from regular service in 1957.

● **LEFT**
The Southern Pacific's No. 2472 was one of 15 Class-P8 Pacific types in the railroad's passenger fleet. These 1912 Baldwin-built locomotives had a 43,660-lb tractive effort.

● **ABOVE**
A highly polished Pennsylvania Railroad K4 Pacific, No. 5475.

PENNSYLVANIA RAILROAD K4 PACIFIC

Date	1914–28
Builder	Juniata Shops, Baldwin, Pennsylvania, USA
Client	Pennsylvania Railroad
Gauge	4 ft 8½ in
Driving wheels	80 in
Capacity	2 cylinders 27 x 28 in
Steam pressure	205 lb
Weight	468,000 lb
Tractive effort	44,460 lb

Shays and Switchers

American logging railroads had special locomotive requirements because their track, often crudely built, used very sharp curves and negotiated grades as steep as 10 per cent. Also, these railroads required locomotives that could haul relatively heavy loads at very slow speeds.

● Shays and Other Geared Locomotives

To meet these requirements, three builders specialized in constructing flexible, high-adhesion steam locomotives that operated with a geared drive, rather than the direct drive used on conventional locomotives. These builders were Lima, at Ohio, with the Shay-type; Heisler Locomotive Works, at Eire, Pennsylvania, and Climax Locomotive and Machine Works at Corry, Pennsylvania. Each builder used the same basic principle – a cylinder-driven shaft that connected to the driving wheels using bevelled gears – but each approached the concept slightly differently.

● **ABOVE**
This is a stock Shay, built by Lima in 1928. It was sold to the Mayo Lumber Company and operated in British Columbia, Canada. It is preserved, with other Shays, at the Cass Scenic Railroad, West Virginia, USA.

Lima's Shay was the most popular type. It used a row of vertical cylinders on the fireman's side, that is the right-hand side of the engine, to power a shaft that connected two or three sets of driving wheels. Two-cylinder Shays had two sets of driving wheels; three-cylinder Shays had three sets of driving wheels. The Shay-type was first constructed in the 1880s.

Heisler used two cylinders facing one another crosswise, one on each side of the locomotive, forming a V-pattern. These cylinders turned a shaft to power two sets of driving wheels. Climax used two parallel, sharply inclined cylinders, one on each side of the locomotive, to power a shaft connecting two sets of driving wheels.

● Switchers

Most railroads used specialized locomotives of a conventional design for switching service at yards, terminals and industrial sites. Because most switchers were relatively small locomotives, operated at slow speeds, and needed high adhesion to move long cuts of cars, they normally did not have pilot or trailing trucks – commonly used on road locomotives.

The smallest switchers were 0-4-0 types. This sort of locomotive, however, had low adhesion and a notoriously bad ride quality, so locomotives with more driving wheels were generally preferred. The 0-6-0 switcher was the most popular for general switching and about 10,000 were built. Some railroads used 0-8-0 switchers for heavier switching duties and, after the turn of the century, 0-10-0 switchers saw only limited service in hump yards.

Specialty tenderless switchers, with water-tanks built over the boilers, and "fireless" steam engines saw limited use in areas where conventional locomotives were inappropriate.

TYPICAL 0-6-0 SWITCHER

Date	About 1905
Builder	American Locomotive Co. (Alco)
Gauge	4 ft $8^1/_2$ in
Driving wheels	51 in
Capacity	2 cylinders 19 x 24 in
Steam pressure	180 lb
Weight	163,365 lb
Tractive effort	26,510 lb

● **OPPOSITE**
Heisler's geared locomotives use two cylinders in a V position. This Heisler was built in 1912 for the Louise Lumber Company of Hawkes, Mississippi. It operates on the Silver Creek & Stephenson Railroad in Freeport, Illinois, USA.

● **RIGHT**
The last of the Lima-built Shay-types were heavy, three-cylinder locomotives built in 1945. The Western Maryland railroad in the USA owned several of these big Shays. They weighed 324,000 lb and generated a 59,740 lb tractive effort.

● **ABOVE**
Locomotive 2-8-0, No. 207 (formerly Southern 630), and North American Rayon Company's fireless 0-6-0T, No. 1, on the East Tennessee and Western North Carolina Railroad, USA.

● **BELOW**
Surrounded by lumber, this Ely Thomas Lumber Company's Lima-built Shay-type No. 2 waits for its next run in 1958 near Gauley, West Virginia, USA.

American Exports

Nations around the world relied on the locomotive prowess of the United States of America to supply their motive-power needs. Of some 175,000 steam locomotives built in the USA in the 120 years between 1830 and 1950, about 37,000, more than 20 per cent, were built specifically for export. Many varieties of locomotives were sold, depending on customers' needs, but five types were particularly popular in the export market and represented the lion's share of those sold.

● CONSOLIDATIONS

The most popular export model was the 2-8-0 Consolidation. More than 10,000 were sold outside the USA. This model was the second most-popular domestic locomotive, too. More than 22,000 were built for use in the USA where only the 19th-century 4-4-0 American-type was more popular.

A distant second to the Consolidation was the 2-8-2 Mikado-type. More than 4,000 were exported. This type was specifically designed by Baldwin Locomotive Works for Japanese Railways in 1897. Later, it was adapted for domestic use. Many were used for freight service in the USA.

● DECAPODS FOR RUSSIA

The 2-10-0 Decapod was the third most-popular model. Many of the heavy locomotives went to Russia and to the Soviet Union during World Wars I and II. The Decapod was also popular in Germany, Greece, Poland and Turkey. Oddly, it was not very popular in the

MACARTHUR 2-8-2 USATC

Builder	Baldwin Locomotive Company, Eddystone, Pennsylvania, USA
Client	United States Army Transport Corps (USATC)
Gauge	Metre
Driving wheels	4 ft
Capacity	Cylinders 16 x 24 in
Weight in full working order	112 tons

● LEFT
One of the last surviving MacArthur 2-8-2s. These metre-gauge engines were built for the United States Army Transport Corps (USATC) for operations during World War II. They saw wide service in India, Burma, Thailand and the Philippines. After the war, survivors remained active. In India, they were classified MAWD (McArthur War Department) and found in the country's Northeast Frontier region.

● ABOVE
Cuba's Manuel Isla sugar mill is host to this vintage Baldwin 0-4-2 tank believed to have been built in 1882. A retired employee at the mill, 88-year-old Jose Alfonso Melgoragio, remembers knowing the engine all his life. He worked on it for 25 years.

● LEFT
This classic American ten-wheeler, built by Rogers of New Jersey in 1896, pictured at the San Barnado Locomotive Works near Santiago, Chile, where the veteran was ending its days as works pilot.

● ABOVE LEFT
A night scene in the mountains of the Philippines island of Negros. Two last survivors of their respective types are seen at the Insula Lumber Company. On the left, a Baldwin-built, four-cylinder compound Mallet; on the right, a vertical-cylinder Shay. These are classic American locomotives of the American Pacific Northwest.

domestic market. Only the Santa Fe and Pennsylvania Railroad owned large numbers. The Frisco picked up Decapods intended for Russia and used them successfully for many years. Of the 4,100 American-built Decapods, 3,400 were exported around the world.

● LEFT
A rare Baldwin 2-6-2 saddle-tank, known as the "Lavras Rose", which as Baldwin export order No. 372 of 1927 operated as a works shunter at Lavras in Mina Gerais State, Brazil.

● EXPORTS OF MOGULS AND TEN-WHEELERS

Nearly 3,000 2-6-0 Mogul-types were built for export. This locomotive was popular for heavy freight in the mid-19th century. Some 1,600 4-6-0 ten-wheeler types were also exported, nearly 10 per cent of American production. Of 3,800 geared locomotives built in the USA for use on steep grades and for specialty railroads, such as logging, 600 were exported.

● BELOW LEFT
This classic American switcher once worked for the 5 ft 3 in gauge Paulista Railway serving the city and Pernambuco state in eastern Brazil. It was built by Baldwin of Philadelphia, Pennsylvania, USA, in 1896. The veteran is pictured here pensioned off to industrial service at the Cosim Steelworks at São Paulo, Brazil.

Streamlined Steam

In 1934, at the height of the Great Depression, the Burlington railroad's Budd-built stainless-steel streamlined Pioneer Zephyr streaked across America.

● **STREAMLINING TAKES OFF**

Everywhere Pioneer Zephyr went, it inspired railroad managers and the riding public. In a similar vein, Union Pacific's streamlined City of Salina toured the West. These Winton engine-powered diesel articulated "trains of the future" soon resulted in the streamlining of a great many steam locomotives for passenger service. New locomotives, steam, diesel-electric and electric, were ordered as well, along with whole streamlined trains of luxurious passenger cars.

● **DRESSING UP THE OLD GUARD**

The railroads were quick to send crack passenger locomotives to shop for a fancy new dress. In 1936, Pennsylvania Railroad hired noted industrial designer Raymond Loewy to improve K4 No. 3768 aesthetically. The result was a flashy-looking locomotive. Many railroads dressed up their older locomotives with elaborate shrouding, though in some cases with less than superlative results. In many cases, shrouding hampered maintenance and was later removed.

● **BELOW**
The Chesapeake & Ohio railroad operated four Class L1 streamlined 4-6-4 Hudson types in passenger service. These odd-looking, yellow and stainless-steel adorned locomotives were nicknamed "Yellowbellies".

● **NEW STREAMLINERS**

The Milwaukee Road was one of the first railroads to order new streamlined steam locomotives. In 1935, it ordered high-speed 4-4-2s with 84 in driving wheels and shrouds designed by Otto Kuhler. Assigned to its Hiawathas, these fast engines would regularly zip at more than 100 mph between Chicago, Illinois, and Milwaukee, Wisconsin.

Beginning in the late 1930s, Southern Pacific's fleet of semi-streamlined 4-8-4 Northern types, painted in its flashy orange, red and silver "Daylight" scheme, marched about California. The epitome of this famous class were the 30 GS-4s and GS-5s built by the Lima works in 1941–42. These powerful engines exhibited some of the finest styling found on any North American locomotive.

Among the last types of streamlined locomotive built were the Norfolk & Western's J Class 4-8-4s, for service with its passenger-trains.

● **RIGHT**
The Norfolk & Western Railroad's Class-J Northerns, Nos. 600 to 612, were its most famous streamliners. These powerful locomotives could operate to a top speed of 110 mph but rarely needed to. N&WR operated other streamline steam as well, including its 800 Series Class K-2, 4-8-2 Mountains. Two N&WR Js pause for servicing in 1958.

● ABOVE
Canadian National Railway 4-8-4 No. 6402 passing through Toronto.

● BELOW
Southern Pacific owned a fleet of semi-streamlined, "Daylight"-painted 4-8-4 Northern types for fast passenger service. Of these, the best performing and most aesthetically pleasing were 30 Class GS-4s and GS-5s built in 1941–42.

SOUTHERN PACIFIC GS-4

Date	1941
Builder	Lima, Ohio, USA
Client	Southern Pacific
Gauge	4 ft 8½ in
Driving wheels	80 in
Capacity	2 cylinders 26 x 32 in
Steam pressure	300 lb
Weight	475,000 lb
Tractive effort	78,650 lb

The Network Expands – Decapods, Mountains, Santa Fes and Overlands

The railroads of the United States of America had an insatiable appetite for ever-larger, more powerful and more efficient locomotives. It stemmed from their belief that more powerful locomotives would produce lower operating costs through the ability to haul more goods, faster, with fewer crews and locomotives.

In the 19th century, locomotive output was limited to the size of the firebox and the fireman's ability to shovel coal. Early attempts at producing big locomotives usually resulted in curious behemoths that did not steam well and languished for lack of power. The development of superheating (recirculation of steam through a locomotive's firetubes, significantly increasing power) and of the trailing truck (enabling an increase in firebox capacity) allowed for significant increases in practical locomotive size and for the development of several large new locomotive types. The further development of devices such as the mechanical stoker (moving coal from tender to firebox without a shovel) allowed for maximum performance from new larger locomotives.

CHESAPEAKE & OHIO CLASS J1 MOUNTAIN TYPE

Date	1911–12
Builder	American Locomotive Co. (Alco)
Client	Chesapeake & Ohio Railroad
Gauge	4 ft 8½ in
Driving wheels	62 in
Capacity	2 cylinders 29 x 28 in
Steam pressure	180 lb
Weight	499,500 lb
Tractive effort	58,000 lb

● DECAPOD AND MOUNTAIN-TYPES

The 2-10-0 Decapod-type, first introduced in 1870 by the Lehigh Valley Railroad, Pennsylvania, proved too big for its time. After 1900, it was built with limited success for several American railroads. It was most successful in the export market.

The 4-8-2 was introduced in about 1910 for use on the Chesapeake & Ohio railroad and soon proved a very popular design. This versatile type of locomotive was well suited for fast passenger-trains.

● SANTA FE AND OVERLAND-TYPES

Western railroads, which operated over great distances across the open plains, mountains and deserts, had a special need for large, powerful locomotives and

● **ABOVE**
The 2-10-0 Decapod type was not popular among American railroads, but Pennsylvania Railroad owned more than 500. The Decapod was used for heavy, slow-speed freight service.

● **RIGHT**
The Norfolk & Western Railroad operated streamlined 4-8-2 Mountain types in passenger service. These locomotives, Class K2, looked very similar to the J Class Northern types.

were better able to handle those with a long wheelbase. Shortly after the turn of the century, the Santa Fe Railway took delivery of 2-10-2 locomotives called Santa Fe types. This type did not attain popularity with other railroads until World War I, when changes in technology made it more appealing and the type was mass produced. In the 1920s, the Union Pacific railroad took delivery of a three-cylinder 4-10-2 locomotive named after that railroad's primary corridor, the Overland Route. Southern Pacific also ordered this type and referred to it as the Southern Pacific type. The 4-10-2 was not very popular. Fewer than 100 were built.

● **ABOVE**
This Baltimore & Ohio railroad's 4-8-2 brand new Mountain type poses for its builder's photograph. This locomotive had 74 in driving wheels, 30 x 30 in cylinders, operated at 210 lb per sq in and produced a 65,000 lb tractive effort.

American Superpower

American locomotive builders were constantly looking to improve the steam locomotives' output and fuel economy, and in doing so developed many important innovations.

● FOUR-AXLE TRAILING TRUCK KEY TO POWER

The development of the four-axle trailing-truck or -tender allowed for a larger firebox, and thus increased the heating surface and power. "Superpower" also took advantage of other improvements, such as automatic stokers, superheating and, later, roller bearings.

The first locomotive exhibiting the radial, outside-bearing, four-axle truck and enlarged firebox was a Lima 2-8-4 built in 1925 for the New York Central railroad. It was designed for heavyfreight service. NYC used its 2-8-4s on the Boston & Albany (B&A) line in western Massachusetts. This line featured the steepest grades on NYC's system. As a result, this new type was named the "Berkshire", after the mountain range in which it operated. The Berkshire type was the logical progression from the Mikado type, long popular for freight service. NYC was pleased with the Berkshires' performance and ordered a fleet of them for service on the B&A line. There they served for more than 20 years, until the introduction of diesel-electric.

● SUPER PASSENGER POWER

The four-axle trailing-truck and larger firebox principle worked so well on the freight-hauling Berkshire that the same principle was tried on fast passenger locomotives. In 1927, NYC took delivery of its first 4-6-4 locomotive from Alco. This type was named after the Hudson River, NYC's famed Water Level Route, which runs parallel to the line between New York City and Albany, the state capital.

● LEFT
One of the most impressive types of steam locomotive ever built was Atchison, Topeka & Santa Fe's 2900 Series, 4-8-4 Northerns. They weighed 510,000 lb, operated at 300 lb per sq in and had 80 in driving wheels. They regularly ran at more than 100 miles an hour.

● **OPPOSITE**
In 1945, Reading Railroad built eight 4-8-4 Northerns, Class T1, at its shops in Reading, Pennsylvania. Designed for freight service, the T1 weighed 809,000 lb, had 70 in driving wheels and operated at 240 lb per sq in.

● **RIGHT**
The Baltimore & Ohio Railroad's 4-6-4 Hudson type. Many American railroads used Hudsons in passenger service. The superpowered Hudson was the natural progression from the Pacific type.

READING 4-8-4 NORTHERN TYPE CLASS T1

Date	1945
Builder	Reading Shops, Reading, Pennsylvania, USA
Client	Reading Railroad
Gauge	4 ft 8½ in
Driving wheels	70 in
Capacity	2 cylinders 27 x 32 in
Steam pressure	240 lb
Weight	809,000 lb
Tractive effort	68,000 lb

Continued development of the Hudson type produced some of the finest passenger locomotives ever built. About 500 Hudson types were built for service in America.

● **ABOVE**
Milwaukee Road took delivery of Class S-3 Northerns from Alco in 1944. These powerful locomotives were used for freight and passenger service but were too heavy to operate on some routes.

● **NORTHERNS**

The 4-8-4 Northern type was first developed in 1927 for the Northern Pacific. The Northern was an excellent locomotive for high-speed passenger service and fast freight service and remained in production throughout World War II. Some of the finest examples of the Northern type were Union Pacific railroad's 800-class, built by Alco in 1937; Milwaukee Road's S-Class, built by Alco in 1944; Santa Fe's 2900 Series, built by Baldwin that same year; and NYC's 6000 Series locomotives, built in 1946 and usually referred to by the railroad as Niagaras rather than as Northerns.

Some Northerns were delivered in streamlined shrouds, notably Norfolk & Western Railroad's J Class and Southern Pacific's GS-2 to GS-6 Class. (SP's Class GS-1, GS-7 and GS-8 did not feature streamlining.)

More than 1,000 Northern types were built for North American railroads. Union Pacific has the distinction of maintaining a Northern well past the end of steam in the 1950s. In 1996 its famous Northern No. 844 emerged from a multi-million dollar overhaul and paraded around the system in excursion service.

● **RIGHT**
Union Pacific has maintained No. 844. While used mainly for excursion services, it occasionally hauls freight. In September 1989, it led a westbound freight across Nebraska from Omaha to North Platte.

American Electric and Early Diesels

The first use of electric locomotives in the United States of America was in the Baltimore Railway Tunnel, by the Baltimore & Ohio Railroad (B&O) in 1895.

● ELECTRICS

Electrification gained popularity after the turn of the century and through the 1930s many American railroads electrified portions of their main lines. Most notable were the Pennsylvania Railroad (PPR) extensive 11,000-volt alternating current (a.c.) electrification in New York, New Jersey, Maryland and Pennsylvania; the New York Central (NYC) 660-volt direct current (d.c.) third-rail electrification; New Haven's 11,000-volt a.c. suburban main-line electrification in Connecticut; and Milwaukee Road's famous 3,000-volt d.c. overhead electrification through the mountains of Montana, Idaho and Washington State. PRR owned many classes of electric locomotives, from the small 0-C-0 switchers, Class B1, to the famous Raymond Loewy-styled 4-C+C-4, Class GG1. The GG1 served PRR and its successors for nearly 50 years.

NYC operated several classes of motors in the New York City area. Its first electric, Class S1, No. 6000, was in service from 1904 until the 1970s.

New Haven's electrics could operate from both 660-volt d.c. third rail and 11,000-volt a.c. overhead wire. New Haven used EF-class motors in freight service and EP-class motors in passenger service. Its last passenger electrics were 10 EP-5s, delivered by General Electric in 1955.

PENNSYLVANIA RAILROAD CLASS GG1 ELECTRIC LOCOMOTIVE

Date	1934–43
Builder	Baldwin, General Electric, Juniata Shops
Client	Pennsylvania Railroad
Gauge	4 ft 8½ in
Voltage	11,000 volts a.c.
Power	4,680 hp
Weight	460,000 lb
Tractive effort	75,000 lb

● BELOW

The PRR operated 139 GG1 electrics in freight and passenger service on its electrified lines. These Raymond Loewy-styled locomotives operated for nearly 50 years.

● ABOVE

A PRR GG1 leads a high-speed passenger-train through Frankford Junction, near Philadelphia, Pennsylvania, in 1959.

● LEFT

The Rio Grande Zephyr on the Denver & Rio Grande Western Railroad, seen at Thistle, Colorado, in 1982.

Milwaukee Road's most famous electrics were its 6-D+D-6, Class EP-2, Bipolars, built by GE in 1918 for use on its Washington State lines; and its 1949 GE-built Little Joes for its Montana and Idaho lines. These double-ended, baby-faced locomotives were intended for operation in Russia but not delivered because of the start of the Cold War. Hence their nickname, after Joseph Stalin. Milwaukee discontinued the last of its electric operations in 1974, and six years later abandoned its tracks to the Pacific Coast.

DIESEL-ELECTRIC INTRIGUE

America's first successful commercial diesel-electric was a 60 ton, 300 hp boxcab built by Alco-GE-Ingersol Rand for the Central Railroad of New Jersey in 1925. At first, the diesel-electric was primarily used for switching, but its passenger application became evident with the introduction of the Budd-built Pioneer Zephyr on the Burlington railroad in 1934. This articulated, streamlined, stainless-steel wonder changed the way railroads viewed the diesel-electric.

In 1939, General Motors Electro-Motive Corporation introduced the FT, a 1,350-hp, streamlined locomotive designed to be operated in sets of four in heavyfreight service. This amazing locomotive outperformed contemporary steam locomotives in nearly every service in which it was tested. The diesel had proved it could handle all kinds of service and, in most respects, in a more cost-efficient way than steam. Only World War II prolonged the inevitable. Following the war, the diesel-electric quickly took over from the steam locomotive. By the mid-1950s, many railroads had completely replaced locomotive fleets with new diesels. By 1960, the steam locomotive was relegated to the status of a historical curiosity.

The diesel-electric enabled American railroads to "electrify" their lines without stringing wires. In some cases, the diesel-electric replaced true electric operations as well.

LEFT
One of the New Haven railroad's EP-5 passenger electrics leads a train through Sunnyside Yard, in Queens, New York, in 1960. New Haven's 10 EP-5s, built by General Electric in 1955, were the railroad's last new passenger electrics.

BELOW TOP
The Electro-Motive E7 was one of the most popular passenger locomotives. More than 500 were built. Here, a pair of the Louisville & Nashville railroad's E7s rest at Louisville, Kentucky, in 1958.

BELOW BOTTOM
Electro-Motive Corporation's EAs built in 1937 for the Baltimore & Ohio railroad were the first streamlined passenger diesel-electrics not part of an articulated-train set.

American Interurbans

Between the 1890s and World War I, lightweight interurban electric railways were built throughout the United States of America. Their greatest concentration was in the Northeast and Midwest.

● ABOVE
The North Shore operated two articulated, streamlined electric train sets called Electroliners on its high-speed line between Chicago, Illinois, and Milwaukee, Wisconsin. An Electroliner is seen here on the streets of Milwaukee – on 19 July 1958.

● INTERURBANS' PERFORMANCE ACROSS AMERICA

Interurbans were mainly passenger carriers, but many developed freight business as well. Interurbans were badly affected when automobile travel became popular, and very few interurban companies survived the Great Depression of the 1930s. A handful of interurban lines operated passenger services into the 1950s and early 1960s. Others survived as freight carriers. Only a few segments of the once-great interurban system exist today, mostly as freight carriers. Three are still electrified, and one line, the Chicago, South Shore & South Bend, still carries passengers.

● INTERURBAN CARS

Early interurban car design emulated that of steam railroad passenger cars. Ornate, heavyweight, wooden cars prevailed until about 1915 when steel cars became standard. Interurban cars were built by several companies including the American Car Company, Brill, Cincinnati Car Company, Holman Car Company and the Jewett Car Company, most of which also built street cars and elevated rapid-transit cars.

● BELOW
The Chicago, South Shore & South Bend Railroad operated a fleet of Standard Steel Car interurban cars. Here, a typical South Shore interurban is seen at Gary, Indiana, in 1958.

● **RIGHT**
The North Shore painted some of its heavyweight interurban cars to make it appear as if they were modern, stainless-steel, streamlined cars.

CHICAGO, SOUTH SHORE & SOUTH BEND INTERURBAN COACH

Date	1929
Builder	Standard Steel Car
Client	South Shore & South Bend Interurban
Gauge	4 ft $8\frac{1}{2}$ in
Voltage	1,500 d.c.
Axles	Four
Weight	133,600 lb
Propulsion	Westinghouse
Seating	48 seats

A few interurbans ordered high-speed, lightweight cars in the 1930s, notably the Fonda, Johnstown & Gloversville railroad in New York State, which acquired five streamlined Bullet cars from Brill in 1932; the Cincinnati & Lake Erie railroad, which acquired 20 high-speed cars from the Cincinnati Car Company in 1932; and the Northern Indiana Railway, which acquired ten lightweight cars from Cummings in 1930.

● ARTICULATED STREAMLINERS

The Chicago, North Shore & Milwaukee (the North Shore) received two streamlined, articulated interurban train sets from the St Louis Car Company in 1941. Named Electroliners, these flashy trains were painted in a unique emerald-and-salmon multistriped scheme. The North Shore was one of few interurbans integrated with a city rapid-transit system. For more than 20 years, the Electroliners zipped between Milwaukee, Wisconsin, and Chicago's "L" Loop. After the North Shore's demise in 1963, the Electroliners were sold to Philadelphia, where they operated for another ten years as Liberty Liners on the Norristown Highspeed Line (the former Philadelphia & Western). The Illinois Terminal also operated St Louis Car streamlined articulated interurbans.

● **RIGHT**
The Chicago, Aurora & Elgin (CA&E) railroad's No. 20 was built by the Niles Car & Manufacturing Company in 1902. It weighs 85,000 lb and seats 52 passengers. The CA&E powered its cars by third-rail and overhead wire.

Canadian Passenger

In 1948, about 4,100 steam locomotives were serving Canada's two main railroads, Canadian National (CN) and Canadian Pacific (CP).

● LOCOMOTIVE BUILDERS

Two commercial Canadian builders provided most of these locomotives. The Montreal Locomotive Works (MLW), a subsidiary of the American Locomotive Company (Alco), built more than 3,600 steam locomotives between the turn of the century and the early-1950s when it switched to producing diesel-electric locomotives. The Canadian Locomotive Company (CLC), founded in the 1850s, built more than 2,500 steam locomotives, including about 500 export models. In 1950, CLC was given the licence to build Fairbanks-Morse diesel-electric locomotives.

● CANADIAN NATIONAL

The CN railroad introduced the 4-8-4 to Canada in 1927, only a few months after Northern Pacific first tried it in the United States of America. CN called the 4-8-4 the Confederation type and during 20 years ordered more than 200 for freight and passenger service. Of CN's 4-8-4s, 11 were streamlined. One of the most impressive types of 4-8-4 was CN's Class U-2-h, intended for dual service. They operated at 250 lb per sq in,

● ABOVE
Canadian Pacific's most famous locomotives were its Royal Hudsons, built by the Montreal Locomotive Works from 1938. Like many CP steam-locomotives, they were semi-streamlined and had recessed headlights.

● BELOW
Canadian Pacific Railway G-5 4-6-2s, Nos. 1246 and 1293, pictured at Brockways Mills, Vermont, USA.

weighed 400,300 lb, featured 73 in driving wheels, and produced a 56,000 lb tractive effort. CN also maintained a fleet of 4-8-2 Mountain types, many working exclusively in passenger service.

● CANADIAN PACIFIC

The late-era steam locomotives of CP feature several distinctive hallmarks. Most were semi-streamlined and featured centred, recessed headlights. As with CN locomotives, CP used vestibule cabs to give crews greater comfort when operating in extremely cold temperatures.

CANADIAN PACIFIC CLASS H1D, 4-6-4 ROYAL HUDSON

Date	1938
Builder	Montreal Locomotive Works
Client	Canadian Pacific
Gauge	4 ft 8½ in
Driving wheels	75 in
Capacity	2 cylinders 22 x 30 in
Steam pressure	275 lb
Weight	628,500 lb
Tractive effort	45,300 lb

CP preferred 4-6-2 Pacific types and 4-6-4 Hudson types for its passenger service. It began buying Pacifics in 1906 and continued acquiring them until 1948. Its Hudsons were notable locomotives, with outstanding performance records and excellent aesthetic qualities. Some CP Hudsons regularly operated on 800-mile-long runs. Its best-known 4-6-4s were its H1 Royal Hudsons, so named because two of their class hauled the special trains that brought King George VI and Queen Elizabeth across Canada in 1939. The Royal Hudsons were decorated with an embossed crown.

● ABOVE
A Canadian National 4-8-4, No. 6218, races with a passenger excursion. CN owned more 4-8-4s than any other railroad.

● ABOVE
A Canadian National 4-8-4, No. 6218, rolls a passenger-train off a bridge in 1964.

● LEFT
Canadian National railroad preferred four-coupled steam locomotives and owned many Mikados, Mountains and Confederations (known elsewhere as Northerns). Here, a 4-8-2 Mountain Class N-7b, No. 6017, rests at Turcot Yard, Montreal.

Canadian Freight

Canadian National was a publicly owned company formed in 1922 from a number of failing railroad lines. It was the larger line of the two Canadian systems and spanned Canada from coast to coast.

● LEFT
While CN preferred four-coupled steam locomotives such as 4-8-2 Mountains, CP embraced three-coupled locomotives. CP had many 4-6-2 Pacifics and used them in all sorts of service. Here, a CP 4-6-2 leads a mixed train at Jackman, Maine, USA, in 1958.

● LEFT
A 40-ton Shay "Old One Spot", standard gauge, built in 1910: the last of the woodburners.

● CANADIAN NATIONAL

In the 1920s, the unified CN acquired many 4-8-2 Mountain types and smaller 2-8-2 Mikados. In 1927 it was one of the first railroads to adopt the 4-8-4 Northern type, which it called the Confederation type. CN and its American subsidiary, Grand Trunk Western (GTW), eventually owned more than 200 4-8-4s, far more than any other North American railroad. These high horsepower 4-8-4s were ideal suited for heavy freight service and passenger service.

In 1929, CN experimented with an alternative form of motive power. It ordered two diesel-electrics from Westinghouse and was the first North American railroad to use the diesel in main-line service. However, these experimental locomotives were unsuccessful and not duplicated. Ultimately, CN converted from steam to diesel operations, but at a more gradual rate than railroads in the USA.

● CANADIAN PACIFIC

Privately owned CP took a different approach to its freight locomotives from CN. Where CN used many four-coupled locomotives, 4-8-2s, 4-8-4s, etc., CP preferred three-coupled locomotives for many applications. It owned many 4-6-2 Pacific types and 4-6-4 Hudson types. It used light Pacifics in branch-line freight service as

● RIGHT
A Canadian National 4-8-4, No. 6168, leads a mixed train near Brantford, Ontario, in 1959. CN used many 4-8-4s in freight and passenger service.

CANADIAN PACIFIC CLASS T1b, 2-10-4 SELKIRK TYPE	
Date	1929–49
Builder	Montreal Locomotive Works
Client	Canadian Pacific
Gauge	4 ft $8\frac{1}{2}$ in
Driving wheels	63 in
Capacity	2 cylinders 25 x 32 in
Steam pressure	285 lb
Weight	447,000 lb (engine only)
Tractive effort	76,905 lb

well as in passenger service. CP was also one of the few railroads to employ its Hudsons in freight service. Most railroads used this type exclusively for passenger trains.

CP did own some big locomotives. In 1928 it built two 4-8-4s but acquired no more. However, for heavy freight service in the Canadian Rockies, it owned 36 semi-streamlined 2-10-4 Texas-types that it called Selkirks. These locomotives were well suited for steep grades and heavy tonnage and performed well. In 1931, CP built an experimental three-cylinder 2-10-4. This locomotive was not particularly successful, CP did not bother to duplicate it and it was eventually scrapped.

● ABOVE
A Canadian National 2-8-0 Consolidation sits at Turcot Yard, Montreal. Most CN steam locomotives were built by Montreal Locomotive Works.

● ABOVE
A 45-ton, two-truck Climax logging locomotive, No. 9, built in 1912.

● LEFT
In the 1920s, the newly formed Canadian National began buying many 2-8-2 Mikados.

The Prussian Influence

Prussian influence is seen by many to be confined to the large class of 4-6-0 locomotives known as the P8. After Germany's unification in 1871 as an imperial power, Prussia continued to go its own way in railway matters. Other states in the German Empire followed suit under Prussia's sway.

● THE EARLY DAYS

At the end of the 19th century, most railway locomotive authorities were trying to cope with the pace of advance in design, Prussia included. Because of the fairly level nature of Prussian territory, lightweight locomotives with a fair turn of speed lasted for many years and in various guises. Compounding was in fashion and classes were turned out seemingly almost at random, some being compound locomotives and others simple locomotives.

● ABOVE
The Prussian P8 also lasted to the end of the days of steam in West Germany. Here, in the late 1960s, No. 038 509-6 trundles under a bridge.

PRUSSIAN P8

Date	1906
Builder	Schwarzkopff, Berlin
Client	Prussian State Railways
Gauge	1,435 mm
Class	Prussian P8; Deutsche Reichsbahn (DR) 38
Type	4-6-0
Driving wheels	1,750 mm
Capacity	2 cylinders 575 x 630 mm
Weight in working order	78.2 tonnes
Maximum service speed	100 kph

● THE SCHMIDT SUPERHEATER

Then came a most important event for Prussia and railway administrations worldwide. This was the development of a successful superheater. Steam was dried in a further set of tubes in the boiler to remove water drops in suspension. This superheated steam worked far more efficiently than those preceding it.

In the early 1890s, a Prussian physicist working in this field, Dr Wilhelm Schmidt, was encouraged to try out his results on the Prussian State Railways (PSR) system, by Mr Geheimiath Garbe of PSR. The first Schmidt superheater was fitted in 1897, but, as with many innovations, there were problems of lubrication and leaks. Further, locomotives fitted with superheaters cost more to build. In 1900, a simple 4-4-0 was fitted with the Schmidt superheater and achieved much interest and some success. Compared with nonsuperheated compound 4-4-0s of the same class, the nonsuperheated machines used 12 per cent more coal and 30 per cent more water.

● THE PRUSSIAN P8

The cost-savings of a simple machine against a compound being most

● **RIGHT AND OPPOSITE BOTTOM**
Turkish State Railways (TCCD) operates a system separated from the main network to take coal from collieries in the Armutçuk Mountains to the docks at Eregli on the Black Sea. On shed at the port, these Prussian G8-2, two-cylinder 2-8-0s, dating from 1919, are ready for the night's work.

attractive, superheaters began to be fitted more widely and to more types of locomotive, including a class of sturdy 2-6-0 mixed-traffic locomotive. Compounding was not abandoned, however, for high-speed work. PSR had gained experience of the De Glehn compounds and developed their own compound 4-6-0 version. When a simple two-cylinder version for mixed traffic came out in 1906, the scene was set for the expansion of the Prussian Class P8. The first was built by Schwarzkopff of Berlin. Between 1906–21, the PSR bought 3,370 machines. Many others were constructed, including for export. More than 6,000 were built in total. After World War I, reparations demanded from Germany led to the arrival of the P8 in many other countries including Belgium and France.

● **THE WIDER IMPLICATIONS**

Several other classes of Prussian-designed locomotive were also distributed widely, including to Germany's allies, especially Turkey. This distribution and the reparations possibly extended Prussian influence far wider, and interest in these relatively simple and robust designs grew. The German locomotive-building industry's need to gear up to replace stocks distributed elsewhere increased its design and production capacity. From this, German builders outside Prussia also benefited while, in Germany, the foundations were laid for German State Railways – the Deutsche Reichsbahn (DR) and, after 1945, the Deutsche Bundesbahn (DB).

● **BELOW LEFT**
The Deutsche Bundesbahn (DB) Class 078 4-6-4T lasted right to the end of the days of steam, in the early-1970s in then-West Germany. One of the class is pictured in a familiar role on a light passenger-train. This class, as Prussian Class T18, was built in batches between 1912-27.

● **BELOW**
Also on shed at Eregli in Turkey, in the 1970s, a driver is oiling round on a Prussian Type-G8 44071, an 0-8-0 dating from 1902, before moving off to pick up his train.

The Reichsbahn Standards

After World War I, Germany's need to reorganize its railways led in 1920 to formation of a national system, the Reichsbahn. It is not surprising that Prussian management and methods were prominent.

● RIGHT
This unmodified 01-798 had a trailing load of 450 tonnes as it neared Grossenhain, in the then-East Germany, on the 06.37 hours express from Berlin to Dresden in 1977.

● THE FOUNDATIONS

An engineering-management centre was set up in Berlin. One of its decisions was to produce a series of locomotive classes that would operate across the network. A man called Wagner was placed in charge. In the years to 1939, at least, Wagner's stature as an engineer and manager grew.

● FIRST STEPS

One of his first decisions was to categorize all the locomotives from various sources under his control. This was so successful that its basic tenets were widely followed elsewhere in the operation. It pointed to strengths and weaknesses in the stock. Once more, Prussian influence emerged.

This is not to say that the other German States' railways had little to offer. Saxony and Württemberg were well advanced. Further, private locomotive builders contributed high technical input to many designs.

KRIEGSLOK – DEUTSCHE REICHSBAHN (DR) CLASS 52

Date	1942
Builder	Borsig of Berlin
Client	Deutsche Reichsbahn
Gauge	1,435 mm
Class	52
Type	2-10-0
Driving wheels	1,400 mm
Capacity	2 cylinders 500 x 600 mm (stroke)
Weight in working order	85.3 tonnes
Maximum service speed	80 kph

● **RIGHT**
A Class 050 2-10-0, No. 050 383-9, pulling away from Freudenstadt Station in the Black Forest, in the then West Germany of the late 1960s.

● **DESIGN CRITERIA**

Compounding was on the way out. Two-cylinder, simple expansion locomotives were to be adopted, although, in the 1930s, three small specialist classes had three cylinders. Robust engineering was assisted by raising the axleload on main lines to 20.4 tonnes. Ease of maintenance was improved by mounting ancillaries on the boiler and adopting bar-frames as favoured by the locomotive-builders, J.A. Maffei of Munich. Commodious cabs eased the lot of footplate crews. Many other decisions affected components and fittings, some of which carried on Prussian practice. Despite radical changes to external appearance, the Prussian style continued to dominate.

● **OPPOSITE**
A Kriegslok of Turkish State Railways (TCDD), No. 56533, pictured about to move off to pick up a freight train in the nearby yard.

● **RIGHT**
Class 01 Pacific 4-6-2s were still working between Berlin and Dresden, Saxony, in the then East Germany, in 1977, when this rural scene was briefly disturbed near Weinböhla.

● **STANDARDS AT HOME AND ABROAD**

No fewer than 29 classes were brought into service between 1925–45. They ranged from small classes of 0-6-0T and 2-4-2T, to the 6,292 Class 52 Kriegslok introduced in 1942. These ranged far and wide across Europe, surviving well beyond designers' expectations.

Standard designs proved attractive to other countries. Some bought almost identical designs from German builders, or built them under licence in their own works. For example, Poland had modified Prussian P8s in 1922; Turkey had a range of types in regular use in the 1970s and, in small numbers, even later than this.

Many examples remained in regular use in the former East Germany until the late 1980s. A substantial number, especially of Kriegsloks, have been recovered for restoration and use on special trains in European countries.

GÖLSDORF AND THE AUSTRIAN EMPIRE

The Austro-Hungarian Empire, before its eventual collapse in 1918 as a result of World War I, was one of the most powerful political and economic entities in continental Europe.

● BACKGROUND

Its railways' main axis ran generally east-west with few topographical problems in the easterly direction from Vienna, in Austria, to Budapest, in Hungary. To the south, the only real geographical challenge between Vienna and Graz, in Austria, was surmounted by the opening in 1853 of the Trieste Railway line over the Austrian Alps and through the 980 m (3,215 ft) high Semmering Pass. A similar problem faced railway builders for the line going southward to Italy from Innsbruck in Austria. This crossed the mountains through the 1,369 m (4,494 ft) high Brenner Pass whose railroad was completed 1867. Apart from the relatively level lines to the German border to the west, other lines westward tended to be regarded as secondary. Moreover, they faced the main European Alpine barrier. The best route was a single line through Austria's Tirol and Vorarlberg. This reached Buchs, Kanton St Gallen on the Swiss border, with hard climbing on both sides of the 1,798 m (5,900 ft) high Arlberg Tunnel, 6 km (3¾ miles) long and opened in 1884.

● DR KARL GÖLSDORF

Karl Gölsdorf was born into a railway family in 1861. By the age of 30 he was chief mechanical engineer (CME) of the Austrian State Railway. In the early 1900s, he was made responsible for all mechanical engineering under the purview of the Austrian Railway Ministry, which also influenced the notionally independent Hungarian railways. His achievements include the rack-and-pinion Erzberg line. The 1,533 m (5,032 ft) high Erzberg Mountain, rich in iron ore, stands above the mining commune of Eisenerz in Austria's Styria province.

● DESIGN PROBLEMS AND SOLUTIONS

The empire's level routes required locomotives capable of sustained high speed, while the curving, mountainous lines called for machines capable of a long, hard slog. Both criteria needed free steaming. However, Gölsdorf faced the severe limitation of lightweight track and, consequently, a maximum axleload of no more than 14.5 tons.

He achieved high power:weight ratios by relatively high boiler pressures and by applying his own dictum that it is easier to save weight on each of a thousand

● LEFT
This scene in Strasshof locomotive depot north of Vienna in 1987 includes BBO, Bundesbahnen Österreich, class 30.33. This engine dates from 1895 and is sporting two steam domes and joining-pipe.

● **ABOVE LEFT AND RIGHT**
These locomotives are Gölsdorf designs or derivatives active as late as the 1970s in what was then Yugoslavia.

● **BELOW RIGHT**
The elegance of Gölsdorf's express passenger locomotives is well known. Less well known is this class of three rack-and-pinion locomotives. Its life was spent mostly on trains loaded with iron ore from the Erzberg, the Iron Mountain at Eisenerz, in Austria's Styria province, to the point where trains were handed over to pure adhesion traction at Vordernberg.

GÖLSDORF'S DESIGN FOR THE RACK AND PINION ERZBERG LINE

Date	1912
Builder	Dr Karl Gölsdorf
Gauge	1,435 mm
Class	BBO 269; OBB 197
Type	BBO category F: Whyte notation 0-12-0T
Capacity adhesion:	2 cylinders 570 x 520 mm
pinion:	2 cylinders 520 x 450 mm
Coupled wheel diameter	1,030 mm
Weight in working order	88 tonnes
Maximum service speed	Adhesion, 30 kph; rack, 15 kph

small parts than on a few large ones. Wide firegrates helped to ensure a plentiful supply of steam. Very large driving wheels on express locomotives, up to 7 ft in diameter, gave the opportunity for high speed. Up to 12 small coupled wheels offered the adhesion and formed part of the tractive-effort calculations for heavy hauling in the mountains.

● **COMPOUNDING**

Gölsdorf's designs are often regarded as unusual. One obvious feature was visible early on. Two domes were mounted on the boiler barrel, both to collect steam. They were linked by a large pipe through which steam from one passed to the regulator in the other. More important was a hidden device. Gölsdorf was a great proponent of compounding, often using just two cylinders, one high- and the other low-pressure. Difficulty was often experienced in starting compounds from rest. Instead of the usual starting-valve requiring skilled operation, high-pressure steam was automatically admitted to the low-pressure cylinder when the valve gear was fully in fore or back gear.

His designs were generally adopted by the Hungarian railways, although in some cases they used simple machines based on Gölsdorf's compounds. After the empire's break-up, many of his numerous types of locomotive could be found in Czecho-slovakia, Hungary and Yugoslavia where, as in Austria, some can be seen today.

The French Influence – Steam

1900 to 1950 truly was the "Golden Age" for steam in France. Designers were pushing at the frontiers of knowledge of locomotive design and performance. The age also bred a class of driver who not only had to learn about the new technology but also had to adapt driving techniques to take best advantage of it. The French *mécanicien* was an outstanding footplate technician.

● RIGHT
French railways had a wide range of tank locomotives for local passenger and freight work. These Class 141TAs are former Paris-Orleans railway machines built between 1911–23.

● COMPOUNDING

To a railway historian, compounding is immediately identified with France and two names: Alfred De Glehn and André Chapelon. De Glehn was born in Britain.

Compounding works like this. A basic steam locomotive creates steam under pressure in its boiler. The steam expands in cylinders to drive the pistons and is then exhausted to the atmosphere. But a lot of power is still left in the exhausting steam. If this steam is channelled to a larger, low-pressure cylinder, this power, otherwise wasted, can be used to save fuel and water.

As with much engineering, there are disadvantages. The machines are more complicated. They demand top-quality maintenance and skilled driving.

● DESIGNERS AND THEIR WORK

Other French engineers who made great contributions to worldwide development included Gaston Du Bousquet, a contemporary of De Glehn, and, towards the end of the steam era, Mark de Caso. Chapelon always acknowledged Du Bousquet's groundwork, which led to some of his successes.

As always, locomotive designers had to work under constraints. In France, where railways have been strictly controlled since 1857, there was a requirement before World War II for the shortest possible journey-times to be achieved without exceeding 75 mph. This meant that uphill speeds with heavy loads had to be high. The De Glehn compounds built up to 1914, economical and free running, were more than adequate in their day. As loads increased and they had to be worked harder, however, efficiency fell away, and little real work was obtained from a four-cylinder compound's low-pressure cylinders.

● LEFT
Much painstaking work was required to restore this classic "Mountain", No. 241A 65, to working order. It was built by Fives-Lille (Works No. 4714/1931) and is shown on shed at St Sulpice, Neuchâtel, Switzerland, in 1994.

● **ABOVE LEFT**
This former Paris-Orleans railway's 231E Pacific heads the Flêche d'Or Calais-Paris express in the later days of steam, as shown by the standard rolling stock. In its heyday, it was a luxury train, but the locomotive, a Du Bousquet/Chapelon design for the Paris-Orleans railway, is truly from the golden age.

● **ABOVE RIGHT**
These 2-8-2 tanks simmering on shed recall scenes once familiar in a typical French roundhouse.

SNCF (ETAT) 241A	
Date	1927
Builder	Compagnie de Fives-Lille, Fives, France
Client	Société Nationale des Chemins de Fer (SNCF)
Gauge	1,435 mm
Type	241 (Whyte notation, 4-8-2)
Driving wheels	1,790 mm
Capacity	2 cylinders 510 x 650 mm 2 cylinders 720 x 700 mm
Weight in working order	114.6 tonnes
Maximum service speed	120 kph

● REDOUBLING POWER AND EFFICIENCY

In the late 1920s, Chapelon began to stand out as a great railway engineer. He had entered railway service in 1919 but in 1924 joined a telephone company. His research abilities, recognized while he was a student, then led to him accepting an appointment in the Paris-Orleans railway's research department. There, Monsieur Paul Billet charged him to improve specific machines' exhaust systems. This was the platform on which his career really began.

Studies had confirmed that power was being wasted in getting steam from boiler to cylinder. The reasons included inadequate and indirect steam passages. Redesign under Chapelon's expert guidance led almost to redoubling the power and efficiency of rebuilt compound locomotives.

However, these improvements applied equally to simple expansion locomotives, and the techniques were eagerly adopted across the world. They strengthened the argument of those who considered that simple locomotives with high superheat were, overall, more economical. To Chapelon's credit, he was not a slavish devotee of compounding, and he caused similar significant improvements to classes of simple expansion locomotives.

● **LEFT**
231 G 558 drifts into the port of Le Havre, northern France, with a train of 1930s stock. Were it not for the overhead-line equipment, the scene might have been soon after 1935 when the SNCF rebuilt this 1922-constructed Batignolles Pacific. In fact, the picture was taken in 1992.

THE FRENCH INFLUENCE – ELECTRIC

Most major European countries dabbled with electrification in the early 1900s with varying degrees of success.

In 1903, the 31 km (19 mile) long, steeply graded line from St Georges de Commiers to La Mure was electrified by Sécheron, the Swiss firm. It was the first high-tension main line electrified at 2,400 volt d.c. supplied through two wires to Bo-Bo locomotives which were capable of handling 110 tonne trains on the 1:38 gradients.

● THE EARLY YEARS

In 1910, French engineers Auvert and Ferrand together developed a single-phase a.c./d.c. 2Bo+Bo2 locomotive which was built by the Alioth works, Münchenstein. Current at 12,000-volt 25 Hz was fed through converters to vertically mounted traction motors. Trials proved successful and another locomotive was designed but not built.

Southern France's Midi Railway also saw electrification as a solution for effective traction in mountains. Between 1902-08, 12,000-volt a.c. single-phase 162/3 Hz was installed on the 54 km (34 mile) long metre-gauge line in the Pyrénees Orientales of the Roussillon between Villefranche-de-Conflent and Bourg-Madame on the Franco-Spanish border and on the standard-gauge section between Villefranche and Ille-sur-Tet. Six locomotives were ordered from different builders for comparative trials. One established that regenerative braking with single-phase current was practicable. The builder, Jeumont of France, was one of two companies selected for a small production contract. The other was Westinghouse of the USA.

As for multiple-unit operation, the Paris Métropolitan (Métro), opened for

2-D-2 SERIES 5401-23 (ETAT 501-23)

Date	1937
Builder	Fives-Lille, Fives, France
Client	SNCF
Gauge	1,435 mm
Class	2D2 5400
Type	2-D-2
Voltage	1,500v d.c.
Drive	Buechli
Length	17.78 m
Weight in working order	88 tonnes
Maximum service speed	140 kph

● ABOVE
BB 915, a former Etat Railway loco, built in 1935 by Alsthom, standing at Le Mans depot in 1970. It is one of a class of 35 and operates on 1,500-volt d.c.

● LEFT
The 253 trains of Luxembourg Railways were built by MTE in France in 1975 yet all showed the salient characteristics of the Budd cars referred to in the main text when introduced on the Le Mans line. One is pictured entering Esch Alzetle station, southern Luxembourg, in 1995.

● LEFT
BB 209, formerly on the Paris-Orleans line, was built in 1938 by Alsthom and retains the very angular bodywork of earlier years. It is pictured shunting at Paris Austerlitz Station in 1970.

● ABOVE
No. 2D2 5534, formerly on the Paris-Orleans line, heading a train of postal vans at Paris Austerlitz Station in 1970. It was built in 1934 by Compagnie-Electro-Mécanique, at Le Havre, the Channel port in northern France.

traffic on 14 July 1900, was early in the field, two months after the Paris Invalides to Les Molineaux services.

● THE AGE OF DEVELOPMENT

Between 1918–39, basic experimentation gave way to the desire to achieve speed, tractive power and efficiency using technology that was growing apace.

A difficulty facing designers was the disparity of current-supply systems. This was largely created by haphazard development and the autonomy of the regional railways. These showed little desire for standardization. This may have been good for Europe as a whole, because multi-current locomotives were developed capable of crossing boundaries between countries whose electrical supplies differed from those of France.

Locomotives' shapes and sizes were legion. Various drive systems were adopted. Again, as for steam locomotives, the vehicles either looked awkward, being boxes on wheels, or were the more attractive bonnet-ended machines.

In the mid-1930s, softer outlines appeared, as on the Paris-Orleans Type 2-D-2 5100s. In the 1940s, the short body with a generally rounded outline established the French look, especially for Bo-Bos. A final development was the cab with a prominent top overhang, possibly unique to French builders.

● MULTIPLE UNITS

In 1937, the Société Nationale des Chemins de Fer (SCNF) ordered 27 sets of multiple units for the Paris-Versailles-Le Mans electrification, using the Budd corrugated stainless-steel body construction. This set a pattern that was to last for many years, and similar units can be seen today.

● BELOW
Number 5406 about to leave Le Mans, a railcar-production centre in north-western France, on an express to Paris in 1961.

THE SWISS INFLUENCE – MOUNTAIN RAILWAYS

Mountain railways are usually powered either on the funicular principle (the weight of a descending car pulls another up) or on the "rack-and-pinion" principle of toothed rails.

● **THE RIGGENBACH SYSTEM**

The first successful rack-and-pinion system was developed not in Switzerland but in the USA. Development was proceeding in both countries, but neither of their two respective engineers knew of the other's work.

In Switzerland, Niklaus Riggenbach took out a patent on 12 August 1863 but did not develop it then. In 1869, he heard about the railway up 800 m (2,624 ft) high Mount Washington, in Berkshire County, USA, with its rack system designed by Sylvester Marsh. He visited that railway and on his return successfully developed his "ladder rack". Its first application was to a short quarry line at Ostermundigen, near Bern, in 1870. The locomotive that worked the line, "Gnom", has been preserved.

The success was soon followed by another when his system was applied to the Vitznau-Rigi Bahn (VRB), a standard-gauge line linking Vitznau, on Lake Lucerne, with the isolated 1,800 m (5,906 ft) high Rigi Mountain. This line

RIGI BAHN NO. 7

Date	1873
Builder	Swiss Locomotive and Machine Works (SLM), Winterthur
Client	Rigi Bahn
Gauge	1,435 mm
Rack system	Riggenbach
Capacity	2 cylinders 270 x 400 mm
Weight in working order	15.1 tonnes (as built)
Maximum speed	7.5 kph

● BELOW

Switzerland's Vitznau-Rigi Bahn (VRB) owns two steam locomotives that regularly operate on vintage trains. H2/3 No. 17 built by SLM in 1925, is pictured at Rigi Kaltbad in 1986. The sturdy nature of Riggenbach's ladder rack is shown.

● BELOW

The first SLM-built steam railway locomotive, Rigi Bahn No. 7, was taken from Luzern Transport Museum in 1995 and restored by SLM for the 125th anniversary of Switzerland's Vitznau-Rigi Bahn (VRB) in 1996, when it was pictured pushing a fully loaded vintage coach from Rigi Staffel to Rigi Kulm summit station.

● RIGHT
There is no difficulty in fitting pinion gear to electric vehicles. The 800 mm-gauge Wengernalp Bahn (WAB), which provides the intermediate stage of the journey from Interlaken to the 4,758 m (13,642 ft)-high Jungfrau Mountain in central Switzerland's Bernese Alps, uses the Riggenbach-Pauli rack to reach Kleine Scheidegg. These trains are pictured at Grindelwald Grund in 1989 before tackling their climb. Some stock dates from 1947.

● BELOW
The Locher rack's unique construction is shown in this picture, taken in 1991 from the traverser well at the Pilatus railway depot, Alpnachstad, at the foot of Mount Pilatus, near Luzern.

● LEFT
The opening of the Filisur-Bever section of Switzerland's Rhaetische Bahn in 1903 signalled the conquest of river, valley and mountain to reach a plateau at 1,800 m (6,000 ft). Steam was the original power but in 1921 the 61-tonne electric locomotives pictured here came on the scene.

or system celebrated its centenary in 1996 by operating one of the original vertical-boilered locomotives, No. 7, the first locomotive to be built by the Swiss Locomotive and Machine Works (SLM), of Winterthur, near Zürich.

● THE RIGGENBACH-LOCHER SYSTEM

It was Riggenbach who came up with the germ of an idea from the fitting of hooks that ran under the rails on the funicular from Territet to Glion near Montreux at the eastern end of Lake Geneva. The actual design is credited to Colonel Eduard Locher who became engineer to the Pilatus line in Unterwalden Canton, central Switzerland, with its 1:2 gradients. The design amounted to a pair of horizontally mounted guide pinion wheels with deep, plain flanges which run underneath the specially designed rack-rail. In effect, traction and guidance were performed by the rack-rail and pinion wheels. The rails on which the carriage wheels run are merely for balance.

● ADHESION LINES

Numerous, mostly metre-gauge, lines wind their way into the mountains, in some cases tackling gradients of about 1:13 (7.7 per cent) without rack assistance. Two examples are popular with tourists. One is the Montreux-Oberland-Bernoise, which runs from Montreux through valley and alp to Zweisimmen. The other is the extensive spread of metre-gauge routes on the Rhaetische Bahn, which covers the Rhaetian Alps and Switzerland's largest canton, Graubünden (Grisons).

The Rhaetische Bahn offers spectacular scenery and benefits from remarkable engineering feats, which enable the line to reach the fertile flatlands of the Engadine, that is the 97 km (60 mile) long valley of the River Inn, some 1,800 m (6,000 ft) above sea level. Much of the area is devoted to sports in winter when there is only one reliable means of access and egress – the railway. Spirals and tunnelling had to be used similar to that adopted by Swiss Federal Railways on two earlier lines. The section of the SFR over the St Gotthard Pass, with an inter-cantonal 15 km (9½ mile) long tunnel at 1,154 m (3,788 ft), completed in 1872–81, links Göschenen and Airolo and the Bern-Loetschberg-Simplon line between Frütigen and Brig with the Loetschberg Tunnel.

The 20 km (12½ mile) long Simplon Tunnel built in 1898–1905, between Brig and Domodossola, lies partly in Switzerland and partly in Italy. In its day it was the world's longest railway tunnel, famous for carrying the Simplon–Orient Express, with connections, from Calais, over the Alps at 705 m (2,313 ft), to Istanbul, Athens and Asia Minor.

Southern Europe – Iberian, Italian and Greek Peninsulas

The railways of Peninsular Europe – Iberia (Spain and Portugal), Italy and Greece – have long been concerned not only with national and international services but with intercontinental links between Europe and Africa, across the Western and Eastern Mediterranean Sea. Since 1869, proposals to build a rail-and-road fixed link between Spain and Morocco, across the Strait of Gibraltar, making Tangier the gateway to Africa, have been discussed. (Similarly, proposals to link Eurasia and North America by a rail tunnel across the Bering Strait, between Russia's Siberia and Alaska, have been discussed since 1905.)

● LEFT
A large Mallet-type metre-gauge 2-4-6-0T, pictured at Chaves, northern Portugal, in 1974.

● LEFT
In Greece, the sun glints on a chunky USA-built 2-8-0 of a general type familiar across Europe immediately after World War II.

● SPAIN

In Spain, locomotive design and construction was well developed and most steam locomotives not only entered the 20th century but continued to operate beyond the 1950s – apart from those most heavily used or taxed by mountainous terrain. Nevertheless, from the 1920s, many large and well-proportioned locomotives were obtained for the standard gauge from various domestic and foreign builders, the 4-8-2 wheel arrangement being preferred. There were even Garratts, built in 1930 for passenger work.

Electrification began in 1911 on 21 km (13 miles) of steeply graded line on the Spanish Southern Railway between Gérgal and Santa Fé de Montdújar, in the Sierra Nevada of Almeria province, and was slowly extended to Almeria town, on the coast, 44 km (27 miles) in all. Overhead-line a.c. 5.5kv 3 phase was used. Some massive locomotives were supplied for these lines, including 12 2CC2s in 1928 from Babcock & Wilcox-Brown Boveri.

Steady progress came to a grinding halt with the Civil War (1936–9), but new steam and electrics began operating fairly quickly thereafter. Further, the process of building new lines to make a more effective network continued, forming a firm base for the sound rail system Spain has today.

● BELOW
Locomotives 2-8-2 No. 7108 and doubled-domed Es Class No. 7721 head a special train at Diakofto, Greece in 1980.

● **FAR RIGHT**
Visible on FS Italia 2-8-0 No. 741 046 are the Crosti preheater drum, beneath the smokebox door, and the exhaust replacing the conventional chimney.

● **BELOW**
This Alco 1,500 hp diesel-electric, delivered in 1948, is one of 12 in the van of Portugal's diesel revolution. It is pictured at Tunes, Algarve, in 1996.

F S ITALIA CLASS 741

Date	1911 (rebuilt 1955)
Builder	Breda
Client	F.S. Italia (rebuild)
Gauge	1,435 mm
Class	741 (rebuilt from 740)
Driving wheels	140 (Whyte notation 2-8-0)
Capacity	2 cylinders 540 x 700 mm
Driving wheel diameter	1,370 mm
Weight in working order	68.3 tonnes
Maximum service speed	65 kph

● **PORTUGAL**

At the turn of the century, Portugal's steam-locomotive stock was varied and of good lineage. It included De Glehn compounds built in 1898-1903 and typical Henschel outline 4-6-0s, built at Kossel, Germany. Indeed, most European builders of note were represented. It was 1924 before Pacifics arrived from Henschel. Several series of 2-8-0s for freight came into service between 1912-24, built by Schwarzkopf of Berlin and North British of the United Kingdom. The first 4-8-0 arrived from Henschel in 1930. Tank locomotives ranging from 0-4-0T to 2-8-4T helped to cover remaining duties, including suburban passenger-train services.

The metre gauge had some fine machines, many of them big Mallet 2-4-6-0T tanks. The suburban services around Oporto, the country's second-largest city, were shared by 0-4-4-0Ts and 2-8-2Ts dating from 1931.

● **ITALY**

Italy's steam development was reasonably conventional for the period, subject to disruption in World Wars I and II. The unusual took the form of a novel and effective preheating system for feed water. Dr Ing Piero Crosti designed boilers in which combustion gases pass in the normal way through the main, simple boiler and then in reverse direction through a drum or drums. The feed water introduced into the drum(s) thereby captured more heat from flue gases and reduced scale on the firebox wall. This cut fuel costs but the locomotives' conventional appearance suffered. They had no obvious chimney and exhaust gases were disposed of by a series of pipes near the boiler's rear.

Italy is probably best known in the diesel world for its export of railcars. The names Fiat and Breda are on worksplates across the world. These companies began to develop in this field in the mid-1930s, as did Ganz of Hungary. The Fiat railcar started a vogue in 1935 for wheel spats over the bogie wheels, as in aircraft of the day. FS Italia Class Aln 56 was just one example.

● **GREECE**

In Greece, locomotives were haphazardly obtained from various builders and by purchase of secondhand engines from Germany, Austria and Italy. USA-built locomotives were brought to Greece in 1914 and, again, after damage done to the railways in World War II.

SCANDINAVIAN RAILWAYS

From 1900 the railways of the Scandinavian countries – Norway and Sweden forming the Scandinavian Peninsula and Denmark and Finland respectively to its south and east – were gradually extended, in some cases upgrading from metre to standard gauge, especially in Norway, and moved from steam to electrification, except for Finland whose 805-unit fleet included 766 steam locomotives (95 per cent) as late as 1958.

Apart from Denmark, whose insular component presented other physical difficulties, problems facing the railways were the same as in all cold countries. Frost heave disturbed the permanent way in the level wet areas. Heavy snow, with the ever-present risk of avalanche, was a burden in the mountains of Norway and northern Sweden.

● RIGHT AND OPPOSITE BOTTOM LEFT AND RIGHT
These pictures of steam in Finland capture the sense of an age long past and illustrate Russian design influence. The balloon stack and high stacking-rails on the tender of the wood-burner, No. 1163, can be seen.

● BELOW RIGHT
The simple outlines of this 1-C-1 diesel, No. HP 15, of the Danish Hjörringer Privatbanen, the railway operating in north-east Jutland's Hjörring county, are appropriate for this workhorse. It was built in about 1935 by Frichs and is pictured at Randers, the east Jutland seaport.

● DENMARK

Denmark remains different from the other Scandinavian countries because of its islands, its population density and its closely sited communities. Here, speed and frequency of services became paramount together with the desire, gradually being achieved, to link the mainland Jutland Peninsula to all the islands and to the Scandinavian Peninsula at Malmo by bridge and tunnel rather than conveying trains on albeit very efficient train ferries.

In the 1930s, route length was 5,233 km (3,250 miles), of which only 2,512 km (1,560 miles), that is 48 per cent, was state-owned. The level terrain put no great demands on steam locomotives and it was the light diesel-

● LEFT
This 2-6-0T No. 7 sports typical features of Danish steam locomotives, including the smokebox saddle and the national colours in the band around the chimney. Vintage coaches with clerestorey roofs and torpedo vents enhance the nostalgic scene at Helsingor, near Copenhagen, on the Danish island of Zeeland, in 1980.

● LEFT
One of the later versions of the Lyntog ("Lightning") train pictured at Struen, western Jutland, Denmark, in 1980. The four-car unit is powered by a Maybach diesel engine with Voith (Heidenheim, Germany) hydraulic transmission. The power-car is Class MA, No. 467.

railcar that became attractive for passenger work as an alternative to steam.

Electrification came late to Denmark, starting with the suburban system in the capital, Copenhagen, in 1934 employing a line voltage of 1,500 dc. The state system owned a good stock of steam power, mostly built in Germany, but, to develop high-speed services, three-car diesel-electric units called Lyntog ("Lightning") were introduced, which cut journey times dramatically.

● **FINLAND**

From 1809 to 1917, Finland was part of what was then the Russian Empire and so adopted the Russian 5 ft gauge for main lines and 2 ft 5½ in gauge for minor lines. The terrain was relatively level and, in the earlier part of the 20th century, schedules were not demanding, so that comparatively light, often woodburning, locomotives were sufficient. In the latter days of steam, a small class of coalfired Pacifics with good lines and particularly commodious cabs worked the heaviest passenger services. Local and semifast services around Helsinki, the capital, were served by the neat, most attractive Class N1, built by Hanomag in Germany.

● **SWEDEN**

The "Golden Age" of Sweden's railways may be said to be firmly linked to the enormous supplies of iron ore in the inhospitable mountains on the northern borders of Sweden and Norway. Near the town of Kiruna, at 509 m (1,670 ft) above sea level Sweden's highest, established mines work night and day. Some 16 million tons were produced in 1960, the bulk being moved by rail for export.

Electrification of the lines at 16,000 volt single phase ac 16⅔ Hz began in 1910 with the Frontier Railway between Lulea and Rikseransen. By 1914, the first of the massive electric locomotives 1+CC+1 for freight and B-B+B-B were being delivered by the builders ASEA/Siemens. Electrification continued apace until, by 1923, some 450 km (280 miles) had been completed. Even more powerful locomotives were provided, ten -D- for freight, producing 1,200 hp and capable of working in multiple, as well as two 2,400 hp B-B+B-B passenger machines.

For general electrification, SJ, the Swedish State Railway, decided on a single class of locomotive to work passenger and freight trains. 1-C-1, whose gearing can easily be changed to operate either 500-ton passenger-trains at 65 mph or 900-ton freight trains at 45 mph. Electrification did not supplant steam rapidly. Main routes were electrified in the 1930s with considerable success, including the Stockholm–Gothenburg line.

In the early days, locomotives were bought from Britain. Later, designers adapted and developed them to suit local needs. This may be why inside-cylinders continued to be used long after most mainland countries had adopted the more convenient outside form. The practice continued until in 1930 the

● LEFT
This private Traffic-Ab Grangesberg-Oxelosunds Jarnvagar (TGOJ) operated noncondensing turbine locomotives. Class MT3 71 joins a parade at Stockholm in 1981.

Swedish Motala works built a massive inside-cylinder 4-6-0 for the private Kalmar Railways operating in the south-eastern province of Kalmar.

The private Traffic-Ab Grangesberg–Oxelosunds Jarnvagar (TGO), basically an iron-ore mining company, had three noncondensing turbine locomotives in its stock, which achieved a degree of successful operation.

The three-cylinder locomotive was rare in Sweden. In 1927, Nydkvist and Holm of Trollhättan, Sweden, built a class for the Bergslagernas Railway. This class's golden days on the expresses between Gothenburg and Mellerud, on Lake Vanern, ended with electrification in 1939.

As late as 1955, 10 per cent of train miles were operated by steam and 63 per cent by electricity. The remaining 27 per cent was diesel, but during the period under consideration, up to 1950, diesel traction had yet to become significant.

SWEDISH STATE RAILWAY (SJ) 4-6-0

Date	1918
Builder	Nyakvist and Holm, Trollhättan, Sweden
Client	Swedish State Railway (SJ)
Gauge	1,435 mm
Class	B
Driving wheels	1,750 mm
Capacity	2 cylinders 590 x 620 mm
Weight in working order	69.2 tonnes (excluding tender)
Maximum service speed	90 kph

● NORWAY

Norway, politically linked with Sweden under the Swedish Crown between 1814–1905, is the most mountainous of Scandinavian countries. Its railway lines spread out from the capital, Oslo, like fingers, seeking natural routes to a scattered population.

Norway's railways developed late and in a scattered fashion. In the more benign terrain north of Oslo, steam traction was successful. British designs were the basis for further development.

Locomotives had been bought from the USA since 1879. When purchase of new locomotives became necessary during World War I, Baldwin Works of Philadelphia, USA, were asked to supply 2-8-0s, ostensibly to Norwegian design. Certainly, the boiler fittings and enclosed cab were Norwegian, but the rest was

● LEFT
The beauty of polished wood adorning bodywork is a striking feature of SJ Class Du 1-C-1 E109 as it waits with its train of period coaches at Malmø Central Station, in the southern Swedish seaport, in 1981.

● RIGHT
This HHJ Class H3 4-6-0 No. 21 is pictured assembling its train of vintage coaches at Klippan, southern Sweden, in 1981.

● BELOW
The massive scale of this direct descendant of the earliest "Iron Ore" railway electric locomotives is put into perspective by the people in the foreground. It was joining a parade in Stockholm, Sweden, in 1981.

pure Baldwin. Two 0-10-0 yard-shunters came from the same source in 1916, as well as three 2-8-2 for freight. In 1919, a 2-6-2T arrived, which now had the stamp of real Norwegian design.

Later classes show German influence. An unusual design of 1935 was a 2-8-4, a wheel arrangement previously seen only in Austria for an express-locomotive. The class were four-cylinder compounds for the Dovre line, across the Dovrefjell, the 2,285 m (7,565 ft) high central Norwegian plateau, between Dombås and Trondheim (formerly Trondhjem), the seaport and the country's third largest city. The first engine was called The Dovre Giant. However, much smaller and ageing 2-6-0s and 4-6-0s worked main-line and branch services into the mid-1960s.

Electrification, especially in the far north, followed the Swedish pattern. Because there was plenty of water for hydroelectric power, electrification began in 1922 between Oslo and Drammen, the seaport on a branch of Oslo Fjord. At the same time, work was in hand to link the main centres to Oslo. Trondheim was first in 1921, followed by Christiansand, the seaport on the Skagerrak in 1938 and Stavanger seaport in 1944.

Almost all the route mileage of about 4,300 km (2,700 miles) is state-owned, about a third of which is electrified at 15 kv single phase 16⅔ Hz. Few narrow-gauge systems operated by state and private companies have survived.

Narvik, which exports iron ore, is the terminus for the railway that cuts across the peninsula from the Swedish port of Lulea on the Gulf of Bothnia. It is one of the world's two most northerly railway stations.

● RIGHT
The latter-day Swedish State Railways (SJ) steam locomotive is well represented by Class B 4-6-0 No. 1367 as it hauls a special train at the southern Swedish town of Nassjo in 1981. Note the large, enclosed cab.

INDIAN RAILWAYS

Of all world railways influenced by Britain, those of India best reflected the British presence. Railway development proceeded further in India than in any other part of Asia and by the 1950s 64,400 km (40,000 miles) were operating, comprising broad-gauge trunk lines, connecting large centres of population, and a network of narrow-gauge lines.

In the 19th century, four gauges emerged on the Indian subcontinent: 5 ft 6 in; metre; 2 ft 6 in; and 2 ft. The variety of companies operating these gauges had ordered a diversity of designs, which, with the exception of some metre-gauge standards , were largely unco-ordinated. The Central Provinces (from 1950 Madhya Pradesh), for example, had three railway systems.

● ENGINEERING STANDARDS COMMITTEES

This led the British Engineering Standards Committee (BESA) to appoint a subcommittee, composed of several leading British locomotive mechanical engineers, to prepare a set of standard designs for the subcontinent. In 1905, eight locomotive types were suggested to cover all broad-gauge requirements across India. The designs were classic British products: inside-cylinder 0-6-0s and 4-4-0s with common boilers, Atlantics, 4-6-0s and 2-8-0 heavy goods.

● LEFT
The inside-cylinder 4-4-0 express-passenger hauling version of the inside-cylinder 0-6-0, again with an LNER aura – in this case the Manchester, Sheffield and Lincolnshire Railway's Pollitt 4-4-0s.

In 1924, the newly appointed Locomotive Standards Committee (LSC) was asked to make a new set of designs, in accordance with the need for more powerful locomotives. The committee presented eight basic types. The main ones were three Pacifics, XA, XB and XC, for branch-, medium- and heavy-passenger work; two Mikados, XD and XE, for medium and heavy goods respectively; and XT 0-4-2Ts for branch-line work.

Standard designs for metre and narrow gauge were also produced. Following the prefix X for the broad gauge came Y for metre gauge, Z for 2 ft 6 in gauge and Q for 2 ft gauge.

● AMERICAN INFLUENCE

A dramatic change occurred during World War II, Britain could not supply sufficient locomotives for India's increased traffic requirements and many new designs were ordered from North

● LEFT
A typically British 2-8-0 classified HSM from India's South Eastern Railway. These were once main-line heavy-freight haulers on the Bengal & Nagpur Railway. This last survivor is pictured on tripping duties in the Calcutta area.

● LEFT
An XC Class Pacific 4-6-2 of Indian Railways. These engines bear a striking resemblance to Gresley's Pacifics. Both types were introduced in the 1920s.

● BELOW
The heavy-freight hauling version of the XC was the XE 2-8-2. It bore a striking resemblance to Gresley's P1s of 1925.

● BOTTOM
One of Indian Railways's standard inside-cylinder 0-6-0s. These proliferated throughout many of the broad-gauge systems of the subcontinent. In common with the X types, these engines bear a striking resemblance to LNER classes, in this case the Pom Pom J11s of Great Central Railway (GCR).

America. These designs contrasted dramatically with the British engines and set a precedent for the remainder of steam development in India, because of suitability and popularity.

Three notable designs appeared on the 5 ft 6 in gauge: the AWC, which was an Indian version of Major Marsh's famous S160 of World War II; the class AWE, which was an Americanized version of the XE 2-8-2; and a lighter mixed-traffic Mikado 2-8-2 classified AWD/CWD. These three classes totalled 909 locomotives, 809 (89 per cent) of them being the light Mikado from mixed-traffic work. All entered service between 1943–9.

INDIAN XE CLASS 2-8-2

Date	1930
Builder	William Beardmore Dalmuir, Vulcan Foundry, Lancashire, England
Client	East Indian Railway
Gauge	5 ft 6 in
Driving wheels	5 ft 1½ in
Capacity	Cylinders 23 x 30 in
Total weight	200 tons

Chinese Locomotive Traditions

Railway development came late in China, and an incredible locomotive-building programme and standardization of types occurred in the years following World War II.

LEFT
This streamlined Pacific classified SL7 is of a type built in Japan by Kawasaki and at the works of the South Manchurian Railway. These engines worked the high-speed Asia day-train between Dairen (the Japanese name for Dalian) and Mukden (modern Shenyang). The class was introduced in 1934.

Early Development with Foreign Loans

As recently as 1930, China had fewer than 16,000 km (10,000 miles) of railway. During the early years of the 20th century, China's railways were developed by a number of organizations, but invariably they turned to American imported locomotives of modest proportions. America's vigorous drive to promote the export of locomoties proved effective in China. The similarity in size between America and China, along with the varied terrain which the two countries

USATC S160 2-8-0	
Date	1943
Builders	American Locomotive Company (Alco); Baldwin Locomotive Company; Lima Locomotive Company
Client	United States Army Transportation Corps of Engineers (USATE)
Gauge	4 ft 8½ in
Driving wheels	4 ft 9 in
Capacity	2 cylinders 19 x 26 in
Total weight	125 tons

LEFT
In the years following World War II, a number of Major Marsh's classic S160 2-8-0s were transferred to China in a programme to rebuild the country's railways.

● **RIGHT**
A China Railway's JF Class 2-8-2 Mikado on heavy shunt duties at Sankong Bridge, Haerbain (Harbin), the capital of Heilongjiang Province, north-eastern China.

had in common, rendered the American locomotive relatively easy to sell and well suited to the task in hand.

● THE SOUTH MANCHURIAN RAILWAY

The most developed part of China was Manchuria, and the South Manchurian Railway, although Japanese owned, was almost entirely American in its equipment and operation as a result of America having provided most of Japan's railway. In 1931, Japan took over Manchuria and with it the North Manchurian Railway. Locomotives operated in Manchuria were locally made as well as imported from Japan.

The advancement of railway and industrial operation in Manchuria led to the South Manchurain Railway's introducing the streamlined "Asia" train in 1934, which operated a fast air-conditioned service between Dalian and Shenyang, or Makden as it was then known. Streamlined Pacific locomotives were built for this service both in Japan and South Manchuria.

● RAILWAYS UNDER CHAING KAI-SHEK

Under the nationalist government of Chiang Kai-shek, development of railways was proceeding in other parts of the country in the 1930s. In 1937, the outbreak of the Sino-Japanese War ended new building. As this war went on, 80 per cent of China's railways were either destroyed or fell into Japanese hands. However, China's central government continued to build lines in the west, in areas not occupied by the Japanese.

● **RIGHT**
A former Soviet Union FD Class 2-10-2 engine, introduced in 1931. About 1,250 of these engines were transferred to China in the 1950s. The Chinese railway's standard QJ Class was derived from them. The FDs were themselves derived from an American design.

● **RIGHT**
Little British design influence permeated China's railways. American, Russian and indigenous factors were all the more prevalent. An exception is this Mogul, believed to be designed in Glasgow, Scotland, but built in China.

● KMT: RAILWAYS UNDER COMMUNISTS

Japan's surrender in 1945 found China's railways in an appalling state. Aid came through the United Nations Relief and Rehabilitation Adminstration (UNRRA) scheme, which again brought huge numbers of American locomotives to Chinese soil. The ongoing Chinese Civil War caused further damage.

By the time of Mao's victory in 1949, the railways were in terrible disarray. Only half of the system was active. The following decades provided some stability under a powerful national identity and a centrally planned economy. The railways flowered under this regime. Herein lay the seeds of China's "Golden Age" of railways, expanding from the 1950s to the present day.

South-east Asian Railways

This section covers the railways of Peninsular Malaysia, from 1957 the successor-state to the British-controlled Federation of Malaya; of Thailand proper and Peninsular Thailand, which joins Peninsular Malaysia at the Kra Isthmus; of Indonesia and the Philippines.

● PENINSULAR MALAYSIA

In 1909 the last link of the line between two island cities of the then-British colony called the Straits Settlements, Penang and Singapore, respectively at the north and south ends of Peninsular Malaysia, was opened. Termini were on the mainland, at ferry ports serving the islands. The engines used on this line were the Pacifics, which, although small by British and continental standards, were robust machines weighing about 76 tons. With a 4-6-4 wheel arrangement, the locomotives had large headlights and cowcatchers.

In 1938, three-cylinder Pacific express-passenger locomotives were introduced on the Malayan metre-gauge line between Singapore, Kuala Lumpur, capital of Perak State, and Prai, the railway terminus and seaport on the mainland, opposite George Town on Penang Island. Part of this line ascended the 1,000 m (3,300 ft) high Taiping Pass near Ipoh, the commercial centre of the Kinta Valley tin-mining region of Perak. These heavy gradients called for a special type of locomotive. The three-cylinder 4-6-2 Pacifics had a relatively small boiler but at high pressure provided the latent energy needed for developing a high tractive power.

The Pacifics were used on long runs but there were branch lines on which a tender-engine was unsuitable. For these, a 4-6-4 two-cylinder tank-engine was

● ABOVE
The Insular Lumber Company on the Philippine island of Negros operated the world's last four-cylinder compound 0-6-6-0 Mallet. It was built by Baldwin in the 1920s.

● ABOVE
One of South-east Asia's most remarkable systems is the stone railway at Gunung Kataren in northern Sumatra, Indonesia. The line conveys stones from a riverbed to a crushing plant for use as track ballast. Built to 60 cm gauge, this veteran came from Orenstein & Koppel in 1920.

● LEFT
Three standard Japanese 3 ft 6 in gauge designs. Left, a Government Railway Class DT595 2-8-0 (Japanese National Railway 9600 Class); centre, a Class CT192 Mogul (JNR Class 8620); right, a Class DT673 Mikado (JNR Class D51) – 1,100 of these mixed-traffic 2-8-2s were built between 1936–45.

● **RIGHT**
A 4-6-0 built for metre-gauge Royal Siamese State Railways in 1919 by North British of Glasgow, Scotland.

4-6-0	
Date	1919
Builder	North British Glasgow, Scotland
Client	Royal Siamese State Railways
Gauge	Metre
Driving wheels	4 ft
Capacity	Cylinders $14\frac{1}{2}$ x 22 in

used. It was fitted with cowcatchers at both ends so that it was suitable for running in both directions. Like the Pacifics, these 4-6-4Ts were fitted with Caprotti valve gear.

● **THAILAND**

In Siam (Muang-Thai to Thais and since 1949 Thailand), in the rice-growing and jungle country, the metre-gauge railway was laid with relatively light rails on a soft road bed. Powerful locomotives were needed, and in 1925 26 Pacific 2-8-2s were bought from the USA. They were woodfired, and routes were arranged so that the engines would travel out and back to their home station on one tenderful of fuel. The round trips were 193–225 km (120–140 miles) long. This arrangement meant frequent engine changes *en route*.

● **ABOVE**
A battered, hybridized, American-built Mikado, believed to have been constructed by Alco in 1921, at work on the metals of the Ma Ao Sugar Central railway on the Philippine island of Negros. These locomotives draw freshly cut sugar cane from the fields to the mills.

● **RIGHT**
A Thai railways metre-gauge Pacific 4-6-2, No. 823, which, with the MacArthur 2-8-2s, was one of Thailand's last steam locomotives.

Australasian Railways

New South Wales (NSW) entered the 20th century with a scheme to have main-line traffic handled by standard classes for passenger services, the P6 (later C32) Class 4-6-0; for goods traffic, the 1524 (later D50 Class) 2-8-0, of which 280 were built; and for suburban working the S636 (later C30) Class, numbering 145 units.

● LEFT
K167, an example of Australia's Victorian Railways K Class Consolidations introduced in 1922, pictured with a tour-train at Bandiana, near the New South Wales (NSW) border, in 1965.

● LEFT
After 1924, the P96 Class was reclassified as the C32 class. With regular floods in the Hunter Valley, in eastern NSW, this class was able to maintain traffic in conditions no diesel-electric could handle. The cover over the crosshead keeps out dust in the almost desert country in the far west of NSW.

● NEW SOUTH WALES

In the mid-1920s, as traffic grew, 75 C36 Class units took over major passenger services. From 1929, 25 4-8-2 D57 Class units were introduced for heavyfreight. With extreme traffic during World War II, 30 new C38 Class Pacifics were built, becoming the foremost express-locomotive. With the need for new goods locomotives after the war, 42 4-8-4+4-8-4 Garratts were obtained to carry the brunt of the load prior to the arrival of diesels.

● TASMANIA

Tasmania also used Garratts – the 2 ft gauge K Class of 1910 being the first Garratt in the world. The 3 ft 6 in lines followed, with the L Class 2-6-2+2-6-2 for goods traffic and the M Class 4-4-2+2-4-4s for passenger traffic.

● SOUTH AUSTRALIA

In South Australia, ten 4-6-2 passenger, ten 2-8-2 goods and ten 4-8-2 mixed-traffic locomotives entered service in 1926. These were of American design but built in England. On the narrow gauge, the T Class were the mainstay of the traffic, almost to the end of steam.

● WESTERN AUSTRALIA

Western Australia introduced 57 F Class 4-8-0s in 1902. These were accompanied by 65 E Class 4-6-2s for passenger services. Larger Pacifics entered service from 1924 onwards. Following World War II, the fleet was augmented by 60 light-line Beyer Peacock 4-8-2 W Class and 25 heavy 2-8-2 V Class from Robert Stephenson & Hawthorn.

● AUSTRALIAN NETWORK AND THE TCR

The development of Australia's railway network was complicated but striking. The gauge was not uniform (New South Wales was mostly the standard 4 ft 8½ in, South Australia mostly broad 5 ft 3 in gauge and all Queensland was narrow 3 ft

● LEFT
Imported from the North British Works, Glasgow, Scotland, in 1950, this Pmr726 Pacific is pictured outside the Midland workshops in 1968. Unsuccessful at speed, these locomotives did excellent goods-traffic work.

● **RIGHT**
The pride of Australia's NSW Railways, No. 3801, introduced in 1943, waiting to depart with an air-conditioned passenger-train in 1963.

SAR RX 4-6-0	
Date	1909
Builder	SAR Islington/NBLC Walker (SA)
Client	NSWGR
Gauge	4 ft 8½ in
Wheels	5 ft 9 in
Capacity	Cylinders 18 x 24 in
Weight	201 tons

● **RIGHT**
In 1899, South Australian Railways (SAR) started converting 30 R Class 4-6-0 locomotives to Rx Class by providing higher-pressure boilers. An additional 54 were newly built in 1909. This example, RX93, is pictured at the Mile End depot in 1965.

6 in gauge). Of the continent's some 45,000 km (28,000 miles) of railway, all but about 3 per cent, 1,290 km (800 miles), was state-owned by the 1950s. Of that length, 1,694 km (1,052 miles) were occupied by the Transcontinental (East-West) Railway completed in 1917. The TCR crosses South Australia and Western Australia, linking Port Augusta, at the head of the Spencer Gulf, and Perth with its port of Fremantle on the Indian Ocean. It crosses the Great Victoria Desert and the Nullarbar Plain, serves the goldfields of Kalgoorlie and the agricultural industry, and runs link lines to Port Pirie and to Alice Springs in the Northern Territory.

● NEW ZEALAND

New Zealand's main claim to fame is the development of the world's first true Pacific locomotive, 13 of which were supplied by Baldwin in 1901. These engines had a long life, the last being written off in 1957. The Pacific was further developed, eventually to the Ab class of 1915, of which 141 were built, and to a tank-engine, the Wab class. The Ab Class is claimed to be the first locomotive in the world to have been capable of 1 hp for each 100 lb of weight.

Tank engines played a major part on the lines of this small nation, the 4-6-4T W Class of 50 units being one of the more prolific. Garratts were also tried in 1928 but failed, due less to design faults than to the light drawgear on New Zealand rolling stock and the short crossing loops, making economical running almost impossible. Heavier conventional locomotives followed.

● **BELOW**
Designed for traffic on light lines, this example of a J Class was one of 40 delivered to New Zealand at the start of World War II. A modified Ja Class supplied in 1946 is in front. The two locomotives are pictured at Fielding-Marton in 1972.

African Railways

The years before the start of World War I were exciting and dynamic on South Africa's railways, many designs being produced. The 20th century brought a foretaste of the giants to come, powerful 2-8-2s, 4-8-0s and 4-8-2s being put into traffic with some racy Pacific designs.

● UNION OF SOUTH AFRICA

The immense distances and sparsely populated country called for strong locomotives, many of which had four-wheeled leading bogies to cope with cheaply laid track beds.

South African Railways (SAR) were formed in 1910 by the amalgamation of Africa's main railway companies. These were the Cape Government Railway (CGR), the Natal Government Railway (NGR) and the Central South African Railway (CSAR).

The country's first articulated locomotives were 2-6-6-0 compounds built by the American Locomotive Company (Alco). The type was introduced on to Natal's heavily graded, sharply curved routes.

Just as the giant Mallet conquered America, so the Garratt articulated conquered Africa. South Africa's railways were one of the largest users of Garratts from their introduction to the country in 1920. They quickly proved themselves superior to the Mallet on a network that ran through difficult terrain abounding in heavy gradients and curves with relatively lightly laid track.

The Garratt's boiler and firebox are free of axles and so can be built to whatever size is needed. A deep firebox allowed for ample generation of steam and full combustion of gases. By placing the engine's wheels and cylinders under a front water unit and with the rear coal units situated either side of the boiler, the engine's weight is spread over a wide area. With the front and rear units articulated from the boiler, a large, powerful locomotive can be built capable of moving heavy loads over curved gradients and

● ABOVE
In contrast with the typical four- and six-coupled tanks of British industry, South Africa's engines were fully fledged mainliners to haul trains over undulating tracks to SAR connections often many miles from collieries. This North British-built 4-8-2T is one of a standard class exported from Glasgow, Scotland, to South Africa for industrial use.

● LEFT
SAR 3 ft 6 in-gauge 4-8-2s of the 1930s.

● BELOW
Garratts on the Greytown Line in Natal, South Africa. One of SAR's pugnacious GMA Class 4-8-2+2-8-4 Garratts prepares to leave New Hanover, Natal, with full freight for Greytown. These powerful secondary Garratts, descended from the GM Class of 1938, climbed 1:40 gradients with only 60 lb weight.

SAR "BIG BILL" 4-8-2

Date	1925
Builder	Baldwin, American Locomotive Company (USA), Breda (Milan, Italy), North British (Glasgow, Scotland)
Client	South African Railways (SAR)
Gauge	3 ft 6 in
Wheels	5 ft
Capacity	Cylinders 24 x 28 in
Weight	173 tons

● **FAR LEFT**
The SAR Class 15CA, 4-8-2 "Big Bills" were the first large American engines imported to South Africa. They had a profound influence on locomotive development.

● NAMIBIA (FORMERLY SOUTH WEST AFRICA)

In the years following World War II, 100 2-8-4 Berkshires were put into operation for branch-line work, particularly over the 45 lb rail lines in South West Africa (Namibia since independence in 1990). They had cylindrical bogie tenders for long-range operation in waterless areas. The type displaced the ageing Class 7 and Class 8 4-8-0s of half a century earlier.

lightly laid lines. SAR used more than 400 Garratts, mostly British-built.

The 1920s also saw the introduction of large 4-8-2s and Pacifics of pure American construction. These set the precepts for the giants that followed, such as the 15F Class and 23 Class 4-8-2s. These formed the mainstay of steam motive power from the 1930s until the end of steam operations.

● **ABOVE RIGHT**
The Mallett was little used in South Africa but this 2-6-6-2, four-cylinder compound Class MH was one of five built by North British in 1915. At their introduction, they were the largest locomotives in the world on 3 ft 6 in gauge track.

● **RIGHT**
A South African Railways (SAR) Class 23 4-8-2 heads northwards from Bloemfontein, capital of Orange Free State. These American-inspired engines of 3 ft 6 in gauge were constructed in the late 1930s by both British and German builders and totalled 136 examples.

● LEFT
A former Tanganyika Railway ML Class 2-8-2, complete with Geisl ejector and air brakes – and one of Tanganyika Railway's last designs.

● OPPOSITE TOP LEFT
The plate from a locomotive built for Rhodesian Railways by Beyer Peacock of Manchester, England.

● ZIMBABWE

Railways were essential to the rich development potential of landlocked Zimbabwe (Southern Rhodesia until 1964, Rhodesia 1964–78). Routes extended to the Indian Ocean ports, eastwards to Beira in Mozambique, southwards through South Africa to Durban in Natal. A third route was opened up northwards, across the Victoria Falls at Hwange (until 1982 Wankie) and on through the copper belt. This route reached the Atlantic Ocean ports via the Bengeula Railway in Angola. By 1920, when Rhodesia Railways (RR) was formed, a unified 3 ft 6 in gauge was in operation.

Motive power was not dissimilar from that of South Africa, with 4-8-0s and 4-8-2 Mountains. As the national wealth of this vast region was developed, however, the demand for heavier trains became huge and articulated locomotives vital. After a Kitson-Mayer phase, the Garratt phase was introduced to standardize the system. Almost half the locomotives built for Rhodesian Railways were British-built Garratts, embracing all duties from branch-line work, through heavy freights to expresses with the racy 15th Class 4-6-4+4-6-4s. These handled mixed-traffic duties and reached speeds of 70 mph with passenger-trains.

● LEFT
Following the lead by the USA the wide firebox appeared early on Britain's locomotive exports, especially those bound for African countries. A typical example was the Rhodesian Railways 12A Class 4-8-2. The example shown is No. 190, built in 1926 by North British, Glasgow, Scotland.

● EAST AFRICA

In East Africa, the British-built Kenyan and Ugandan lines and the German-built

● RIGHT
A former Rhodesian Railways 16th Class Garratt 2-8-2+2-8-2, built by Beyer Peacock of Manchester, England, in 1929, working at the Transvaal Navigation Colliery, South Africa.

railways of neighbouring Tanzania (formerly Tanganyika) were metre gauge. The Ugandan railway in its early years used early Indian metre-gauge types, notably E Class 0-4-2s and the celebrated F Class 0-6-0s. Invariably, motive power

CLASS 54 2-8-2+2-8-2 GARRATT	
Date	1944
Builder	Beyer Peacock, Manchester, England
Client	Kenya & Ugandan Railway (via UK Ministry of Supply)
Gauge	Metre
Wheels	3 ft $9\frac{1}{2}$ in
Capacity	4 cylinders 19 x 24 in
Weight	185 tons

● **RIGHT**
A typical African plantation-train during the early 20th century at Lugazi, Uganda. The unidentified engine, with ornate spark-arresting chimney, is of European origin.

blossomed and embraced a Mallet stage and some Garratts, although the 4-8-0 was adopted as a general standard, many examples being to Indian BESA designs.

By the time the Kenya & Ugandan Railway (KUR) was formed in 1926, extremely powerful 2-8-2s worked the line linking the Kenyan Indian Ocean port of Mombasa and the Kenyan capital at Nairobi. The network also had a wide variety of Garratts, although these remained in a minority compared with the conventional locomotives, many of which were used on lighter sections of this vast area of Africa.

● ANGOLA

The 1,347 km (837 mile) long Angola Railway (Benguela Railway) was built by the Portuguese to link their then west and east coast possessions in southern Africa, respectively Angola and Mozambique. From the west, it runs from the Atlantic Ocean ports of Lobito and Benguela, to the Democratic Republic of Congo (formerly Zaire), linking to Port Francqui (Ilebo), the Copper Belt of Zambia (formerly Northern Rhodesia) and Zimbabwe, and on to the Indian Ocean ports of Sofala (formerly Beira) and Maputo (Lourenço Marques until 1975) in Mozambique, and Durban, then on to the Cape.

It achieved world renown for the eucalyptus-burning Garratts, which worked over one of the sections climbing the steep coastal escarpment inland from the Atlantic. These red-liveried mammoths shot columns of fire into the sky at night and were regarded by some as one of the railway sights of the world.

Northern African Railways

● LEFT
Nameplates from former Gold Coast Railway's steam locomotives commemorating British governors, tribes and slaving forts.

Railway development in Africa was essential to open up the industrial potential of the continent's interior and provide vital lifelines for the movement of materials. Africa has benefited vastly from her railways but their piecemeal, often parochial, building defied the obvious ideal of a Pan-African system. Had the railways been built with this vision, Africa would be an infinitely more prosperous continent than she is today.

● ALGERIA

Algeria's railways were built and engineered by the French from the mid-19th century. A large network of lines of various types emerged, including through links with neighbouring Tunisia and Morocco. The standard gauge, fed by metre-gauge lines, saw many 0-6-0s. Moguls and standard De Glehn compounds of types commonly seen in Europe.

In the 1920s, 2-10-0s appeared for hauling heavy mineral trains. Famous types working in Algeria included some Prussian G8s and three-cylinder G12s. Most celebrated, however, were the Algerian Garratts. These, built in France in 1932, were the most powerful express-passenger-locomotives ever to operate outside the USA.

By the 1950s, a rail network of more than 4,800 km (3,000 miles) penetrated all parts of Algeria. Two lines stretched into the Sahara to link with motor routes stretching to then French West Africa.

EGYPTIAN STATE RAILWAYS (ESR) ATLANTIC 4-4-2

Date	1906
Builder	North British, Glasgow, Scotland
Client	Egyptian State Railways (ESR)
Gauge	4 ft 8½ in
Driving wheels	6 ft 3 in
Capacity	Cylinders 17 x 26 in

● TUNISIA

Tunisia had both standard- and metre-gauge lines, although no standard-gauge locomotives were delivered into the country after 1928. During World War II, American S160 2-8-0-s, British Hunslet Austerity 0-6-0STs and some British Great Western Dean goods were all introduced for military operations.

● MOROCCO

Morocco's railways were also French-dominated, the country having become a French protectorate in 1912. Through-services were run between Marrakech in

● BELOW
These British-styled Atlantics were delivered to ESR in 1906 from the North British Works in Glasgow, Scotland, for operation on Egypt's standard-gauge network.

● LEFT
Two 0-6-0 well-tanks made by Orenstein & Koppel at the Nsuta Manganese System in Ghana, West Africa. The engines' Works Nos. 10609/10 respectively were exported to Ghana (until 1957 the British colony called Gold Coast) in 1923.

the west and Tunisia in the east, a distance of 2,400 km (1,491 miles).

● EGYPT

The Egyptian State Railway (ESR) is the oldest in Africa and blossomed following British occupation of the Nile Valley in 1882. The railway was built and run by the British. Though the ESR operated a vast diversity of types, British operating methods and many British designs were in evidence. Much of Egypt's express-passenger work was handled by the Atlantic 4-4-2s, backed by either 0-6-0s or Moguls for mixed-traffic work.

World War II's North African Campaign demanded movement of really heavy freight trains. Many British Stanier 8F 2-8-0s were sent, of which 60 were adopted by the ESR after the war.

Egypt's rich locomotive tradition ended with a class of oil-burning, French-built Pacifics delivered as late as 1955.

● SUDAN

Egypt's standard-gauge lines contrast with the 3 ft 6 in gauge network of neighbouring Sudan where railway building proper began around the turn of the century. One of the earliest systems ran from the Nile Valley to the Red Sea then southwards through the capital, Khartoum. Although much of this early railway building had a military purpose, the beginnings of a national railway were established. Sudan has a great will to operate a good, viable railway system. Additions to the network were being made as late as 1960.

Pacifics and Mikados, many with light axle loadings, were a mainstay of Sudan's motive power. Sudan also operated 4-6-4+4-6-4 Garratts pulling 1,600 ton trains between Atbara, Khartoum and Wad Medani. In contrast, English-looking 0-6-0Ts handled shunting and local tripping work. The last of these was not built until 1951, notwithstanding Sudan received diesel-shunters as early as 1936.

The pièce de résistance of conventional Sudanese motive power came with the 42 500 Class 4-8-2s delivered by North British, of Glasgow, Scotland, in 1954.

● WEST AFRICA

In West Africa, Britain, France and Germany all introduced railways to their colonial possessions.

● ABOVE
The spinning driving wheels of a Class 500 4-8-2 of Sudan Railway.

● BELOW
A mixed train on Sudan State Railways headed by a standard oilburning Mikado 2-8-2 built by North British, of Glasgow, Scotland.

Latin American Railways

Latin America's railways are of great diversity, reflecting the vast geographical contrasts of a continent that ranges from the tropical rain forests of the Amazon, to the passes of the Andes standing at 4,266 m (14,000 ft), through to the verdant beef-rearing flatlands of the Argentine pampas.

● **ARGENTINA**

Argentina had by far the greatest density of railways, with over 100 different types of locomotive operating over five different gauges. The British-owned railways of Argentina constituted the largest commercial enterprise ever to operate outside an investing nation. With many of the country's railway systems operated by Britain, Argentina was a huge recipient of British products. British-built steam locomotives fired on Welsh coal gave Argentina one of the world's most successful economies, exporting vast tonnages of meat, grain and fruit.

● **URUGUAY**

The railways of neighbouring Uruguay were also British-owned. Beyer Peacock of Manchester, England, was a principal builder over many years. Manchester was connected with the vast Fray Bentos meat corporation based on Fray Bentos town in Uruguay.

● **BRAZIL**

The vastness of Brazil, with its network of 5 ft 3 in and metre-gauge lines and a huge diversity of secondary routes, plantation and industrial railways, also ensured an incredibly rich locomotive heritage. American-built locomotives predominated with British classics on the metre-gauge Leopoldina system.

● **PARAGUAY**

Neighbouring Paraguay's standard-gauge main-line railway linked the capital and chief port, Asunción, with Encarnación

● **LEFT**
Mixed freight to Fray Bentos, in Uruguay. The Uruguayan Railway's last-surviving T Class 2-8-0 named Ing Pedro Magnou is heading a train bound for the meat-canning port on the Uruguay River. This 2-8-0 has a distinctive Scottish Highland Railway aura about it.

● **OPPOSITE**
A 5 ft 6 in gauge survivor of the Chilean Railway's 38 Class on pilot duties at San Bernardo works, outside Santiago in Chile. It is probably the last survivor from Roger's of New Jersey, USA, having come from those works in 1896.

● **LEFT**
The last surviving Kitson-Meyer 0-6-6-0 – known as "The Dodo of the Atacama" – at work in Chile's Atacama Desert. These locomotives once brought gold and nitrates to Pacific coast ports.

386 km (240 miles) away on the Argentine border. This railway was also British-owned and operated. The main motive power for much of the present century has been provided by woodburning Edwardian Moguls, exported from the North British Works in Glasgow, Scotland.

● BOLIVIA AND CHILE

The railways of Bolivia, South America's other landlocked nation, connected Chile, over the Andes to the west, with Brazil and Argentina, over the humid lowlands to the east. The country's locomotive heritage was diverse, with a rich mixture of European, American and British schools of design.

● TRANS-ANDEAN RAILWAY (TAR)

The Trans-Andean Railway (TAR) completed in 1910 links Valparaiso, Chile's greatest seaport, with Buenos Aires, the Argentine capital, crossing the Andes and desolate Patagonia at the Uspallata Pass between Mendoza in Argentina and Santiago in Chile. The near 3 km (2 mile) long Trans-Andean RR tunnel crosses at the pass's highest point, at 3,986 m (13,082 ft), near the Western Hemisphere's highest peak, 6,958 m (22,835 ft) high Mount Aconcagua. The link cut the 11-day journey by boat via the Magellan Strait to 40 hours overland. The line climbs hills so steep that part of it uses cog-wheel apparatus.

BUENOS AIRES & GREAT SOUTHERN 11B CLASS 2-8-0

Date	1914
Builder	Beyer Peacock, North British and Vulcan Foundry
Client	Buenos Aires & Great Southern Railway (BAGS)
Gauge	5 ft 6 in
Driving wheels	4 ft $7\frac{1}{2}$ in
Capacity	Cylinders 19 x 26 in
Total weight	105 tons

● COLOMBIA, ECUADOR AND PERU

Colombia, Ecuador and Chile drew their locomotive traditions mainly from American builders. Peru had a mixture of American and British designs.

There were no locomotive-building traditions in South America or Africa. Both these continents were entirely dependent on the building traditions developed in Britain, Europe and America.

● **OPPOSITE MIDDLE**
A woodburning Edwardian Mogul from North British, of Glasgow, Scotland, heads along the standard-gauge main line from the Paraguayan capital Asunción to Encarnación on the Argentine border. This railway is the last all-steam worked international main line in the world.

● **RIGHT**
A 2-8-2, No. 183, of Guatemalan Railways, at Gualán in 1971.

AN 2
X 32

The 1950s to 2000

The second half of the 20th century saw the decline of the railway as the premier form of transport. Competition from roads and airlines was intense, and vast amounts of railways were closed worldwide. Half-way through the period, the steam locomotive disappeared from much of the world, and in Western countries it became almost extinct. However, railway administrations sought to stave off competition with super hi-tech trains, and today we are seeing a vigorous international movement away from roads and back to rail. Increasing congestion and population are helping railways to make this resurgence.

● ABOVE
An 8,100-hp Class 103 Co-Co, built for the Deutsche Bundesbahn's IC and TEE network, threads through the Rhine Gorge between Bonn and Mainz in the Rhineland-Palatinate state of Germany.

● OPPOSITE
An Australia National (formerly Commonwealth Railways) locomotive resting beside a platform.

British Main-line Shunters and Industrials

The evolution of British main-line steam shunting-locomotives ended in effect in the 1950s. It fell to the Great Western Railway (GWR) to end the tradition formally with its 1500 Class/9400 Class 0-6-0-Ts. Building of the 9400 Class continued until 1956 when it totalled 210 engines. These were the last examples of a pre-nationalization design built by British Railways.

With many 0-6-0Ts inherited from the "Big Four" companies, British Railways had little need for any more shunting-tanks. Downgraded goods-engines became evermore available and gravitated to shunting yards in hundreds. The contemporaneous advent of diesel-shunters in the 1950s saw the standard British Railways diesel-electric 350-hp 0-6-0 produced in profusion from Derby Works, in Derby, Derbyshire. Many remain in service, fulfilling the modest shunting opportunities left on the main-line system.

● LEFT
American-built diesels are being used on Britain's railways, on the main lines and in industrial service. This example, built for Foster Yeoman, is preparing rakes of aggregates at the company's Merehead quarry.

● BELOW LEFT
Several Great Western Railway (GWR) 5700 Class 0-6-0 pannier tanks passed into industrial service, to receive a further lease of life, like this one working at a colliery in South Wales.

● Diesels Replace Steam Shunters

It had long been recognized that diesels were superior for shunting. Their ability to switch on and off for work often involving long idle periods showed a clear advantage. Also, the even torque provided sure-footed starts with heavy loads.

Since 1966, there has been a huge fall in the number of shunting-engines. Certainly fewer diesel engines are needed than steam. Far more significant, however, has been the erosion of sidings and marshalling yards as freight has been transferred from rail to road. Instead of the shunter being an everyday sight with thousands operating nationwide, sight of one now is a rare occurrence that often draws comment.

● RIGHT
A 16- in Andrew Barclay 0-4-0 saddle-tank draws a rake of freshly lifted coal out of the washery at Pennyvenie Mine, near Dalmellington, Ayrshire, Scotland.

● PRIVATE USE DECIMATED

Steam-shunters survived in industrial environments many years after disappearing from main-line service. The last did not entirely disappear until the mid-1980s. Although diesels, including some early British Railway engines, readily infiltrated industrial networks too, the massive decline in Britain's heavy industry and increasing dependence on roads decimated the number of private organizations using their own locomotives. Those remaining, at collieries and power stations mostly, adopt the merry-go-round principle in which main-line trains serve the industry direct.

Fifty years ago, thousands of steam locomotives were working in hundreds of British collieries. Today there are no steam locomotives and only a handful of active collieries.

● LEFT
Cadley Hill Colliery, near Burton on Trent, Staffordshire, central England, was part of the Derbyshire Coalfield and one of the last locations in Britain to use steam locomotives. In this view, with Drakelow Power Station in the background, a standard Hunslet Austerity 0-6-0St (right) shunts beside Progress, a Robert Stephenson & Hawthorn 0-6-0 saddle-tank with inside-cylinders.

CLASS 08 DIESEL SHUNTER

Builder	Derby Locomotive Works, Derby, England
Client	British Railways
Gauge	Standard
Engine	English Electric 6-cylinder 350 brake horsepower (bhp) (261 kW)
Total weight	50 tons
Maximum tractive effort	35,000 lb
Maximum speed	15–20 mph

● RIGHT
Penzance, Cornwall, is one location of the British Railway network that retains a shunting-engine – a standard 08 Class Diesel Electric 0-6-0.

BRITISH MAIN-LINE FREIGHT

● LEFT
A British Railway's standard Class 9F 2-10-0s, No. 92084, reposes at Cricklewood Depot, north London, in 1960. This class totalled 250 engines.

● LEFT
An ARC's Class 59 Co-Co diesel-electric built in the USA by General Motors. Heavyfreight locomotives for Britain in future are likely to be American-built and of similar proportions to these aggregate-haulers.

In the 1950s, many 2-8-0s firmly controlled main freight hauls on the newly formed British Railways. The most numerous were the Great Western Railway's 2800s; the LNER's 01, 02 and 04 classes; Stanier's LMS Class 8F 2-8-0 and their Ministry of Supply version from World War II. In all, these totalled about 2,000 locomotives. The 2-8-0 was supported by a vast array of 0-6-0s and 0-8-0s, which in themselves handled trains little short of 1,000 tons, especially the 0-8-0s of the former North Eastern and London's North Western railways.

The 0-10-0, widely used in Europe, was avoided in Britain. Its light axleload was of little benefit. Its potential power and adhesion for hill-climbing were not generally necessary. The 2-8-0's greater flexibility was preferred.

Similarly, the 2-8-2 and 4-8-0 were not applied. The 2-8-2's wide firebox capacity did not have to be exploited, because of the good quality coal available. The 4-8-0's powerful hill-climbing capacity was not needed on Britain's main lines. Outside the mainstream of typically heavyfreight designs were some mighty 2-8-0 tanks Churchward produced, to work coal-trains from the valleys of South Wales to the docks.

● BELOW
Brush of Loughborough's Class 60 Co-Co diesel-electric No. 60061 Alexander Graham Bell heading oil-tanks along the West Coast main line beneath the 25 kV a.c. catinery. The 100 Class 60s, an advanced diesel-electric design, perform heavy haulage with trainloads up to 3,000 tons.

● NATIONALIZATION BRINGS STANDARDS

Fast mixed-freights were pulled by Moguls, 2-6-2s or 4-6-0 types generally regarded as mixed-traffic designs. The LMS Crabs and Gresley K3s were typical Moguls. The V2s were the main design of 2-6-2. The 4-6-0s were epitomized by Stanier's Black 5s of the LMS, Thompson's B1s of the LNER and Collett's Halls of the GWR. The antecedent of the 4-6-0 fast mixed-traffic goes back to the early years of the century with Robinson's Fish engines and Fast Goods types.

Following nationalization of Britain's railways in 1948, 12 standard designs – the Standards – were prepared for the

● **RIGHT**
British Railways Class 56 Co-Co diesel-electric locomotives were introduced in 1977 to handle heavy, slow-speed merry-go-round trains. The first 30 were built in Romania. A further 75 were built at Doncaster, South Yorkshire, and Crewe, Cheshire. The Class 56s have a 16-cylinder Ruston four-stroke diesel engine. The type has become a main heavyfreight hauler on the British Railways network.

CLASS 47 CO-CO DIESEL ELECTRIC

Date	1962
Builder	Brush of Loughborough, Leicestershire, and BR Crewe Works, Crewe, Cheshire, England
Client	British Railways
Gauge	Standard
Engine	Sulzer 1920 kW (2,580 hp)
Total weight	125 tons
Maximum tractive effort	60,000 lb
Maximum speed	95 mph

entire country. Among them was the Class 9F 2-10-0 heavy-mineral engine. So the evolution of the British goods-engine had at the eleventh hour aspired to ten-coupled traction some 50 years after the type had become prevalent in America and 40 years after its inception in Austria and Germany.

The trusted British 0-6-0 drudge had finally turned into a highly sophisticated engine. The 9F presented a perfect climax to British freight-locomotive development. Considering the inside-cylinder 0-6-0's major role over 125 years, it is amazing that its absolute displacement came within such a narrow space of time – the Southern Railway's Q1s appearing only 11 years before the first 9Fs.

The last 9F 2-10-0 was built in 1960. What a contrast these ultimate British freight haulers made with Stephenson's Locomotion No. 1 of 1825.

The diesel engine was invented in 1892 by French-born, German-educated engineer Rudolf Diesel (1858–1913). The first diesel engines were used in ships in 1903. The first diesel locomotive was built at the works of Sulzer in Switzerland in 1913.

● **RIGHT**
The Class 47 Co-Co diesel-electric's versatility is shown in this scene at Harbury Cutting, as one heads a Rail-freight Distribution container-train operating between Birmingham, West Midlands, and Southampton Docks, Hampshire.

British Diesel Multiple Units (DMUs)

The diesel multiple unit (DMU) descended from steam railcars working on the LMS and LNER in the 1920s and 1930s. These consisted of a single coach with a driving-compartment at either end and a steam-engine encased in a compartment at one end of the coach.

Britain's diesel-cars were introduced by GWR in 1933 for excursion traffic, branch-line and local services. Initially they worked between Paddington in west London and Didcot, about 80 km (50 miles) away in Oxfordshire. In 1934 they were used in an express service, mainly for businessmen on the 155 km (100 miles) between Birmingham in central England and Cardiff in Wales. The trains comprised two railcars with a restaurant-car between. This formation anticipated the first generation of DMUs in having two motor-units with a trailing car between and the later InterCity 125s with a power-car at both ends.

CLASS 158 EXPRESS DMU

Date	1990
Builder	British Rail Engineering Ltd. (BREL), England
Client	British Rail
Gauge	Standard
Engine	One Cummings 260 kW (350 hp) or 300 kW (400 hp), alternatively Perkins 260 kW (350 hp)
Maximum service speed	90 mph

● **ADVENT OF DIESEL-RAILCAR**

The advent of the diesel-railcar proper was in the 1950s, as part of the British Railways 1955 Modernization Plan. The theory was that diesel-units could serve more stations efficiently, effect rapid starts and use high speeds between stations separated by only a few miles. No sooner had DMUs taken over many steam-stopping services than a vast

● **ABOVE**
A brand-new Turbo Class 165 for working the Chiltern lines between London Marylebone Station and Birmingham reposes outside the Aylesbury depot, Buckinghamshire. These trains were introduced in 1992 as part of the Chiltern lines' total route modernization.

● **LEFT**
A Class 158 two-car BREL express unit. This design has bridged the gap between local/cross-country work and express services and is used on many long-distance runs across Britain.

● **ABOVE LEFT**
First-generation heritage DMUs, in Network South East livery repose at London Marylebone depot while working the Chiltern line. These units have been replaced on Thames and Chiltern lines by Class 165 Turbo-DMUs operating from the new depot at Aylesbury, Buckinghamshire.

● **ABOVE RIGHT**
A Class 141 Leyland Pacer in West Yorkshire (Public Transport Executive [PTE]) livery. These units were built from Leyland National Bus parts on four-wheeled underframes at the Derby works, Derby, in 1984.

number of stations were closed nationwide under Beeching.

Early, steel-bodied DMUs ran as two-, three- or four-coach units. Two-car ones generally comprised two motor-units. Three-car ones had a trailing unit in between. Four-car ones had a motor-unit at both ends. The diesel engine sat beneath the motorized cars, providing direct drive.

Many designs appeared in the 1950s and 1960s, particularly from the works at Derby and Swindon, Wiltshire, and from private builders such as Metro Cammell, Birmingham Railway Carriage and Wagon Co. and Cravens. These early units were known later as Heritage DMUs. Their numbers ever dwindle but several classes remain in service.

● **SECOND GENERATION**

The second-generation DMU was introduced in the mid-1980s as the Sprinter series. These have sliding doors, hydraulic transmissions and offer great advance in riding qualities over the earlier trains. The main classes are the 150s and the 156s. Both are usually seen in two-car formations and have a Cummins 285 hp engine beneath each car.

In contrast came the Pacers embraced by Classes 141, 142 and 143/144. These are lighter, four-wheeled vehicles with each car motorized. The absence of bogies made these units rougher to ride in and probably accounts for why they have not been popular.

The pièce de résistance of British DMUs is the Class 158 express unit. This first appeared from British Rail Engineering Ltd (BREL) in 1990. The 158s consist of two car units with an advanced bogie design and a 350 hp engine per car. They perform well on medium- and long-distance runs, are extremely comfortable and have a 90 mph top speed.

This second generation of DMUs has gone into widespread service nationwide and all but replaced traditional locomotive-hauled trains.

● **BELOW**
A green-liveried Heritage DMU "bubble car" heads an afternoon local service between Bletchley, Buckinghamshire, and Bedford, in the Midlands. Classified 121, these units date from 1960.

British Electrical Multiple Units (EMUs)

The electrical multiple unit (EMU) predated the diesel multiple unit (DMU) by many years for the City & South London Railway, which used EMUs when it opened in 1890. Power-collection was from a third rail carrying 450 volts. Apart from London's Underground, it was the Southern Railway – following the 1923 Grouping – which truly exploited the EMU's potential with an expanding network of electrification based on a third-rail system at 600 volts d.c.

In 1923, Britain's railway companies had been reorganized into four groups – the "Big Four": London, Midland & Scottish (LMS); London & North Eastern (LNER); the Great Western (GWR) and the Southern Railway (SR).

EMUs' high power:weight ratio provides the rapid acceleration needed on busy suburban services. Most EMUs consist of four-car sets including a motor-coach. As traffic demands, these trains can be run as either four-, eight- or 12-coach combinations.

● LEFT
Among British vintage overhead EMUs are Class 302s. One is pictured leaving Fenchurch Street Station, London, for Essex on the London-Tilbury, Southend-on-Sea section. These date back to the 1950s.

● ABOVE
A former Network South East Class 415/6. These are among the oldest units left on Britain's railways. They are slam-door stock with 750 volt d.c. third rail and date back to 1959.

● BELOW
Class 323s were introduced in 1992 for the West Midlands Public Transport Executive (PTE) and Greater Manchester PTE areas. They have aluminium bodies, thyristor control and sliding doors.

● NEW GENERATION

As main-line electrification spread across Britain from the late-1950s, a new generation of EMUs emerged with overhead pantographs collecting from 25 kV a.c. More recently dual-voltage units have appeared, capable of running on 25 kV a.c. overhead and 750 volt d.c. third rail. In this category, Thameslink Class 319 and 319/1s operate between Bedford, in the Midlands, and Brighton, the Sussex seaside resort, through the heart of London.

In the 1950s, DMU and EMU features were combined to produce several classes of trains with a diesel-engine in the motor-coach to generate electricity to drive the traction motors. These diesel electrical multiple units (DEMUs) run on sections of non-electrified railway.

● SUPERFAST EXPRESSES

In common with the DMU, the EMU soon developed into express units, the Brighton Belle being an early example. More recently, the Wessex Electrics have been introduced and operate superfast services between London Waterloo and Southampton in Hampshire and Bournemouth and Weymouth in Dorset. Later, the Networker Express Class 365, with aluminium bodies, advanced bogie design and regenerative braking, were introduced. These are 100 mph express units of comfort and sophistication.

● **RIGHT**
An express Class 325 parcels unit for postal services, with roller-shutter doors, heads south through the Lune Gorge with a West Coast postal train. These units operate on 25 kV a.c. overhead, 750 volt d.c. third rail.

● **BELOW**
Class 465 Networker EMUs replaced ageing units on Kent Link services. The new units have aluminium bodies, sliding doors and regenerative braking. They entered service in the early-1990s when building of new trains was at an all-time low. In 1996, the Class C1365 Networker Express was launched by Connex South Eastern. These 100-mph trains have dual-voltage capability, 2+2 seating layout (2+3 on Kent Link), a toilet for the disabled and carpeting throughout.

● **BELOW**
The Wessex Electrics Class 442 is a most prestigious EMU. These 100 mph units were built for the Waterloo-Bournemouth-Weymouth services and also worked to Portsmouth Harbour, Hampshire. Unusually for British EMUs, many are named. These comfortable riding units were introduced in 1988 as a partial refurbishment of older stock, a precedent likely to be followed in preference to building new trains.

Class 325 express postal units were introduced in 1995. Apart from their dual voltage, these 100 mph trains are compatible with diesel-locomotive haulage over non-electrified sections, giving access to the entire railway system.

Many units on the 750 volt d.c. lines of southern England are ageing. In 1996, Adtranz proposed the Networker Classic, a "half-life, quarter-cost solution" to unlock the potential of existing vehicles more than 25 years old by refurbishing the underframe, traction system and running-gear with the latest body design, including automatic sliding doors and crashworthy front ends.

● **BELOW RIGHT**
A ThamesLink dual-voltage Class 319 climbs the steep gradient into Blackfriars Station, London, with a Bedford-to-Brighton service. These 100 mph units work on 25 kV a.c. on the Midland main line and on 750 volt d.c. on the London-Brighton section.

CLASS 319 EMU

Date	1987
Builder	British Rail Engineering (BREL), York, England
Client	British Rail
Gauge	Standard
Engine	Four GEC of 247.1 kw
Maximum tractive effort	35,000 lb
Maximum service speed	100 mph

British Steam Standards

On nationalization of the "Big Four" railway companies – LMS, LNER, GWR and SR – in 1948, the new administration inherited hundreds of different locomotive types. Many of these had come down from the multiplicity of private companies that existed before the 1923 Grouping. This was untenable for a new, centralized administration and so it was proposed to build 12 standard types – the Standards – to fulfil most functions across the network.

● 1955 MODERNIZATION PLAN

Within four years of the Standards' introduction, the Modernization Plan for 1955 decreed the end of steam in favour of diesel and electric traction. This resulted in the Standards adding even more design variety. The new engines were designed on experience gained by the locomotive exchanges of 1948, in which the Big Four's leading types were tested across one another's territories to ascertain best-performance characteristics. Mechanically and aesthetically, the new designs showed a distinct departure from traditional British practices, towards those of America.

The 12 types comprised three Pacifics (the Britannia for fast express work, the Clans for fast mixed-traffic work and the solitary Duke of Gloucester intended as forerunner of a new generation of heavy express-passenger-locomotives), two classes of 4-6-0s, three of Moguls, one powerful 2-6-4 tank, two 2-6-2 tanks and the Class 9F mineral-hauling 2-10-0s.

Except for Duke of Gloucester and the 9Fs, the new Standards were all mixed-traffic designs, because by this time the concept of different locomotives for freight and passenger work had all but

● LEFT
British Railways Standard 80000 Class 2-6-4Ts were based on earlier LMS engines by Stanier and Fairburn. Powerful, with a turn of speed, they were to be found on many parts of Britain's railway network. The class totalled 155 examples.

BR BRITANNIA PACIFIC 4-6-2

Date	1951
Builder	Crewe Locomotive Works, Crewe, Cheshire, England
Client	British Railways
Gauge	Standard
Driving wheels	6 ft 2 in
Capacity	Cylinders 20 x 28 in
Total weight in full working order	150 tons

● **RIGHT**
British Railways Standard Pacific No. 71000 Duke of Gloucester reposes outside the paintshop at Crewe Works, Cheshire.

● **BELOW**
British Railways Standard Class 4 4-6-0s were for light passenger and general duties. The class numbered 80 engines. Their clean, modern lines, with distinct American characteristics, are shown in this picture.

● **OPPOSITE BOTTOM**
British Railways Standard Britannia Class Pacific No. 70042 Lord Roberts at Willesden, west London, in 1962.

disappeared. In principle, the 9Fs were the exceptions to this rule. In practice, their balanced proportions enabled them to undertake fast running with passenger-trains. Stories abounded of them reaching 90 mph – until their use on such work was forbidden.

● BRITANNIA AT THE FESTIVAL OF BRITAIN

In terms of easy accessibility to moving-parts and labour-saving devices, the Standards were an improvement on most previous designs. In terms of overall performance, they were little different from their Big Four counterparts on which they were largely based.

The first engine, No. 70000 Britannia, appeared at the Festival of Britain in 1951, attracting much interest and admiration. This was justified by the Britannias' performance over their relatively short lives. They proved extremely fast engines and put in scintillating performances, not least on the former Great Eastern main line between London Liverpool Street and Norwich, Norfolk.

Perhaps the biggest disappointment, at least initially, was the Duke of Gloucester, sluggish in service and heavy on coal. This engine passed into preservation, having been rescued from Woodhams Scrapyard in Barry, Glamorganshire, South Wales, and renovated to full working order. Computer calibrations of the Duke's valve settings proved, in the light of contemporary experience, that these were incorrectly set during the engine's main-line years, and the modifications made under preservation have enabled the Duke to climb the notorious Shap Bank with a 450-ton train at a speed hitherto unknown and to top the summit at 51 mph. This gives insight into the potential of steam and of this express-passenger design destined to remain as a solitary engine.

● **BELOW**
British Railways Standard Class 3 Mogul, No. 76005, one of a class of 115 engines for light intermediate work, at Bournemouth Shed, Dorset, in the mid-1960s.

British Diesel

The decision to dieselize came rather late in Britain. Not until 1955, when the government announced the Modernization Plan, was the end of the steam age seriously suggested. Even then, prolific railway experts like Cecil J. Allen confidently said steam would last until the end of the century.

The modernization programme was rapidly implemented. This resulted in many classes of diesel appearing, not all of which proved satisfactory. From the outset, diesel-electric was the preferred mode, following extensive trials of the LMS's 1947-built 10000/10001. The brief visit to the concept of diesel-mechanical, as epitomized by H.G. Ivatt's 4-8-4 No. 10100 introduced in 1951, and visits to gas turbines were not continued.

Diesel-hydraulic gained acceptance, especially on former Great Western lines, but the classes concerned, revered as they were, had a short life.

● LEFT
H.G. Ivatt's twin diesel-electrics Nos. 10000/10001 appeared in the late 1940s and paved the way for main-line dieselization. This proved to be a milestone in the evolution of British locomotives. A unit is pictured receiving attention in Derby works, Derbyshire.

● LEFT
The Class 47 Co-Co diesel "Maid of all Work" has been a familiar sight on Britain's railways since the early 1960s, with hundreds still operating. Here, one leaves Birmingham in the Midlands at the head of a cross-country express.

● Early Experiment

Another early experiment was the blue English Electric Deltic, prototype for the Deltics on the East Coast main line. These were highly admired, extremely successful and proved worthy successors to Gresley's A4 Pacifics.

Fine general-purpose mixed-traffic haulers are the Brush Sulzer Class 47s, which proved worthy successors to the 842 Stanier Black 5s. The 47s proved themselves equally at home with 90 mph passenger-trains or 1,000 ton freight-hauls. About 500 went into service; many remain active.

Other notables include Class 40 English Electrics, which moved most trains on the West Coast main line before electrification, and the Sulzer 12-cylinder Peaks introduced in 1959, which also proved themselves on passenger and freight. The 40s and Peaks are history but the Class 37, a 1950s design built from 1960 onwards, remains an important class engaged on such diverse services as EPS sleeping-car trains, locals, all types of mixed-freight operations and engineers' service trains.

● BELOW
One of the oldest diesel types left on British Railways is the Class 31 Brush Type 2s, introduced by Brush Traction at Loughborough, Leicestershire, in 1957. Over the years, they have been used on a wide variety of duties but are now almost entirely relegated to engineers' trains.

BR CLASS 37 CO-CO DIESEL ELECTRIC

Date	1960
Builder	English Electric Company, Vulcan Factory, Newton-le-Willows, or Robert Stephenson & Hawthorn, Darlington, Durham, England
Client	British Railways
Gauge	Standard
Engine	English Electric 1,300 kW (1,750 hp)
Total weight	108 tons
Maximum tractive effort	55,500 lb
Maximum service speed	80 mph

● ABOVE RIGHT
English Electric Type 3 Class 37 Co-Co diesel electrics were built in 1960-65 by the English Electric Co. at its Vulcan Foundry, Lancashire, and by Robert Stephenson & Hawthorn in Darlington, Durham. They truly are maids of all work, fulfilling many functions. One of their most prestigious services is the sleeping-car run through the Scottish Highlands to the tourist attractions of Fort William and Inverness.

● LEFT
A Class 50 Co-Co English Electric Type 4 diesel. Built in 1967–68 by the Vulcan Foundry at Newton-le-Willows, Lancashire, these engines originally worked the northern reaches of the West Coast main line between Crewe, in Cheshire, and Carlisle, in Cumbria, but ended up on the South Western main line between London Waterloo and Exeter, Devon.

● LEFT
The InterCity 125, one of the most successful trains in British railway history, revolutionized long-distance passenger services. Introduced in 1976, the 125s have a maximum speed of 125 mph, hence their name. A set on the Midland line is seen passing Milepost 92½, south of Leicester, with a Sheffield-to-London train.

● MIXED-TRAFFIC CONCEPT

The concept of mixed-traffic locomotives established by the British Railways Standard steam designs has continued through the diesel age, but since 1976 the classes 56, 58 and 60 have been put into operation mainly for mineral- and aggregate-haulage.

The next batches of new diesels for Britain's railways are tipped to come from North America when EWS begin their mighty restocking of British freight-motive power. The new engines may follow the lead begun with Foster Yeoman and ARC's Class 59 General Motors Co-Cos.

British Main-line Electric

● BELOW
A Class 73 Bo-Bo electro-diesel in InterCity livery working the Gatwick Express between London Victoria and Gatwick Airport – London, in West Sussex. Built at Eastleigh, near Southampton, Hampshire, in 1962, these engines operate from 660 to 850 volt d.c. third rail and are equipped with an English Electric diesel engine for running over non-electrified sections.

Although it is fashionable for electrification to be thought of as the ultimate railway modernization, it is a form of motive power extant in Britain since the 1880s. In the 19th century, two locomotive engineers, George Stephenson and F.W. Ebb, predicted that one day Britain's railways would run on electricity.

In 1905, the first freight-hauling electric locomotive appeared, on the North Eastern Railway (NER). After that, many adventurous schemes were proposed, including electrification of the NER's main line between York and Newcastle upon Tyne following World War I. However, the Depression in the 1930s, followed by World War II, prevented many projects being started. In 1948, only 17 main-line electric locomotives were inherited by British Railways.

● GREAT CENTRAL MAIN LINE ELECTRIFIED

In the early 1950s, a project was continued that had been held over in the war years. This was the electrification to 1,500 volt d.c. overhead of the steeply graded Great Central main line between the English industrial centres of Sheffield in West Yorkshire and Manchester in Lancashire. This highly acclaimed, much-publicized project operated Bo-Bo locomotives for freight and Co-Co for passengers.

Simultaneously, in the mid-1950s there was a development with Southern Region's electro-diesels. The traction motors were fed from either a third rail or by current generated from an on-board diesel engine, enabling them to run across non-electrified sections. Many of these Class 73s remain active today and can be seen on the Gatwick Express service from London Victoria to Gatwick Airport – London, in West Sussex.

● RIGHT
The 30-year-old Class 86 electric, built by English Electric at the Vulcan Foundry, remain the mainstay of services on the West Coast main line. Here, one approaches Crewe from the south, beneath the 25 kV a.c. overhead catinery.

● WEST AND EAST COAST MAIN LINES ELECTRIFIED

The West Coast main line, from London Euston Station, is Britain's busiest. It was an early candidate for electrification to 25 kV a.c. under the 1955 modernization scheme. The locomotives were designated mixed-traffic and designed to haul 475-ton trains at 90 mph on level track, with maximum speed of 100 mph, and 950-ton freight-trains at 42 mph, with a 55-mph maximum. The West Coast fleet's mainstay are Class 86s, dating back to 1965. The 86s and later

● **RIGHT**
Driving-van trailers (DVTs) used on Britain's East Coast and West Coast main lines simulate the design of Class 91 electrics. On both routes, southbound trains are headed by DVTs, as in this London-bound service waiting to leave Crewe, Cheshire.

● **OPPOSITE MIDDLE**
In the mid-1990s, Class 92 Bo-Bo electrics were introduced for through-services between Britain and Europe. The picture shows No. 92.019 at Crewe Station, Cheshire.

BR CLASS 91 BO-BO ELECTRIC

Date	1988
Builder	British Rail Engineering Ltd. (BREL),Crewe Works, Cheshire, England
Client	British Railways
Gauge	Standard
Traction motors	General English Electric (GEC) G426AZ
Total weight	84 tons
Continuous Rating	4540 kW (6090 hp)
Maximum speed	140 mph

87s are augmented by powerful Class 90s introduced in 1987.

Completion of the East Coast main-line electrification brought the Crewe-built Class 91s with an outstanding 140-mph top speed. These are Britain's most powerful locomotives capable of running across the East Coast racing-ground to reach Edinburgh, Scotland, in under four hours from King's Cross Station, London.

Almost all West Coast and East Coast main-line electric services have the locomotive at one end and a driving-van trailer (DVT) at the other. These are basically a luggage-and-parcel van with a driving console that enables the train to be driven in either direction without turning around.

Soon after completion of the 91 class came the dual-voltage Class 92s for operating freight- and passenger-trains through the Channel Tunnel between Britain and France. Apart from being another technical triumph, the 92s open up the possibility of running through freight-trains from many parts of Britain directly into Europe.

● **RIGHT**
A GEC-designed Class 91 Bo-Bo electric at King's Cross Station, London. These powerful locomotives revolutionized services on the East Coast main line.

British Light Rail

● BELOW
Supporting the regeneration of Birkenhead's docklands in Merseyside is a Heritage tramway featuring traditional double-deck trams, but built in Hong Kong to the British style.

Britain's first electric tramway ran in Blackpool, Lancashire. It was the only British urban tramway to survive the abandonment completed nationwide in Britain by 1962. This traditional system continues to modernize its infrastructure and trams. It is one of only three systems in the world to use double-deck cars.

● TRAMWAYS AND MASS-TRANSIT SYSTEMS

In addition to tramways, mass-transit systems were built in London and Glasgow, Scotland. London Underground is one of the world's largest metro systems, with two sizes of rolling stock used, on subsurface and tube lines respectively. The Glasgow underground is a city-circle line built for cable traction but electrified in the 1930s. New rolling stock was delivered as part of complete modernization in 1978–80.

● TYNE & WEAR METRO

After a decade when it seemed that most of Britain's towns and cities would have to make do with buses and increasing traffic congestion, the late 1970s saw planning start for flexible and cost-effective light-rail systems (LRS). In Tyneside, north-east England, the closure of run-down local rail services offered the Passenger Transport Executive (PTE) the opportunity to create a rail-based integrated system in 1980–84 by the introduction of light rail and new subways under the city centre. The successful Tyne & Wear Metro has been extended to Newcastle Airport, and also from Sunderland to South Hylton, using the disused Sunderland to Durham line.

● LONDON'S DLR

A different version of light rail was installed in London's Docklands in 1984–7. The Docklands Light Railway (DLR) was built as a fully segregated system (mostly on new or existing viaducts) with third-rail current collection and automatic train operation. Designed to carry 2,000 passengers an hour in single cars, the system soon had to be rebuilt to carry up to 12,000 passengers an hour with multiple-unit trains. The line now extends from Tower Gateway to the Royal Docks Victoria, Albert and King George V on Plaistow Marshes; from Canning Town to Beckton and King George V; to Lewisham; and to

● LEFT
Blackpool's Promenade tramway is just the place for a summer ride on an open-top tram. No. 706 is the only double-decker rebuilt to its original, 1935, condition.

SOUTH YORKSHIRE LOW-FLOOR TRAM

Date	1993–4
Builder	Siemens-Duewag, Germany
Gauge	1,435 mm
Power supply	750 v or kV
Bogie arrangement	B-B-B-B with 4x277 kW motors
Overall length	34.75 m
Width	2.65 m
Body height	3.64 m. Floor height 480 mm (880 mm over bogies)
Unladen weight	46.5 tons
Passengers	Seated 88; standing 155
Maximum speed	80 kph

● LEFT
South Yorkshire Supertram's steep gradients are easily handled by its German-built low-floor trams. This scene shows the Woodburn Road crossing in the background.

Stratford in East London. The system is operated by Serco Docklands Ltd, a company formed jointly by Serco and the former management company, the London Docklands Development Corporation (LDDC).

● MANCHESTER METROLINK

In Manchester, light rail was created in 1990–93 by the PTE taking over the rail lines to Bury, Lancashire, and Altrincham, Cheshire, and linking them with new street-track through the city centre. The system was built and operated by the Metrolink consortium, using articulated trams made by Firema, Italy.

● SOUTH YORKSHIRE, WEST MIDLANDS AND CROYDON

In South Yorkshire, a tramway was created in 1992–5 to link Sheffield city centre with outer suburbs and the Meadowhall retail centre. The system's steep gradients required articulated trams with all axles motored. German-built, they are the first trams in Britain to feature low-floor boarding and alighting at all doors. After a slow start, caused by population shifts, poor traffic priorities and bus competition, Sheffield Supertram saw a 40 per cent rise in use in the second half of 1996.

● BELOW LEFT
London's Docklands Light Railway (DLR) expanded when the towering office complex at Canary Wharf was built. The complex is served by this station incorporated in the tower.

● BELOW RIGHT
The Tyne & Wear Metro in north-east England has taken over local rail services, around Newcastle upon Tyne, including this former freight line to Callerton. It is seen here at Fawdon. The cars were built by Metro Cammell and based on a German design.

British Train Preservation

Britain's railway preservation movement was created on 11 October 1950 when a meeting in Birmingham presided over by L.T.C. Rolt declared its intention to save the Talyllyn Railway in Brecknockshire, Central Wales (now Powys). There were no precedents for such action and tremendous opposition came from many sources declaring "enthusiasts could never run a railway". This pioneering endeavour's success is well known among railway enthusiasts.

GREAT WESTERN KING CLASS 4-6-0

Date	1927
Builder	Swindon Locomotive Works, Wiltshire, England
Client	Great Western Railway (GWR)
Gauge	Standard
Driving wheels	6 ft 6 in
Capacity	4 cylinders (16 x 28 in)
Total weight in full working order	136 tons

● **BELOW**
Before Deltics were introduced, A4s held sway on the East Coast main line. Here, preserved, is No. 4498 Sir Nigel Gresley, named after the famous locomotive designer. Sir Nigel Gresley (1876–1941) was chief mechanical engineer of England's Great Northern Railway (GNR) and its successor LNER. He designed Mallard.

● **RIGHT**
Former British Rail Class 55 Co-Co Deltics were a production version of the Deltic prototype locomotive of the mid-1950s. They worked the heaviest long-distance trains on the East Coast main line for many years. Their popularity rendered them a perfect subject for preservation.

● **BELOW**
Great Western Railway's King Class 4-6-0 express-passenger-engine. Apart from one engine in 1908, GWR did not use Pacifics. Nothing larger than the 4-6-0 was needed, because of the high-quality Welsh coal they burned and the relative flatness of their routes. Several have been preserved. No. 6000 King George V, the original engine of 1927, pictured during "GWR 150" celebrations in 1985.

● **RIGHT**
A former Southern Railway (SR) King Arthur Class 4-6-0, No. 777 Sir Lamiel, *en route* for Leeds and York with the Red Rose Special train.

● **BELOW**
This former LMS Jubilee class 4-6-0, No. 5690 Leander, is one of many examples of preserved locomotives running on British Rail's main lines.

● **BOTTOM**
Unrebuilt "Bulleid Pacific" No. 34092 City of Wells is prepared for the Golden Arrow trip to Leeds, Yorkshire.

● PRESERVATION AND THE LEISURE INDUSTRY

So began a movement that over the next 50 years created a vast new leisure industry and saved part of the railway heritage in living form for future generations to enjoy.

Once the 1955 railway modernization programme took effect, class after class of Britain's locomotive heritage was scrapped. A limited selection of locomotives was earmarked for static display in museums, but this would have done little justice to the heritage, and the joy and wonder of seeing steam trains in action would have been but a dream.

Nationwide, thousands of enthusiasts united to save locomotives, rolling stock and sections of railway. Following the Beeching programme, innumerable closed branch lines were available. Over the years, dozens became the subject of preservation schemes. The movement gained momentum at the ending of steam operation on British Railways on 11 August 1968, after which it was announced that no preserved locomotive would be allowed to run on the national system.

● STEAM EXCURSIONS

Today, Britain has more than 100 centres where steam-trains can be enjoyed. They attract millions of visitors every year. More than 2,000 locomotives have been preserved.

Railway preservation is a creative, ongoing process. As the first generation of diesels began to slip into history, examples were saved and put to work on preserved lines – often beside the very steam-locomotives they had replaced.

The decision to ban steam was rescinded in 1971. Many historic locomotives returned to the main line, including examples borrowed from the National Railway Museum in York. In 1985, a total of 235 steam-excursions operated on British Rail, attracting many people to linesides and promoting awareness of the railway among the general public.

A visit to any preserved line is an unforgettable experience, for enthusiast or lay person alike. These centres achieve authenticity and fascinate all ages.

The union of free enterprise and enthusiasm provided a catalyst for achieving the impossible. Britain's railway preservation movement has been little less dynamic in spirit than Victorian industrialists of a century earlier. The number preserved contrasts with the "handful of stuffed and mounted exhibits" proposed by the Government when the dismantling of the railways began.

EUROSTAR

The idea that steam is exciting while modern traction is dull and lifeless is disproved for ever by Eurostar. This train combines the romance of the 1930s' streamlined era and the cutting edge of technology. London's St Pancras International Station is as magnificent as its Victorian counterpart and the Channel Tunnel, within the 37.5 km (24 mile) terminal-to-terminal fixed link between Folkestone and Calais, is one of the world's greatest civil-engineering feats.

● WORLD'S MOST COMPLEX TRAIN

The connecting of Britain's 16,000 km (10,000 miles) of railway with Europe's 185,000 km (116,000 miles) in 1993 has provided a much-needed and massive boost for railways. Eurostar competes with airlines between the cities of London, Paris and Brussels.

Eurostar is the world's most complex train. It operates on four different signalling systems and three different power-supply systems – 750 volt d.c. 25 kV a.c. in Britain; 25 kV a.c. in the

● ABOVE
Three Eurostar units in repose at the former Eurostar terminal at Waterloo International, London, England.

● BELOW
A Eurostar train speeds through the countryside of northern France on the high-speed line.

● **LEFT**
A Eurostar train from London approaches the Channel Tunnel. The Dolland's Moor freight complex is in the background and a new Class 92 locomotive in the left foreground.

● **BELOW**
Eurostar trains waiting to leave Waterloo International for France and Belgium.

● **BOTTOM**
Eurostar design details.

EUROSTAR	
Date	1992
Builder	GEC Alsthom at various works
Clients	British Rail (BR); Société Nationale des Chemins de Fer Français (SNCF); Société Nationale des Chemins de Fer Belges (SNCB)
Gauge	Standard
Traction motors	Six XABB 6PH
Maximum service speed	187.5 mph

tunnel, France and on high-speed lines in Belgium and 3,000 kV d.c. on Belgium's conventional network.

● **HIGH-SPEED LINK**

Eurostar trains comprise 18 coaches. The trains, at 394 metres (1,293 ft), are almost a quarter of a mile long. Eurostar runs at 186 mph on Europe's high-speed lines but is restricted to below 100 mph in Britain.

Eurostar's coaches are joined by bogies. No bogies are set beneath the passenger seating. This and pneumatic suspension ensures a smooth, quiet ride. The train is comfortable and has footrests, reading-lights and air-conditioning. First-class has areas for business meetings.

There are two bar-buffets and a trolley service. Eurostar trains are serviced in London at the dedicated depot at Temple Mills, which is located near Stratford International station.

● **OVERNIGHT TRAVEL REVOLUTION**

The Eurostar service was augmented by two developments. Firstly, day trains began to run between Edinburgh, Manchester, Birmingham and Paris. Second, night trains now operate with sleeping-cars. These services revolutionized long-distance overnight travel in Europe. Passengers are now able to go to bed in departure cities and awake at their destination the very next morning.

American Switchers

Switchers, that is engines to transfer rolling stock from one railway track to another, are relatively small, lightweight locomotives in the 300 hp to 1,500 hp range, designed to work at slow speeds, often on poor or winding track.

● **BELOW**
Southern Pacific Lines embraced the switcher longer than other Western railroads and ordered larger numbers of EMD's SW1500s. The 1,500 hp SW1500 was eventually replaced in EMD's catalogue by the MP15, also rated at 1,500 hp.

● **ABOVE**
Baldwin switcher S-12 No. 16 is lettered for the Feather River & Western railroad. Baldwin built more than 550 S-12 diesel-electric switchers of 1,200 hp between 1951-56.

● FIRST SUCCESSFUL DIESEL-ELECTRIC

The first successful application of diesel-electric locomotives was as switchers. Central Railroad of New Jersey, USA, operated the first commercially successful diesel-electric in 1925. By the 1940s, builders were constructing low-horsepower diesel-electric switchers for yard switching, industrial switching and passenger-terminal work. General Electric (GE), Baldwin, the Electro-Motive Division (EMD) of General Motors, American Locomotive Company (Alco), Fairbanks-Morse, Whitcomb, Porter and Davenport all built switchers in the 1940s and 1950s.

● CHANGING DEMAND

As traffic patterns changed between the 1950s and 1970s, fewer switchers were needed. American railroads discontinued

● **LEFT**
A former Alco S-1 switcher of the United States Army poses as Western Pacific Railroad's No. 512. More than 500 S-1s were built for use in the USA and Mexico between 1940-50. The locomotive features a six-cylinder 539 prime mover that delivered 660 hp.

● **RIGHT**
Western Pacific Railroad's NW2u shows off a coat of orange paint at Portola, California. Electro-Motive built 1,119 NW2 switchers of 1,000 hp. Many were later rebuilt, using the "u" designation.

many passenger-trains and thus had a greatly reduced need for switchers at terminals. Carload-freight declined as railroads switched to intermodal operations, that is using different modes of conveyance in conjunction. By the mid-1970s, railroads had stopped ordering large numbers of new switchers. Instead, they either rebuilt existing switchers or downgraded older road-switchers.

● **SWITCHER MODELS**

Electro-Motive began building switchers in the 1930s. An early model that gained popularity was the 1,000 hp NW2 made in 1930–49. The SW1, a 600-hp switcher, was made between 1939-53. Other SW-type switchers, ranging from the 700-hp SW7 to the 1,500-hp SW1500, were made through the 1970s. In the mid-1970s, EMD introduced its 1,500 MP line of switchers.

Alco made many S Series low-horsepower switchers between 1940–60. General Electric built switchers for many years before entering the heavy road locomotive market in 1960. Its most popular switchers were its 44-ton and 70-ton models.

In the 1990s, builder Morrison-Knudsen entered the new-switcher market with conventionally powered diesel-electrics and natural gas-powered locomotives. By 1996, it had not sold more than a handful of locomotives.

SW8 DIESEL-ELECTRIC

Date	1950–54
Builder	General Motors (Electro-Motive Division)
Engine	8-cylinder 567B
Capacity	567cc per cylinder
Power	800 hp

● **RIGHT**
An SW8 of the Wellsboro & Corning Railroad leads a train south of Gang Mills, New York. The EMD's 800-hp SW8 was built between 1950–54. Many short lines prefer switchers to larger road-switcher locomotives.

American Trains in the 1950s

American freight railroads have relied on diesel-electric locomotives to move the bulk of their tonnage since America saw the end of steam in the 1950s. Builders have implemented many improvements in locomotive design in the last 40 years. Locomotive-builders – now just General Motor's Electro-Motive Division (EMD) and General Electric (GE) – have been working on single-engine, single-unit locomotives with ever-greater pulling power.

● LEFT
General Electric (GE) surpassed its main competitor, EMD, in new-locomotive sales with the introduction of the DASH-8 line. One of Santa Fe Railroad's 4,000 hp DASH 8-40Bs rests in Corwith yard, Chicago, Illinois.

● ABOVE
Brand-new EMD SD70MAC locomotives in Chicago. Burlington Northern Railroad prefers these powerful a.c.-traction locomotives for coal-train service in Wyoming, USA.

● BELOW
The carbody-style locomotive, popular in the 1940s and 1950s, was displaced by the more versatile road-switcher type. Only a few railroads now use this older style, including LTV Mining, which has a fleet of antique EMD-made F7As.

● **HORSEPOWER RACE**

In the 1950s, EMD's GP9 road-switcher and F9 carbody locomotives were state-of-the-art designs, each developing 1,750 hp with a 567-series 16-cylinder prime mover and traditional d.c. traction motors.

In the early 1960s, EMD increased the 567 prime mover's horsepower by adding a turbocharger, featured on its GP20 and SD24 models. Meanwhile, General Electric entered the new heavy-haul diesel-electric locomotive market with its U25B. The U25B road-switcher developed 2,500 hp with its 16-cylinder, 7FDL-series prime mover. Following GE's entry into the market, a horsepower race was on. To meet North American railroad's demands, EMD, GE and Alco (which has since, in 1969, ceased locomotive production) began to develop both four- and six-axle road-switcher locomotives of ever-increasing output. EMD's most popular models were: the four-axle 2,000-hp GP38, the six-axle 3,000-hp SD40 and the 20-cylinder, 3,600-hp SD45. GE peaked with the 3,600-hp U36C. Both builders dabbled in high-horsepower dual-prime mover eight-axle monsters, but this big locomotive's limited flexibility resulted in weak sales.

● **DESIGN IMPROVEMENTS**

The 1970s saw many electrical improvements. The 1980s brought microprocessor control. In the mid-1980s, GE introduced the DASH-8 line, a successful 4,000-hp design that put GE at the forefront of the locomotive market. In the mid-1990s, improvements in

● RIGHT
GE introduced the a.c. traction motor with its AC4400CW, a model that closely resembles earlier, d.c. traction locomotives. This model proved popular with Western railroads, which use them mainly to haul heavy mineral-trains in the mountains.

SD45-DIESEL-ELECTRIC	
Dates produced	1965–71
Builder	General Motors (Electro-Motive Division)
Engine	20 cylinder 645 cc per cylinder
Power	3,600 hp

microprocessors enabled both builders successfully to apply a.c. traction motor technology to North American freight locomotives. This was the most significant improvement to American locomotive design since the advent of the diesel-electric. By using a.c. traction, locomotive builders were able to improve dramatically the tractive effort of a single locomotive. In 1996, the first 6,000 hp a.c. traction locomotives were being tested and sales of 4,000–5,000 hp a.c. locomotives dominated the new locomotive market.

● ABOVE
In 1996, the Union Pacific Railroad (UPR) took delivery of EMD's latest a.c.-traction locomotives, the "upgradeable" SD90MAC. These locomotives have a 4,000 hp prime mover and can accept a 6,000 hp prime mover that is being developed.

● RIGHT
A new EMD SD75M, featuring a safety cab and colourful warbonnet paint-work, rests between runs at Corith Yard, Chicago, Illinois. Despite a trend towards a.c. traction motors, the Santa Fe Railroad has remained committed to the traditional d.c. motor.

American Short Lines

American short-line railroads are those smaller carriers that operate fewer than 350 route miles (560 km) and produce revenue of less than $40 million.

● MANY NEW SHORT LINES

Since the mid-1970s, many new short-line railroads have been formed. These new lines are mainly branch and secondary main lines disposed of by larger railroads in recent downsizing. Traditionally, healthy short lines had a choice of buying secondhand locomotives from larger railroads or new ones from builders. Through the mid-1970s, builders offered a variety of low and medium horsepower, switchers, road-switchers and specialty diesel-electric locomotives that appealed to short-line needs.

● TOP
New Hampshire & Vermont (NHV) Railroad operates on several branch lines formerly operated by Boston & Maine and Maine Central. It uses Alco RS-11s and EMD GP9s. NHV RS-11 switchers are pictured at Whitefield, New Hampshire.

● BELOW
Green Mountain Railroad (GMR) runs freight- and passenger-trains in Vermont. Usually, EMD's GP9s handle freight-trains and its Alco RS-1 road-switcher is used on passenger-trains.

● ABOVE
Many American short lines operate with obscure locomotives. Massachusetts Central railroad has a rare EMD NW5, one of only 13 built. This 1,000 hp road-switcher was originally owned by Southern Railway.

● EMD SWITCHERS AND "GEEPS"

General Motors (Electro-Motive Division), the main builder of new locomotives, offered a line of switcher-type engines featuring a short wheelbase that were popular with both short lines and larger railroads for use in yards and on secondary track. This range began with the 600 hp SC and SW locomotives

CENTURY-425

Dates produced	1964–6
Builder	American Locomotive Company (Alco)
Engine	251C
Gauge	4 ft $8^1/_2$ in
Power	2,500 hp
Capacity	16 cylinders

in 1936 and ended with the 1,500 hp SW1500 and MP15 in the mid-1980s. Another EMD locomotive popular with short lines was the GP series commonly known as "Geeps", particularly the lower-horsepower, non-turbo-charged 1,500 hp GP7, 1,750 hp GP9 and 2,000 hp GP38.

● LEFT
In the 1970s, the Santa Fe railroad converted many of its EMD-made F7 cab-units to road-switchers designed as CF7s. The Massachusetts Central Railroad bought one CF7 from Santa Fe in 1984. The CF7 has been popular with short lines looking for secondhand locomotives.

● SHORT LINES PRICED OUT OF NEW LOCOMOTIVES

As the price of new locomotives began to climb, more short-line railroads began to buy used and remanufactured locomotives. Also, as the large railroads disposed of branches, they had less need for the types of locomotives required for branch-line service, glutting the used market with switchers and "Geeps". By the late 1970s, few short lines were placing orders for new locomotives; instead, they operated with hand-me-downs. As a result, short lines are operating with a great variety of old, secondhand locomotives, long discarded from main-line service. As a group, short lines feature the greatest diversity of locomotives in the USA. Locomotives built by Alco, which ceased production in 1969, and many other curious and obscure models can be found working on short lines around the USA.

● ABOVE
Sierra Railroad was one of the last short lines to use Baldwin locomotives regularly. To operate its 80 km (50 mile) railroad, it owned several Baldwin S-12 diesel-electrics. Many short lines held on to Baldwins long after larger railroads discarded them.

● LEFT
New Hampshire & Vermont GP9 No. 669 switchers at Whitefield, New Hampshire. NHV, like many modern short lines, operates "first-generation" diesels – those that replaced steam locomotives – on lines let go by larger railroads.

American Passenger Trains

The diesel-electric made its passenger début in 1934 with the Burlington Northern railroad's Pioneer Zephyr and Union Pacific Railroad's M-10000 City of Salina.

● LEFT
Cal-Train operates commuter-rail services between San Francisco, San Jose and Gilroy, California. The agency uses EMD's 3,000-hp F40PH locomotives in push-pull mode. The locomotives always face outbound (south).

● PIONEER ZEPHYR INTRODUCES THE PASSENGER DIESEL

After World War II, American railroads began ordering diesel-electrics in quantity for general passenger service. As with the freight market, the General Motors Electro-Motive Division (EMD) dominated the market for new passenger-locomotives. Its most popular models were its E series, streamlined locomotives featuring twin 567 prime movers and A1A trucks. Each truck had three axles but the centre axle was not powered. The E7, rated at 2,000 hp, was introduced in 1945; the E9, rated at 2,400 hp, was introduced in 1954 and remained in production until 1963. While other builders also produced passenger locomotives – notably Alco with its PA series – none was particularly successful in the USA. The PA was well liked by enthusiasts for its superior aesthetics but generally disliked by railroads for poor performance and high maintenance.

FL9 DIESEL-ELECTRIC/ELECTRIC	
Dates produced	1956–60
Builder	General Motors (Electro-motive Division)
Engine	20 cylinders 567C or 567D1
Power	1,750 hp or 1,800 hp
Capacity	567 cc per cylinder

EMD also made four-axle F Series locomotives for passenger service. Western railroads preferred F units, mainly because of their pulling ability in heavily graded territory.

Beginning in 1956, the New Haven Railroad (NHR) took delivery of FL9s (dual-mode diesel-electric/electric) from EMD for use in electrified territory around New York City. These versatile locomotives use a diesel engine or electric third rail.

● THE AGE OF AMTRAK

Amtrak, America's National Railroad Passenger Corporation, an American government-owned body set up in 1970,

● LEFT
Amtrak maintains several dual-mode FL9 diesel-electric/ electric locomotives for service between New York City and Albany, New York. The now-defunct New Haven Railroad (NHR) ordered 60 of these specialty locomotives between 1956–60.

● OPPOSITE
Amtrak locomotives in Chicago, Illinois, await assignment. On the left, No. 828 is a General Electric AMD-103. On the right are EMD-made F40PHs.

● RIGHT
In the Northeast Corridor – between Washington, DC and New Haven, Connecticut – Amtrak operates AEM7 electrics in a high-speed service up to 130 mph.

assumed responsibility for most intercity passenger runs in 1971. By the 1980s, governmental operating agencies relieved most railroads of commuter-train responsibilities. A new generation of motive power was developed for Amtrak and the commuter lines. In the early 1970s, EMD made a passenger version of its successful SD40 freight-locomotive, but the six-axle passenger SDP40Fs, with full cowl hood, proved largely unsatisfactory for passenger service. Many were later sold to the Santa Fe railroad for fast freight service. In 1976, EMD introduced the F40PH, a turbo-charged 3,000 hp, four-axle locomotive well received by Amtrak and the commuter lines. Several hundred were sold in the USA and Canada. Meanwhile, General Electric offered its six-axle 3,000 hp P30CH, with limited success.

● LEFT
Two General Electric Genesis AMD-103s lead Amtrak's California Zephyr westbound at La Grange, Illinois.

● ELECTRICS AND TURBOLINERS

Amtrak's Northeast Corridor is mostly electrified. In the 1970s, General Electric made about 30 E60 electrics to replace 40-year-old former Pennsylvania Railroad GG1 electrics operating on that route. In the early 1980s, EMD licensed the Rc4 electric locomotive from the Swedish company Allmänna Svenska Elektriska Aktiebolaget (ASEA), and from that design made more than 60 high-hp AEM7 electrics for high-speed service on the Northeast Corridor.

Amtrak has had limited success with articulated turboliners. In the mid-1970s, it placed seven streamlined Rohr Turboliners in service in its Empire Corridor, between New York City and Niagara Falls. Each set has a 1,140 hp power-car at both ends.

● THE NEXT GENERATION

In the early 1990s, Amtrak began taking delivery of several new types of locomotives. It received about 20 utilitarian-looking 3,200 hp DASH-8 32PBs from General Electric, followed by several varieties of GE's Genesis Locomotive. The Genesis is a semi-streamlined product that uses a monocoque (frameless) body and a GE prime mover. Amtrak and commuter-operator Metro-North also use dual-mode Genesis locomotives for service in the third-rail electrified territory around New York City. On its Californian routes, Amtrak uses EMD's F59PHIs, streamlined passenger locomotives exhibiting what EMD deems the "swoopy look".

American Metro-Elevated Lines

● **RIGHT**
New York City Transit Authority's logo.

Traditional elevated lines, using steel structures to carry electrified rapid-transit tracks above city streets, can still be found in New York City, Philadelphia and Chicago.

● TRADITIONAL ELEVATED LINES

All of these elevated lines are operated in conjunction with a subway/heavy-rail metro system. In New York and Philadelphia, use of elevated lines is restricted to outside the central, commerical area – downtown. This leaves Chicago as the only remaining American city with a traditional elevated rapid-transit structure at its centre. Its skyscrapers and antique route present an incongruous mix of architecture.

In the mid-1980s, Boston, Massachusetts, replaced most of its Orange Line elevated structure with a modern metro-rail system, leaving the Lechmere-North Station section of Green Line Light-Rail route as the only significant elevated structure in the area.

● **LEFT**
An outbound D train heads towards Coney Island, Brooklyn, Long Island, New York City, in a frigid December in 1993. The New York City Transit Authority (NYCTA) has several thousand rapid-transit cars in its fleet and operates the most extensive rapid-transit system in North America.

● **LEFT**
An inbound train from Flushing, Queens, New York City, heads for Times Square, Manhattan, in 1993. This is one of many elevated lines operating in the borough of Queens.

● **ABOVE**
Chicago's famous "Loop" is the last traditional elevated rapid-transit line to operate in the heart of an American city. A set of Morrison-Knudsen cars negotiates the "Loop" on 4 July 1995.

● MODERN HEAVY METRO-RAIL TRANSIT

Some American metropolitan areas that did not have traditional elevated lines are today served by modern heavy-rail metro transit systems. Like the traditional elevated lines, these systems use electrically powered multiple-unit transit vehicles (usually powered by third rail) on a variety of gradient-separated right-of-ways – underground (subway), in open cuts or on concrete elevated structures. The most extensive modern systems are the Washington D.C. Metro and, serving the greater San Francisco metro area, the Bay Area Rapid Transit, known as BART.

CHICAGO TRANSIT AUTHORITY (CTA) SERIES 2000 CARS	
Date produced	1964
Builder	Pullman Car & Manufacturing Company
Weight	47,400 lb
Propulsion	General Electric
Seating	47/51 seats

● RAPID TRANSIT CARS

New York City and Chicago operate the largest rapid-transit fleets in the USA. In recent years, New York has modernized its rolling stock with new cars from north American builders such as Bombardier, and by having its older cars rebuilt. In the late 1980s and early 1990s, many of New York City Transit cars were built by MK Rail in the former Erie Railroad shops at Hornell in rural western New York state.

New York, with its new and rebuilt cars, has successfully eliminated the colourful graffiti that covered most of its fleet in the 1970s and 1980s. Its cars' spray paint-resistant surfaces are now nearly graffiti-proof.

Chicago's fleet of cars represents a host of different builders. Following discontinuation of streetcar service in the 1950s, Chicago rebuilt most of its large fleet of President Conference Committee (PCC) streetcars for rapid-transit service on elevated and subway lines. In 1964, Chicago took delivery of 180 new cars from Pullman. In 1969, it ordered 75 new stainless-steel cars from the Budd Co. In the 1970s, Chicago took delivery of 200 cars from Boeing-Vertol and another 600 cars from Budd. Chicago's most recent order was in the early 1990s, for 256 cars from Morrison-Knudsen.

● ABOVE LEFT
On Independence Day 1995, in Chicago, Illinois, a red, white and blue set of cars made by Boeing-Vertol heads south on the Howard Street line.

● ABOVE
Into the 1950s, New York City operated a fleet of antique open-platform cars on one remaining Brooklyn elevated route, the Myrtle Avenue Line.

● BELOW
Chicago has one of the largest networks of traditional elevated-metro rail lines. A 3200 Series car made by Morrison-Knudsen heads downtown on the Howard Street Line.

American Light Rail

In the mid-1970s, San Francisco, California, and Boston, Massachusetts, ordered new light-rail vehicles to replace worn President Conference Committee cars (PCCs). This represented the first orders for new cars in several decades and began to reverse a long decline in American light-raise use.

● **ABOVE**
San Francisco's brightly painted, rebuilt PCCs have proved popular with tourists. The cars were regauged to operate on the San Francisco Municipal Railway's light-rail lines. Usually, the PCCs are assigned to the F-Market line, which does not use the Muni-Metro subway. This car is painted to represent Boston's MBTA scheme of the 1950s.

● **OPPOSITE BOTTOM**
An LRV made by Kawasaki, Japan, negotiates the broad-gauge single-track Media Line at Media, Pennsylvania, in suburban Philadelphia, in 1992. Philadelphia was the only city to buy these non-articulated cars.

● **BELOW**
A Type 7 car built by Kinki Sharyo of Japan prepares to turn at Cleveland Circle in Boston, Massachusetts, in 1993. Boston uses three different kinds of LRVs on its system.

● American Light Rail Revival

The new cars, built by Boeing-Vertol, had design flaws. There were no further orders for them. By the mid-1990s, fewer than 20 years after most of the Boeings were delivered, both cities were buying replacements.

● Canadian Lead Followed by San Diego

The real light-rail revival came in 1978 at Edmonton, Alberta, Canada, when the city inaugurated its 4½ mile (7 km) line. This was the first all-new light rail system in recent memory. The system used 14 six-axle Siemens-Duewag U2 light-rail vehicles (LRVs). The USA followed Canada's lead in 1980 when the San Diego Trolley (SDT) began operating in California. Like the Edmonton system,

MASSACHUSETTS BAY TRANSPORTATION AUTHORITY (BOSTON) TYPE 7

Dates produced	1986–8
Builder	Kinki Sharyo
Client	MBTA (Boston)
Voltage	600 kV d.c.
Axles	Six
Weight	84,800 lb
Propulsion	Westinghouse
Seating	50 seats

● LEFT
Boston's Massachusetts Bay Transportation Authority (MBTA) bought 100 Boeing-Vertol light-rail vehicles (LRVs) for its Green Line Light-Rail routes. The Mattapan-Ashmont High-Speed Line, part of the Red Line, still uses older President Conference Committee (PCC) cars.

● SAN FRANCISCO RE-EMBRACES THE PCC CAR

In 1995, San Francisco re-established its long-dormant F-Market line, using rebuilt PCC cars from Philadelphia, Pennsylvania. The cars were completely overhauled by M-K Rail, a division of Morrison-Knudsen, at Hornell, New York, and regauged for San Francisco tracks. To celebrate the PCC design, each car was painted differently, using traditional liveries from American cities that had formerly operated this traditional type of streetcar. The idea made this one of the most colourful fleets of regularly operated streetcars in the USA. San Francisco's once large fleet of PCC cars were mostly retired by the mid-1980s when new Boeing-Vertol cars arrived.

Some American cities have started a trend using low-floor cars. Portland, Oregon, was the first US city to use them, taking delivery of 46 Type-2 cars from Siemens Transportation Systems in 1993.

the SDT line, running from the commercial centre to the Mexican border at San Ysidro, was an entirely new light-rail system and also used six-axle U2 cars, painted bright red. The SDT system proved popular. Extensions and new routes have since been built.

● VARIETIES OF LIGHT-RAIL VEHICLES

Since then, nearly a dozen new light-rail systems have started operating. The latest is in Dallas, Texas, which started operating in June 1996. Its 18 km (11 mile) system uses yellow-and-white cars built by Kinki Sharyo/Itochu International.

LRVs used in the USA have few uniform standards and even the gauge varies somewhat. Most cities use the standard 4 ft $8\frac{1}{2}$ in gauge, but New Orleans in Louisiana and Philadelphia and Pittsburg in Pennsylvania use 5 ft $2\frac{1}{4}$ in and 5 ft $2\frac{1}{2}$ in.

Many builders' cars are in service. They range from traditional American companies, such as Perley Thomas with vintage streetcars built in 1923–4, used in New Orleans, to Bombardier which built cars for Portland, Oregon's light-rail system, and also include many foreign companies such as Italy's Breda and Japan's Kinki Sharyo.

● LEFT
Sacramento, California, the original terminus of the transcontinental railroad, began operating its new light-rail system in 1987. Trains of four-coupled Siemens-Duewag U2A LRVs regularly traverse the streets of the Californian capital.

Tourist Lines in America

In the past 20 years, dozens of railroads have begun operating tourist-trains. Some of these lines are strictly passenger-carriers, often catering to speciality markets such as luxury dinner-trains.

● LEFT
The Green Mountain Railroad (GMR) operates its freight- and passenger-trains with a fleet of well-maintained historic locomotives. In 1993, EMD's GP9 1850 leads a freight up the gradient at Ludlow, Vermont. The GP9 was popular in freight and passenger service.

● LEFT
The East Broad Top Railroad (EBTR) in central Pennsylvania offers an authentic railroad experience. It uses vintage equipment appropriate for its line. It has four operational 36 in gauge Baldwin Mikados. No. 15 is pictured at Rockhill Furnace.

● POPULARITY OF TOURIST LINES

Other tourist trains are short-line railroads looking to supplement freight revenue. The type of motive power used on these lines varies greatly but tends towards the historic, to appeal to the travelling public. Some lines use steam-locomotives, others vintage diesel-electrics. Many lines that use diesels paint them in elaborate schemes reminiscent of the schemes used in the 1940s and 1950s.

● CALIFORNIA'S NAPA VALLEY WINE TRAIN

Napa Valley Wine Train is one of the most successful operations. It runs several trips a day through the Napa Valley and caters for up-market patrons. Guests have dinner and wine-tasting aboard vintage heavyweight passenger cars hauled by FPA-4 diesel-electronics made by Montreal Locomotive Works (MLW), Alco's Canadian subsidiary. Four of these engines, acquired from the Canadian passenger-rail authority Via Rail, entered service in 1989. They have a burgundy-and-gold paint scheme that reflects the colours of California's wine country. Several tourist lines acquired FPA-4s from Via Rail when it upgraded its locomotive fleet and disposed of many of these older models.

● GREEN MOUNTAIN RAILROAD

The Green Mountain Railroad (GMR), a successful short line in rural Vermont, USA, has augmented freight revenue by operating a seasonal excursion-train. For this service it maintains a vintage Alco RS-1 diesel – the precise model used by its predecessor Rutland Railway in passenger service in the 1940s and 1950s. It also uses General Motors Electro-Motive's GP9s when passenger-

● BELOW
In 1989, the Boone Scenic Railway (BSR) took delivery of a brand-new JS Class Chinese-made Mikado, seen here atop the railroad's high bridge, north of Boone, Iowa. The brightly painted steam locomotive is popular with train-riders.

FPA-A

Dates produced	1958–9
Builder	Montreal Locomotive Works (MLW) (Alco)
Engine	251B
Power	1,800 hp
Capacity	12 cylinders

trains are heavily patronized, particularly in autumn when the coloured foliage attracts hundreds of riders daily.

● NEW STEAM PROVES POPULAR

The Boone Scenic Railroad (BSR) operating a former interurban line in central Iowa, USA, has taken a novel approach towards passenger-trains. In 1989, it took delivery of a brand-new JS Class Chinese-made Mikado. Several other American tourist lines have also ordered new steam locomotives. For Boone, which derives all its revenue from excursion-trains, the new steam locomotive has been a great success. Other tourist lines operate with traditional American-built steam locomotives restored for tourist service.

● ABOVE LEFT
A Northern Pacific Railroad (NPR) Ten-Wheeler 4-6-0, Class S-10 328, leads a passenger-excursion train across Wisconsin Central's St Croix River bridge in Wisconsin. This Alco-built locomotive 1907 is the only remaining NPR 4-6-0.

● RIGHT
In autumn 1989, the Napa Valley Wine Train began dinner-train service in the scenic Californian valley. Four streamlined Via Rail, FPA-4 locomotives provide power. They were bought from the Canadian passenger transport authority.

American Train Preservation

Preservationists have rescued and restored nearly 150 steam locomotives to serviceable status in the USA and Canada. Authentic locomotives and replicas from all periods of development are represented – a complete range in age and size, from a re-creation of Peter Cooper's diminutive Tom Thumb of 1830 to World War II-vintage super power, such as Union Pacific Railroad's massive Northern type 4-8-4, No. 844.

● STEAM LOCOMOTIVES

Colorado's preserved narrow-gauge railroads operate vintage steam locomotives. The Cumbres & Toltec, which operates over the 3,048 m (10,000 ft) high Cumbres Pass through the San Juan Mountains of southern Colorado to Toltec in Arizona, maintains three classes of Denver & Rio Grande Western Mikado Type 2-8-2, Classes K27, K36 and K37. The Baltimore & Ohio Railroad (B&OR) Museum, Baltimore, Maryland, has a collection of steam locomotives, including the Tom Thumb replica. The Federal Government has spent millions of dollars preserving vintage steam locomotives from around the USA and Canada, at Steamtown, in Scranton, Pennsylvania. Steamtown, once a private foundation, is now run by the American National Park Service.

Despite the many restored locomotives, considerable work is left for preservationists. Alas, for every serviceable locomotive there are probably a half-dozen others in poor shape and great need of attention.

● TOP
Chicago & Northern Western railroad's No. 1385, a Class R1, Alco-built 4-6-0 Ten-wheeler, is preserved in operating condition at the Mid-Continent Railway Museum, North Freedom, Wisconsin.

● ABOVE
Illinois Terminal GP7 No. 1605 displays a lively paint scheme. The GP7 was Electro-motive Division's first popular road-switcher. This locomotive and many others are preserved in operating condition at the Illinois Railway Museum, Union, Illinois.

● LEFT
Colorado's Cumbres & Toltec Scenic Railroad operates several former Denver & Rio Grande Western Class K36 narrow-gauge Mikado 2-8-2s. It maintains a Class K28 and a Class K37 for occasional use.

NORTHERN PACIFIC RAILROAD (NPR) 4-6-0, CLASS S10 NO. 328

Date produced	1907
Builder	American Locomotive Co. (Alco)
Driving wheels	57 in
Capacity	2 cylinders 19 x 26 in
Steam pressure	190 lb
Weight	153,000 lb
Tractive effort	26,000 lb

● **ABOVE RIGHT**
The Portola Railroad Museum, Portola, California, specializes in preserving diesel-electric locomotives. No. 6946, a Union Pacific Railroad DDA40X, the largest class of diesel ever built, is one of the museum's most impressive displays. EMD built 47 DDA40X for Union Pacific Railroad between 1969–71.

● PRESERVED DIESEL-ELECTRIC AND ELECTRIC LOCOMOTIVES

In the past 30 years, effort has been exerted to acquire and preserve significant examples of diesel-electric and electric locomotives. Several museums are now almost exclusively dedicated to such preservation.

The first commercially successful diesel, a box-cab built by Alco-General Electric-Ingersol Rand in 1926 for the Central Railroad of New Jersey, is preserved at the B&OR Museum. Several examples of the largest type of diesel-electric ever built, EMD's monster, eight-axle, 6,900 hp DDA40X, are preserved in the west. Union Pacific Railroad, sole operator of the big locomotives, still owns and operates one in excursion-service. On rare occasions, UPR still operates it for freight.

Electric locomotives are preserved, too. Several fine examples of the Raymond Loewy-styled Pennsylvania Railroad GG1 are on display. One of the largest collections of preserved railroad equipment – steam, diesel-electric, electric and traction – is located at the Illinois Railway Museum, Union, Illinois, where there is a DDA40A, Pennsylvania GG1 among hundreds of other items.

● **RIGHT**
Northern Pacific Railroad's "Ten-wheeler" 4-6-0 No. 328, made by Alco is operated by the Minnesota Transportation Museum, Osceola, Wisconsin. It has a limited summer-excursion schedule. When the steam locomotive is not running, vintage diesels are used.

Canadian Freight Trains

● BELOW
Two Ontario Northland RS-3s await assignment. These MLW-built engines are almost identical to RS-3s built in the USA by MLW's parent, Alco.

Canadian railroads had a more conservative approach to motive power than had their American counterparts. Canadians preferred tested, established locomotive models rather than innovative ones and continued to rely on steam locomotives through the 1950s.

● THE 1950S

While Canadian railroads' transition to diesel-electrics copied the USA, they began serious conversion to diesel later and were far less experimental in choice of models. In the late 1950s and 1960s Canadian Pacific and Canadian National began taking delivery of mass-quantities of essentially stock American diesel-electric designs. General Motors Diesel Ltd (GMD) and Montreal Locomotives Works (MLW), Alco's Canadian subsidiary, were the main builders. Baldwin and Fairbanks-Morse also marketed their products in Canada.

Canadian railroads bought a few streamlined F units but largely dieselized freight operations with road-switcher-type locomotives had a solid market with Canadian Pacific and Canadian National. Both railroads acquired many MLW S-Series switchers.

● CANADIAN LOCOMOTIVES TAKE ON A DISTINCTIVE LOOK

In the late 1950s, Canadian locomotives took on a distinctive appearance, distinguishing them from their American counterparts. Mechanically, they were the same. For example, Canada bought MLW's 1,800 hp RS-18 that featured a slightly different hood-style from Alco's RS-11 preferred by American railroads. The locomotives were identical in most other respects. MLW continued to make diesels after Alco discontinued American production in 1969. Through the 1970s, MLW built distinctive Canadian locomotives

based on Alco designs. In 1979, Bombardier acquired MLW and continued to build locomotives into the mid-1980s. It has since left the new locomotive market.

● CANADIAN SAFETY-CABS

In the early 1970s, safety-conscious Canadians began ordering road-switcher hood-unit locomotives with full-width, four-window "Canadian safety-cabs", or "comfort cabs". These reinforced cabs were designed to protect the crew in derailments or collisions. Canadian railroads also began equipping locomotives with "ditch-lights", bright headlamps near the rail, for increased visibility. For many years, these were trademarks of Canadian motive power. American lines have since emulated Canadian practice and safety-cabs and ditch-lights are now standard features on North American locomotives.

RS-18	
Dates produced	1956-68
Builder	Montreal Locomotive Works (MLW) (Alco)
Engine	12-cylinder, 251B
Power	1,800 hp

● OPPOSITE
A Canadian Pacific (CP) MLW RS-18 switches at St Martin's Junction, Quebec, in 1993. The Canadian-built RS-18 was not significantly different from the American-built RS-11.

● BELOW
The wide-nosed "Canadian safety-cab", or comfort cab, and ditch-lights were once trade-marks of Canadian National locomotives. Now they are standard features on most North American freight locomotives. Here, a quartet of CN GP40-2s with comfort cabs leads a northbound freight.

● LEFT
Canadian National (CN) acquired SD701 locomotives from General Motors in 1995. In 1996, CN began to receive its first SD751s, part of an order for more than 300.

● THE 1990S

In the mid-1990s, Canadian National and Canadian Pacific began ordering what were essentially stock locomotives from GM and GE, although some assembly was done in Canada. In 1995, Canadian Pacific ordered a fleet of GE AC4400CWs for heavyfreight service in the Canadian Rockies. While Canadian Pacific had experimented with a.c. traction, this investment represented the first commerical application of the new technology in Canada. Meanwhile, Canadian National has remained firmly committed to traditional d.c.-traction motors. Instead of trying a.c. locomotives, it ordered more than 300 General Motors six-axle SD701 and SD751 locomotives.

CANADIAN PASSENGER TRAINS

Steam locomotives were used in passenger service in Canada until the early 1960s.

● 1950S TO 1980S

In the 1950s, Canadian National and Canadian Pacific began acquiring passenger-diesels. Both railroads used Canadian-built General Motors Diesel (GMD) FP7s. FP9s and passenger-equipped road-switchers. These locomotives were in most respects the same as

FPA-A

Dates produced	1958–9
Builder	Montreal Locomotive Works (MLW) (Alco)
Engine	12-cylinder, 251B
Power	1,800 hp

● LEFT
Via Rail, the Canadian passenger-train operating agency, ran a fleet of Montreal Locomotive Works FPA-4s inherited from Canadian National. Four FPA-4s at Central Station, Montreal, Quebec, in 1984.

● BELOW LEFT
Via Rail's LRC locomotives did not always haul the specially designed tilting LRC train sets. In 1985, an LRC locomotive leads a conventional train in Toronto, Ontario.

● BELOW
Toronto's GO Transit was an early user of push-pull commuter train sets. On the end opposite the locomotive is an auxiliary cab. This provides head-end power in addition to comfort for the engineer. Some of GO Transit's auxiliary cabs were built from old F-units.

their American counterparts. Canadian National also used FPA-2s and FPA-4s, the MLW passenger version of Alco's FA freight locomotives. The E unit, popular in the USA, did not catch on in Canada, although Canadian Pacific owned a few.

● TORONTO COMMUTER OPERATIONS

In 1966, Toronto's commuter agency GO Transit ordered specially built road-switchers from General Motors, called GP40TCs, for its passenger runs. The GP40TC is essentially a modified version of the 3,000-hp GP40 freight locomotive, equipped with a headend power generator to operate electric heat and lights on passenger cars.

GO Transit was an early proponent of push-pull commuter trains. Rather than run traditional trains with the locomotive always on the front, GO Transit equipped the rear of its trains with auxiliary power-cabs. The auxiliary cabs, built from the shells of old F-units, provide head-end power and comfortable operating cabs. By using an aux-cab, GO Transit obviated need for a specially equipped locomotive to provide head-end power.

● LIGHT, RAPID, COMFORTABLE

The Canadian passenger agency Via Rail took on the operation of most long-distance passenger-trains in 1997. Looking for a better way to haul passengers, it decided to acquire modern "tilt" trains. Between 1981–4 Via Rail took delivery of LRC trains, powered by 31 specially designed locomotives built by Bombardier's Montreal Locomotive Works. The LRC locomotives proved problematic and are no longer made.

● ABOVE LEFT
Canadian National box-cab electrics lead a commuter-train at Val Royal Station, Montreal. CN's suburban commuter service to Deux Montagnes, Quebec, uses overhead electrification. The traditional electrification and electric locomotives, some nearly 80 years old, were replaced in 1995 with a modern system.

● ABOVE RIGHT
In the late 1980s, Via Rail began replacing its ageing carbody-style locomotives with new F40PHs from General Motors.

● BELOW
Ontario Northland Railroad operated its Northlander passenger-train with FP7m locomotives and secondhand Trans-European Express articulated train sets acquired in 1977.

Canadian Light Rail

Canada's three main light-rail systems are in Calgary and Edmonton, in Alberta, and in Toronto, Ontario. Both the Alberta systems were built new in the late 1970s and early 1980s. The Toronto system evolved from a traditional streetcar system.

Toronto and Montreal both operate underground electrified metro-rail systems. The Montreal system uses an unusual rubber-tyre propulsion. Vancouver, British Columbia, features an elevated metro-rail system called Sky-Train, which uses computer-controlled unmanned cars operating from a 600 volt d.c. third rail.

EDMONTON'S U12 LIGHT RAIL VEHICLES (LRVS)

Dates produced	1978–83
Builder	Siemens-Duewag
Voltage	600 volts d.c.
Axles	Six
Weight	71,585 lb
Propulsion	Siemens
Seating	64 seats

● **EDMONTON**

Edmonton inaugurated its 7 km (4½ mile) line in 1978. By 1992, the system had expanded to 10.6 km (6½ miles). In the 1900s, Edmonton operated a streetcar system. This was discontinued after World War I, in favour of highway transportation. Edmonton's light-rail system began operations with 14 six-axle articulated Siemens-Duewag U2 light-rail vehicles (LRVs).

● **CALGARY**

Calgary followed Edmonton's lead and opened its 12 km (7½ mile) all-new light-rail line in 1981. By 1992, Calgary's

● **LEFT**
In the 1960s, Toronto still operated venerable Peter Witt cars, which seem particularly antique compared to a modern CLRV.

● **OPPOSITE**
Toronto operates 196 four-axle CLRV cars built between 1977–82. A TTC car pauses at Dundas Avenue, Toronto, in 1985.

● **BELOW**
Toronto once boasted a large fleet of President Conference Committee (PCC) cars. In the past two decades, most were replaced with CLRVs.

system was operating more than 27 km (17 miles), with extensions planned. Calgary operates a fleet of more than 80 six-axle articulated Siemans-Duewag U2 cars. It has also operated two experimental U2 cars that feature a.c.-traction motors. Most North American light-rail systems use traditional d.c.-traction motor technology. In the USA, the Baltimore, Maryland, light-rail system also uses a.c. traction.

● TORONTO

Toronto relied on a large fleet of President Conference Committee cars (PCC)s. In 1977, the city began replacing traditional PCCs with new Canadian Light Rail Vehicles (CLRVs). By the early 1990s, Toronto was operating nearly 100 four-axle single-unit CLRVs and more than 50 six-axle articulated CLRVs. Like cities in the USA, Toronto was looking at low-floor cars for future operation.

CUBA'S RAILWAY NETWORK

For many years, Cuba had a huge diversity of classic American steam locomotives, left suspended in time following Fidel Castro's revolution in 1959.

Some of them came from former lines in the USA and their builders' plates read like a who's who of American locomotive history: H.K. Porter, Rogers, Davenport, Alco, Vulcan Ironworks and Baldwin. Small wonder that up until the turn of the twentieth century became a focus for steam lovers worldwide, as traditional outposts of steam in Eastern Europe, South Africa and India have declined.

All of Cuba's steam-locomotive fleet worked on the island's vast sugar plantations but, in the course of work, often travelled over the national railway system's main lines. Far from being the small locomotives found on many of the world's sugar plantations, Cuba's engines were, in many cases, fully fledged main-liners and typical of the engines that many American roads were operating in the early years of this century.

A remarkable variety of gauges exists on Cuba, too, including standard, 3 ft, 2 ft $10\frac{1}{2}$ in, 2 ft 6 in and 2 ft $3\frac{3}{4}$ in.

A remarkable number of centenarian engines were still active until the early 2000s, including Baldwins of 1878, 1882, 1891, 1892 and 1895, and a pair of Rogers of 1894. However, Cuba's reliance on steam locomotives in the twenty-first century is more or less restricted to museum and tourist rides.

● **BELOW**
At the Boris Luis Santa Coloma mill network on Cuba, the flat crossing at Robles has a classic American signal-box on stilts. A Baldwin Mogul built in January 1920 completes the picture.

● **RIGHT**
A German-builder's plate on a Cuban locomotive.

● RIGHT
This Mogul, built by H.K. Porter in 1919, was pictured trundling a yellow caboose, that is guard's van, across the rails of the Carlos Manuel de Cespedes sugar mill in Camaguey Province, Cuba.

● FAR RIGHT
The wreckage of Baldwin 2-8-0 No. 1542 Manuel Fajardo at Obdulio Morales sugar mill's locomotive shed in Sancti Spiritus Province, near the spot where its boiler exploded. The boiler, wasted at the front tube-plate, had been welded. The result was disastrous. The driver, oiling the motion, was killed instantly. The fireman, in the cab, was thrown about 15 m (50 ft) across the depot yard.

4-4-0 WESTINGHOUSE

Builder	Baldwins, New York, USA
Client	Havana Central Railroad
Gauge	4 ft 8½ in
Type	4-4-0
Driving wheels	5 ft 8 in
Capacity	Cylinders 18 x 24 in
Weight	119,600 lb

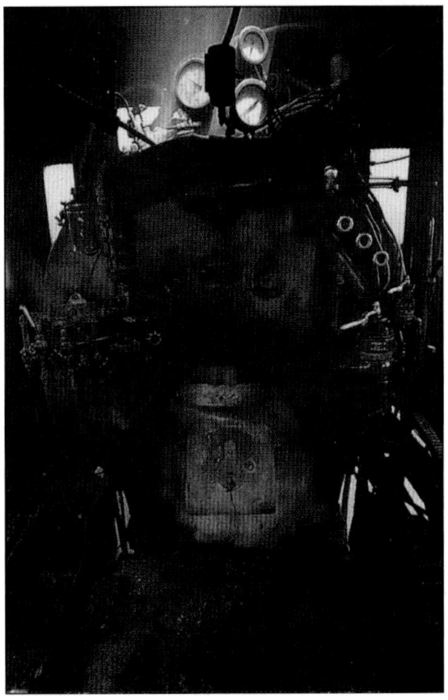

● OPPOSITE
Baldwin-built 2-8-0 No. 1390 eases a rake of freshly cut sugar cane down the Arroyo Blanco line at the Rafael Freyre sugar mill in Holguín Province, Cuba.

● ABOVE
Cuba had several Fireless engines. This huge 0-4-0, built by Baldwin in September 1917, worked at the Bolivia sugar mill, in Camaguey Province.

● ABOVE
Cuba has no coal reserves, so the island's locomotives are oilfired. The cab interior of a Baldwin 2-8-0 raising steam at the E.G. Lavandero sugar mill.

South American Steam

South America was a major area of importance during the worldwide decline of steam from the 1950s and remained so until the mid-1980s.

The area is fascinating because of its diversity of locomotive types, operating terrain and gauge.

● **BELOW RIGHT**
One of the Teresa Cristina's Texas 2-10-4s bursts out of Sideropolis Tunnel on the Rio Florita branch line. The engine, No. 313, was built by Baldwin in 1940.

● ARGENTINA AND URUGUAY

Argentina displayed the British school of design. It had more locomotives than any other South American country – about 1,000 active as late as the mid-1970s. Five gauges operated over 80 different locomotive types. One of the world's most exciting steam lines is Argentina's 75 cm (2 ft 6 in) gauge Rio Gallegos, a coal-carrying line 52 degrees south, near the Strait of Magellan. This route operates 2-10-2s, hauling 1,800-ton coal-trains, and is one of the steam sights of the world.

Uruguay, across the River Plate from Buenos Aires, was another stronghold of classic British designs, rivalling India in faithfulness to the domestic product.

● **ABOVE**
A 4-8-0 15B Class of Argentine Railways. Britain's Vulcan Foundry exported 30 of these two-cylinder engines to Argentina in 1949. Mixed-traffic engines, they gained distinction in hauling seasonal fruit over the 1,200 km (750 mile) run from the Rio Negro Valley to Buenos Aires, working 1,000-ton loads on passenger-train timings.

● **LEFT**
In the 1950s, the Yorkshire Engine Co. of Sheffield sent two Moguls to Paraguay. The engines have a distinct LMS air about them as shown in this picture of No. 152 Asunción in the shed yard at San Salvador.

● BRAZIL

Brazil has long been a land of discovery for rare and unrecorded locomotive types, because of its vast terrain and the relative remoteness of much of the country. Brazil's best-known steam-line is the metre-gauge Doña Teresa Cristina in the south-east where the world's last Texas Type 2-10-4s work. Formerly, they worked across the Mato Grosso, the highlands in eastern Mato Grosso state. These giants of American steam superpower, scaled down to metre-gauge operations, contrast with a plethora of sugar-plantation systems in the area around Campos, north of Rio de Janeiro, and in the north-eastern state of

● ABOVE
Texas Type 2-10-4s and Mikado 2-8-2s in the shed yard at Tubarao on Brazil's metre-gauge Doña Teresa Cristina Railway in south-east Santa Catarina Province.

● BELOW RIGHT
Brazil's Doña Teresa Cristina Railway acquired 6 metre gauge 2-6-6-2 Mallets from Baldwin between 1941–9. They were introduced for the heavily graded, curving route from Tubarao to Lauro Muller.

Pernambuco behind the Atlantic Ocean port and state capital Recife (formerly Pernambuco). These sugar usinas hosted a fascinating variety of metre-gauge veterans, many from Brazil's former main-line railways such as the Leopoldina, Mogiana, Paulista and Sorocabana.

● CHILE, PERU AND PARAGUAY

Chile's waterless Atacama Desert was host to the last Kitson Meyers, weird, double-jointed beasts that bent in the middle and had a chimney at both ends. These engines were an articulated predecessor of the more successful Garratt engine.

The Kitson Meyer's rarity was complemented by the incredible veterans found farther north in Peru where an 1870 classic American Rogers 4-4-0 was active at Puerto Eten.

The wilds of the Paraguayan Chaco were host to a fascinating stud of veterans that hauled *quebracho* from the interior to ports along the River Paraguay for conveying to the Atlantic Ocean at Buenos Aires. The logs were once a major source of tannin, used as tanning agents and in medicines. The flame-throwing woodburners of the Chaco contrasted well with the standard-gauge main line from Asunción to Encarnación with its woodburning Edwardian Moguls, from North British Glasgow and Hawthorn Leslie 2-6-2Ts.

Thus, diversity and exotica have been left over from the great age of steam. Although, by the 1990s, much of the diversity had disappeared, survivors will linger on in ever-diminishing pockets into the new century.

15B CLASS 4-8-0

Date	1949
Builder	Vulcan Foundry, Lancashire, England
Client	Argentine Railways (Ferrocarriles Argentinos; FA)
Gauge	5 ft 6 in
Driving wheels	5 ft 8 in
Capacity	Cylinders 19 x 28 in
Total weight in full working order	154 tons

Modern South American Locomotives

In the past, many South American countries had closer ties with Europe and the USA than with each other. This resulted in at least six different railway gauges being built on the continent.

● Snaking Bulk Traffic in Peru

Peru's railways climb the upper slopes of the highest Andean summits but adhesion only is used, resulting in spectacular sights as long mineral-trains snake up and around grand mountains. Diesel is the established form of motive power. Peru has more than 1,350 km (839 miles) of standard gauge and just 300 km (186 miles) of 3 ft gauge.

Peru's oil-burning steam locomotives were replaced by diesel-electrics, the most numerous being General Motors (GM) Type JJ 26 CW-2B 3,300 hp Co-Cos built by Villanes of Brazil.

● Restructuring in Chile

Chile has just under 2,576 km (1,600 miles) of 5 ft 6 in gauge and more than 1,600 km (1,000 miles) of metre-gauge track still in use after restructuring of the railway system. The metre-gauge lines to the north of Santiago are diesel-operated but the standard-gauge Southern Railway, extending from Santiago south to Puerto Montt, an area of German settlement, has been electrified. Electric locomotives of Swiss origin are being built in Chile. Diesel has taken over the narrow-gauge routes.

● Above
An Alco-built 1,000-hp diesel-electric, No. 107, shunting on a multigauge track in the station yard at Mérida, Yucatan, Mexico. The locomotive belongs to the Ferrocarriles Unidos del Sureste.

● Below
Argentina's changing motive-power character is shown at Constitution Station, Buenos Aires. A diesel-electric stands beside a Class 8E three cylinder 2-6-4 suburban tank, one of the most successful locomotive types ever delivered to the country.

ARGENTINE CLASS 8E 2-6-4T SUBURBAN

Date	1923
Gauge	5 ft 6 in
Client	Buenos Aires & Great Southern Railway
Driving wheels	5 ft 8 in
Capacity	3 cylinders 17 x 26 in
Pressure	200 lb sq in
Axle loading	19 tons
Weight in full working order	101 tons

● ABOVE
A 2-8-0 of Mexico's Southern Pacific Lines threads a freight-train along the West Coast route, which stretches 2,104 km (1,307 miles) from Guadalajara, Mexico's second-largest city, to the border of the United Mexican States (UMS) and the USA.

● BELOW
The nameplate and numberplate of one of the two Moguls delivered to Paraguay from Yorkshire Engineering Co., named Asunción after the country's capital city Nuestra Señora de la Asunción founded in 1538. The sister engine was No. 151, named Encarnación, after Encarnación de Diaz, the agricultural centre opposite Posados, Argentina, with which it is connected by ferry.

The E32 Co-Cos from GAI of Italy are Chile's most numerous passenger-electric locomotives. Most diesels are from GM in Argentina. The DT600, DT1300, DYDT5100, D7.100 and D1600 classes account for more than two-thirds of Chile's diesels. The most numerous diesel classes on the 5 ft 6 in gauge are GAIA 1350, GAIA 1050 and Alco RSD16. Metre-gauge diesels are supplied by General Electric (GE), the most numerous class being the G22CO with more than 100 units in service. The 201 km (125 miles) of electrically-operated track is entirely serviced by Russian-built locomotives.

● DIESEL TAKE-OVER IN ARGENTINA

Argentina has more than 22,500 km (14,000 miles) of 5 ft 6 in gauge, nearly 3,220 km (2,000 miles) of 4 ft 8½ in gauge and more than 14,500 km (9,000 miles) of other gauges. Much of the rail system radiates from Buenos Aires. Because of British influence in the early days, most equipment is British in appearance. Diesel has all but taken over, yet steam is still active on the Esquel and Rio Gallegos lines of Patagonia. On main lines, Fiat-type diesel railcars are common, although freight traffic on the many electrified lines is mainly hauled by British outline diesels. Lines carrying the heaviest commuter traffic around Buenos Aires have been electrified for many years.

● BELOW
An electric locomotive pulls a freight-train through the Argentine-Chilean Pass at Caracoles, near Socompa in Chile's Antofagasta Province.

● HEMATITE, STEEL AND SÃO PAULO IMPACT ON BRAZIL

Brazil is South America's largest and most industrial country. The two main gauges are 5 ft 3 in and metre. Bulk freight has increased and made new export routes a priority, because of vast hematite deposits, which is the chief source of iron, in Minas Gerais state, the steel industry of Volta Redonda town in Rio de Janeiro state, Brazil's first steel-making town from 1942, and the manufacturing potential of the fastest-growing city in the world, São Paulo, itself a great railway centre. Track up-grading and electrification has been in progress for the past 15 years. Diesels work the various narrow gauges and the non-electrified main lines. There are just more than 1,932 km (1,200 miles) of 5 ft 3 in gauge, 24,150 km (15,000 miles) of metre-gauge with just more than 885 km (550 miles) electrified. Freight account for 99 per cent of traffic.

European Shunters

In the days of steam, locomotives for shunting or gravity marshalling-yard work were sometimes specifically designed but many, also, were those pensioned off from main-line duties. To an extent, this practice still applies but from the 1950s increasing attention was paid to efficiency and fitness for purpose.

● **LEFT** Members of the numerous Swiss Federal Railways class of diesel-tractor built between 1950–68, represented by Tm" 736 at Chambrelien in 1996, are often involved with work on the permanent way.

● Shunting within station limits

These shunters come in many shapes and sizes, depending to a degree on whether what is required is casual shunting at a relatively small station or transfer work with moderate loads on the main line from time to time.

For the lighter duties, locomotives are usually four-wheeled and range from about 50 hp to about 300 hp. Propulsion can be diesel or electric. In Switzerland, alternative power sources are provided in the same locomotive and can be selected. For example, in sidings where there is no overhead-line equipment, the diesel engine provides power to the electric-traction motors. Some are fitted for remote radio control, enabling the driver to operate from the lineside, thereby performing the role of the traditional shunter. Small machines can be driven by people without the lengthy, rigorous training needed for a main-line driver, and, when not driving, they perform other station work.

Larger locomotives tend to be six-wheeled or Bo-Bo, diesel or electric. Diesel is usually preferred for its flexibility.

● Marshalling yards and trip freights

The bulk of marshalling-yard and trip-freight work is done by Bo-Bos where the prime power source is a diesel motor or overhead electric supply often giving an output of more than 1,000 hp. At gravity marshalling yards, standard locomotives with special low gearing for propelling wagons over the hump are sometimes used. In more recent years, some gravity-yard shunters have been fitted with radio to permit operation from the control tower. Other specialist shunters include a normal locomotive semi-permanently

● **LEFT** Berne-Loetschberg-Simplon (BLS) No. 401 at Spiez, near Interlaken, Bern Canton, Switzerland, in 1988, with its notable jackshaft drive. These locomotives are similar to shunters on Swiss Federal Railways, Schweizerische Bundesbahnen (SBB), and to others in Sweden. Their power coupled with a reasonable turn of speed enables them to work trip-freights and to act as carriage-shunters.

● **RIGHT**
The trend to make small shunters more versatile is increasing. They have been fitted, for example, with radio control. A new application is accumulators, fitted to this electric-shunter of Switzerland's Spiez-Erlenbach-Zweisimmen Railway so that it can work in non-electrified sidings. Tea 245.021 is at Zweisimmen in 1995.

● **BELOW**
This Deutsche Reichsbahn Class 101 No. 512, almost the classic small diesel-shunter, acts as carriage-shunter at Riesa, Dresden, Germany, in 1991. It was later No.311.512 on the unified German railway system (DBAG).

● **RIGHT**
Older main-line locomotives are downgraded to light duties, performing trip-freight and shunting work as needed. Class 1200 of Portuguese Railways – Companhia dos Caminhos de Ferro (CP) – built by Sorefame in Portugal in 1961–64, do such work in Southern Portugal. Nos. 1213 and 1210 are pictured resting at the railway-junction town of Tunes, Algarve, in 1996.

ELECTRIC SHUNTER: BERN-LOETSCHBERG-SIMPLON RAILWAY (BLS)

Date	1943
Builders	mechanical: Swiss Locomotive and Machine Works (SLM) electrical: SA des Ateliers de Sécheron
Gauge	1,435 mm
Class	Ee 3/3
Axle (wheel) arrangement	030 (Whyte notation 0-6-0)
Catenary voltage	a.c. 15 kV, 16.7 Hz.
Weight in working order	38 tonnes
Rating	One hour, 462 kW (about 619 hp)
Maximum service speed	40 kph

coupled to a similar power-unit without cab or related console. Such units are sometimes called "cow and calf".

Larger, non-specialized shunters can work "trip freights" between their own yard and others in the vicinity, or to factory sidings.

● LARGE PASSENGER STATIONS

At most large passenger stations, the "station pilot", often in gleaming condition, is a familiar sight as it deals with empty stock or remarshals trains. The locomotives are often members of the same class, or a variant of those found in marshalling yards. Sometimes the only difference is the fitting of extra, or different, braking equipment or couplings.

● **ABOVE**
Hungarian State Railways (MAV) has a sizeable class of modern Bo-Bo electrics built by Ganz Mavag from 1983 onward. Their 820 kW (1,100 hp) enables them to cover a wide range of duties, including carriage pilot, heavyfreight shunting and trip-freights. No. V46. 054 is pictured at the river-port of Szeged (Szegedin), on Hungary's border with then Yugoslavia, in 1993.

EUROPEAN FREIGHT

● LEFT
A new country and new livery have brought a striking change to former Deutsche Reichsbahn Class 242, which was bought by Lokoop, a Swiss consortium, and hired out. The engine, working on the Swiss Südostbahn in 1996, is pictured at Schindellegi in a livery advertising transport to a nearby mountain resort.

Reconstruction of Europe after World War II and growing international trade brought a huge resurgence in rail freight. This traffic had to be integrated with equally large volumes of passenger-trains and so locomotives had to be able both to handle heavy loads and to run at relatively high speeds.

Carriage of many classes of freight by rail has steadily declined. New business, however, is arriving as road-freight tractors and trailers are transported by rail across national boundaries, sometimes with drivers accommodated in sleeping-cars on the train. Intermodal traffic, with either swap-bodies or vehicles designed to operate on rail or road, is not a new concept but it is being further developed. The transport of standard-gauge wagons on special metre-gauge bogies or transporter-wagons continues to cut the cost of time delays and trans-shipment, especially in Switzerland.

● ELECTRIC LOCOMOTIVES

As the mixed-traffic locomotive's development progressed along similar lines, the superficial appearance of the motive power on each rail system varied normally only to the extent of front-end body shape and the ventilation grilles' style and position.

Most adopted the Bo-Bo formation. In countries where heavy trains tackle steep gradients, however, locomotives with the Co-Co arrangement were introduced. In more recent years, developments in multiple working and remote radio control have enabled the use of two or more compatible locomotives at the head and a locomotive cut into the train. This is, among other things, to relieve weight on the drawbar between the locomotive and the train's

● ABOVE
Class 140 of German Railways (DBAG) was devised as a freight version of a similar passenger-class. It first appeared in 1957, and to 1973 nearly 900 were built. They handle anything from empty-carriage workings to medium-tonnage freights. No. 140 009-2 is pictured at Murneau, south of Munich, Bavaria, in 1994.

● LEFT
In sharp contrast to the bustle of the French scene, a freight-train in southern Portugal waits to leave the junction station of Tunes, Algarve, headed by Alco-built A1A-A1A diesel-electric No. 1503 in 1996.

● **RIGHT**
Two locomotives look excessive for this light freight-train at Venlo, Limburg Province, in the Netherlands in 1989, but Netherlands Railways-NV Nederlandse Spoorwegen (NS)-diesel-electric No. 6401, built in 1955, is part of the train that is in the charge of NS 2213. It is ironic that it is hauling a member of the class destined to lead to its withdrawal.

FRENCH STATE RAILWAYS (SNCF) CLASS BB 22200

Date	1976
Builder	Alsthom/MTE
Gauge	1,435 mm
Axle arrangement	BB
Catenary voltage	d.c. 1,500 v, a.c. 25 kV single phase (dual voltage)
Wheel diameter	1,250 mm
Weight in working order	89 tonnes
Rating	4,360 kW
Maximum service speed	160 kph

front vehicles. Longer trains also improve line capacity and therefore economic performance of the line.

● DIESEL LOCOMOTIVES

Diesel power, with locomotives working in multiple on heavy trains, is the only practical course on non-electrified lines or where traffic is lighter. The available tractive effort is generally lower than electric locomotives, but continuing use of diesels widely throughout Europe can be foreseen because of the flexibility of operation coupled with, usually, a mixed-traffic availability and, in some cases, lighter axleloading.

● BUILDERS

All the larger and some of the smaller countries of mainland Europe have the capacity to build both diesel and electric locomotives. However, the case now is that few builders design, manufacture and erect a complete locomotive. Credit for the design or manufacture of a particular class of locomotives often goes to the company or works which does the final erection. In practice, the design may well be that of the erecting company but components – bodies, motors, electrical equipment and other items – are likely to have been provided by other locomotive manufacturers.

● **LEFT**
French National Railways (SNCF) BB22288 Louhans leaves the extensive marshalling yards of Villeneuve-St Georges, south-eastern Paris, with a long train of empty car-transporters in 1996.

European Rack Railways

Rack railways are specially built to climb steep gradients in mountainous areas.

● **TOURIST LINES**

Most but not all tourist lines exist to convey skiers in winter and walkers, or just sightseers, in summer high into mountains. Other lines enable the tourist to reach points from which spectacular views can be obtained.

Track gauge varies from 800 mm to standard gauge. Propulsion is generally by an electric power-car pushing a control-trailer up the grade but the touristic value of the steam locomotive has not been lost on some operators who, in recent years, have ordered new steam locomotives using oilfiring and needing only one man in the cab. For obvious reasons, the track of each is relatively short. Examples of both types of line are illustrated.

● LEFT
Austria's metre-gauge Achenseebahn uses both Riggenbach rack-and-pinion and adhesion to climb from Jenbach, in Austria in Tirol, east of Innsbruck, to the lake that gives the railway its name. The locomotives date from 1899. No. 2 and its vintage coaches are pictured leaving Jenbach in 1980.

● LEFT
Switzerland's 800 mm gauge Brienzer-Rothorn Bahn, between Brienz, on Lake Brienz in Bern Canton, and Rothorn, has put into service three new steam locomotives of revolutionary design but conventional external appearance. These are oilfired and can be operated by one man. The first, No. 12, was delivered in 1992 and is pictured at Brienz in 1995.

● BELOW LEFT
The Monte Generoso Railway has been operated successively by steam, diesel and from 1982 electricity. The train is pictured having just arrived at the summit station, which was being modernized in 1989.

ELECTRIC RAILCAR – MONTE GENEROSO RAILWAY

Date	1982
Builder	Swiss Locomotive and Machine Works (SLM)
Client	Monte Generoso Railway
Gauge	800 mm Abt Rack
Class	Bhe 4/8
Axle arrangement	Four of the eight axles of the two-car unit are driven
Catenary voltage	d.c. 650 v
Weight in working order	34.1 tonnes
Rating	810 kW (about 1,086 hp)
Maximum service speed	14 kph

● LEFT
A popular mountain line in Austria is the metre-gauge Schneebergbahn, south of Vienna, from Puchberg to the summit at Hochschneeberg. No. 999.02 of Austrian Federal Railways dating from 1893, pauses at Baumgarten in 1986 before tackling the next stage of the climb.

● BELOW LEFT
The oldest locomotives on the standard-gauge Erzberg line of Austrian Federal Railways (ÖBB) were Class 97, first in service in 1890.

● BELOW RIGHT
Not all rack railways are in mountains. In Hungary, Budapest has an important standard-gauge line that partly serves commuters but is mainly for citizens wishing to reach the hills behind Buda, the old Magyar capital on the west bank of the River Danube. The line was originally steam-worked but Switzerland's SLM works provided the stock when the line was electrified in 1929. Car 55 is pictured leaving the lower terminus in August 1993.

● CONVENTIONAL RAILWAYS WITH RACK AID

The main aim of conventional railways with track assistance is to provide communication between towns and villages for passengers and freight conveyance. Often, tourist areas are served as well. Indeed, if this were not so, the viability of many lines often operating in relatively sparsely populated regions would be at risk.

The track gauge is generally metre and the trains appear at first sight quite conventional with an electric-locomotive hauling a moderately long train of coaches. Other trains might be hauled by single or double electric power-cars, in effect locomotives with passenger or baggage accommodation in the body. If track configuration permits, speeds of more than 75 kph are achieved over the adhesion sections but on rack sections about less than half of that can be expected.

● INDUSTRIAL LINES

A most spectacular example of industrial lines was the "Iron Mountain" railway from Vordernberg, in the Styria, Austria, to Eisenerz. Of standard gauge, there were some passenger services but its main purpose was to bring iron ore from Eisenerz, a mountain consisting almost entirely of iron ore, to a huge iron and steel works at Donawitz, west of Leoben in Styria. Steam was the motive power until the last few years of its existence when specially fitted diesel locomotives joined a rack locomotive purpose-built for the line. These achieved only a modest degree of success. Passenger traffic declined to the point where it could be handled by a single four-wheel, rack-fitted diesel-railcar.

This Austrian Federal Railways – Österreichische Bundesbahnen (ÖBB) – line closed in 1986 because of a fall in demand for steel coupled with the fact that it was cheaper to import ore from outside Austria. The last ore-train ran under diesel power on 27 June 1986. No fewer than seven steam locomotives have been preserved. Five of them are Class 0-6-2 Ts dating from 1890, the most popular with the crews, and one of which stands on a plinth in the town square. One is a 0-12-0T and one a 2-12-2T, built in Germany in 1941 and now standing on a plinth at Vordernmarkt Station.

European DMUs

The diesel multiple unit (DMU), the most flexible of all means of rail passenger transport, is used in Europe on all gauges and in many configurations.

● SINGLE RAILCARS

Single railcars range from a unit capable of coupling to another power-unit, to a control-trailer or just to a freight-wagon or passenger-coach. Operating alone, a single railcar can often be sufficient to maintain the passenger traffic on a narrow-gauge line, such as the Austrian Federal Railways 760 mm gauge line linking the Neider-Österreich (NÖ) towns of Gmünd and Gross Gerungs in the Greinerwald, or standard-gauge routes like the picturesque cross-border route between the Austrian Tirol town of Reutte and the German resort and winter sports centre Garmisch-Partenkirchen in the foothills of the Bavarian Alps.

● ABOVE
Netherlands Railways (NS) diesel-electric Class DE IIs were built by Allan, in 1953 and extensively rebuilt in 1975–82 by NS. This unit had just arrived at Arnhem, in Gelderland Province, in 1989.

● BELOW
The modern appearance of this rebuilt X4300 Series unit of French National Railways (SNCF) belies the fact that the class was introduced in 1963. In 1988, a typical representative, from Dinant, Belgium, awaits its return working at Givet, in the Ardennes Department of north-eastern France, near the border with Belgium.

The ability to strengthen the train quickly, to cope with known or sudden peaks of traffic, by adding a powered vehicle to run in multiple without reducing its line speed, is invaluable on services which share, for part of the route, the tracks of a main line where lengthy track-occupation by slow trains is unacceptable. Such units are capable of 120 kph.

On branch lines or secondary routes with a relatively infrequent service, any cut in speed from hauling unpowered trailers is not serious. However, many modern trailing-vehicles offer relatively

● **RIGHT**
In Bavaria, German Railways No. 614-012 pictured about to leave Hersbruck and head south for Nuremberg in 1985. These sets have self-tilting suspensions.

GERMAN FEDERAL RAILWAYS (DBAG) CLASS 614

Date	1971
Builder	Orenstein & Koppel/Uerdingen
Client	DB
Gauge	1,435 mm
Class	614 three-car set
Power unit	One MAN diesel-engine in each power-car, driving all wheels on one bogie via hydraulic transmission
Weight in working order	123 tonnes total (all three cars)
Rating	670 kW
Maximum service speed	140 kph

little resistance, so speeds can be relatively high, an important factor where the bus is the potential rival for traffic.

● UNITS OF TWO OR MORE CARS

The duties of units of two or more cars can range from branch-line work through local passenger to semifast and, in some cases, high-speed intercity services.

At the lower end of the speed-and-capacity scale are two-car sets in which only one vehicle is powered. At the other end of the scale are sets with two power-cars between which run one or more trailers.

These units are usually used on standard-gauge lines but also run with medium-distance semifast traffic on local and branch-line services. Recent developments in Germany with two-car tilting sets were sufficiently successful for progress to be made to a further class having suspension of Italy's Pendolino type, with a maximum authorized speed of 160 kph. Their value has been particularly appreciated on lines such as the Bavarian one from Nuremberg to Hof, which suffers from stretches of frequent curvature. There, tilting trains can be permitted higher speeds than trains with conventional suspension.

● **ABOVE**
Coachwork made by Budd of USA seems popular with Portuguese Railways for its DMUs. These sets dating from 1989 work Rápidos – expresses stopping at main stations – as well as local trains. One curves away from the railway junction of Tunes, Algarve, in 1996.

● **BELOW**
Austrian Federal Railways (ÖBB) have revolutionized speed and comfort on lesser-used lines with modern Class 5047 railcars built from 1987 onward. Passenger-loads have risen as a result. No. 5047-028 a backdrop of mountains at Reutte-im-Tirol in 1994.

EUROPEAN EMU

The electric multiple unit (EMU) dates back to the turn of the century. In its simplest form, d.c. motors were controlled by robust mechanical tap changers made for relatively low maintenance costs, which balanced the high cost of line power supply. A bonus was that units could be coupled electrically and driven by one person. The main attraction, however, was probably that turnround times at terminuses were significantly cut because no locomotive change was required.

Operators of underground railways and metros found the system attractive not least because, in the restricted environment, a d.c. electric supply could be provided relatively cheaply by third rail.

This simple system saw few dramatic changes until the 1950s when the development of electronics and hi-tech engineering transformed the scene in nearly every aspect of EMU design and construction.

• THE MODERN EMU – LOCAL AND INTERMEDIATE TRAFFIC

In mainland Europe, the Netherlands can probably claim the most concentrated use of EMUs. Few lines are not electrified and the proximity of towns and villages in this densely populated land calls for trains with high-capacity seating and good acceleration and braking.

In 1975, the Netherlands railways coined the term "Sprinter" for a two-car unit. Two- and three-car variants soon followed. The name was quickly copied by British Rail. In Belgium and around the big cities of France, Germany and Italy the EMU is important. The Swiss Federal Railway briefly flirted with EMUs in the 1920s, some of which are still used on departmental duties, but moved from locomotive haulage of short-distance trains to sophisticated EMUs from the mid-1950s. The latest units can be formed of two power-cars with up to three intermediate trailers and are termed Neue Pendel Zug (NPZ). Variants can be seen on the private railways where, in many instances, they form the backbone of the fleets. Thyristor control is well established following the usual difficulties experienced in many countries with development models. Reliability is now such that many of the numerous metre-gauge systems operate power-cars with similar technology.

Austria boasts a similar and sizeable class of attractive three-car sets built between 1978 and 1987 for suburban and middle-distance work.

• **ABOVE**
In contrast with the angular design of recent years, this Austrian Federal Railways two-car EMU epitomized the flowing lines adopted by several European countries from the 1950s. No. 4030.309, one of a batch built by Simmering-Graz-Pauker between 1956–9, is pictured about to leave St Margrethen, Switzerland, for a cross-border run into Austria's Vorarlberg Province, to Bregenz on Lake Constance in 1994.

• **BELOW**
These units, readily strengthened by adding trailers, set a standard for the modern thyristor-controlled EMU able to handle suburban and regional services equally well. They are used throughout Switzerland's Federal railway network. Similar versions have been bought by private railways. A unit is pictured arriving at Lausanne's main station in 1993. A French Train Grande Vitesse (TGV) – a high-speed train – and a former Swiss TEE unit now in grey livery are present.

NEUE PENDEL ZUG (NPZ) – SWISS FEDERAL RAILWAYS

Date	Four prototypes, 1984. Production, 1987-90
Builders	Mechanical: Flug und Fahrzeugwerke AG, Altenrhein, Switzerland; Schweizerische Locomotiv und Maschinenfabrik (SLM), Winterthur, Switzerland; Schindler Waggon AG, Pratteln, near Basel (Basle), Switzerland Electrical: A.G. Brown-Boveri & Cie, Baden, Baden-Württemberg, Germany
Gauge	1,435 mm
Class	RBDe4/4 (now Class 532)
Axle arrangement	All four axles driven on each power-car
Catenary voltage	a.c. 15 kV, 16.7 Hz
Weight in working order	70 tonnes (including driving-trailer)
One hour rating	1,650 kW (about 2,212 hp)
Maximum service speed	140 kph

● THE MODERN EMU – EXPRESS SERVICES

Few genuine EMUs have been designed specifically for long-distance express-services, but in 1965 Austria Federal Railways introduced a class of six-car sets with a permitted speed of 150 kph. All included a dining-car for some of the most prestigious services, including the run between Zurich in Switzerland and Vienna. No longer in the forefront of express travel, they have been refurbished and are usefully employed on expresses over the Semmering Pass.

● ABOVE
The Netherlands has long gone its own way with design. To some, Plan ZO/Z1 (ICM 1/2) "Koploper" three-car units are ugly. However, they are practical: the door beneath the driver's raised cab enables passengers to have unobstructed gangway-access to all vehicles.

● ABOVE RIGHT
The rounded outline of the 1950s is carried through in this four-car EMU of Trafik AB Grängesberg-Oxelosund Jarnvag, a Swedish private railway operating west of Stockholm. It is standing at Katrineholm in 1981. The X20 Class was built in 1956–7. It was ahead of its time, because the power-car is in the train rather than being a motored driving-vehicle.

● RIGHT
The Austrian 4020 Class EMU is similar in appearance to the Swiss NPZ but differs in technology. Between 1978–87, 120 units were built. They have proved most successful in S-Bahn and medium-distance work alike and were built by Simmering-Graz-Pauker, with electrical parts by Brown-Boveri, Elin and Siemens. Four traction motors produce 1,200 kW, about 1,608 hp, for each three-car unit, to permit a 120-kph service speed. No. 4020-116 sits beneath mountains at St Anton in 1990.

European Diesel – Main-line

● BELOW
Diesel locomotive No. 232-231 stands, in 1992, at Brandenburg, former residence of Prussia's rulers, now in Lower Saxony, on a double-deck shuttle train to Potsdam. Brandenburg and Potsdam are respectively 60 km (37 miles) and 27 km (17 miles) south-west of Berlin.

Main-line diesels began to become prominent in the 1950s as steam started to decline. Some countries had seen at first hand diesels operated by the American Army just after World War II. The first large diesels were modelled on American lines. In some cases, virtual copies were made under licence or using imported components. One look at a large Belgian diesel shows from whence came the inspiration. Other examples were in Scandinavia where the Nohab Company of Trollhättan, Sweden, set a style that, externally at least, showed a transatlantic influence, which spread even to countries in the then Eastern Bloc.

The diesel's field of operation was almost universal for freight-trains. Some classes are geared specifically for this work. In passenger service, they tended to work on secondary lines or main lines that could not justify electrification costs. The locomotives can be classified by transmission type.

● ELECTRICAL TRANSMISSION

Electrical transmission is the more popular. A diesel-engine drives a generator to power electric-traction motors. The system is relatively simple, robust and easy to maintain. Proponents of hydraulic transmission, however, claim less precise control and lower efficiency.

The 5100 Class Co-Co of Belgium's national railways, the Société Nationale des Chemins de Fer Belges (SNCB), is powered by an engine producing 1,580 kW (about 2,118 hp) at 650 rpm built by Cockerill/Baldwin and has a 120-kph service speed. Germany, however, is where one of the most popular and sturdy classes of diesel-electrics is in widespread use. It originated at the October Revolution Locomotive Works in Lugansk (Voroshilovgrad, 1939–91), Ukraine, part of the former USSR. A batch of Co-Co locomotives, now Class 230, was built in 1970 for what was then the Deutsche Reichsbahn (DR) of East Germany. Another batch, Class 231, arrived in 1972–73. A final batch of 709 locomotives was delivered between 1973–82. With a massive diesel engine delivering 2,950 hp and a 120 kph top

● ABOVE
This diesel-electric of the Grand Duchy of Luxembourg's railways, the Société Nationale des Chemins de Fer Luxembourgeois (CFL), was built by Brissonneau & Lotz, of Aytre, in 1958. In 1995, standing at Esch/Alzette, in Luxembourg, at the border with France, it shows clear signs of French origin. Its duties include heavy trip-freights in Luxembourg's industrial south.

● ABOVE
The Austrian Federal Railways (ÖBB) Class 2043 and similar Class 2143 are, at 1,100 kW or 1,475 hp, of modest power by European standards. Yet they are the most powerful locomotives in Austria and find work on several non-electrified secondary lines.

DEUTSCHE REICHSBAHN CLASS 132

Date	1973
Builder	October Revolution Locomotive Works, Voroshilovgrad (Lugansk), USSR
Gauge	1,435 mm
Class	132 (now 232 on DBAG, unified German railways)
Axle arrangement	Co-Co
Weight in working order	123 tonnes
Rating	2,200 kw (appox 2950 hp)
Maximum service speed	120 kph

speed, they proved ideal for passenger and freight use.

With the reunification of Germany in 1990, their diagrams gradually spread across the country with favourable comment from drivers of the Deutsche Bundesbahn (DB), operating in what was the former West Germany. An uprated version, Class 234, has a 140 kph top speed. Many of the locomotives are being re-engined and appear to have a long life ahead.

Diesel-electrics have great importance to smaller nations where heavy traffic between major sites of population and commerce is offset by the need, on social if not economic grounds, to provide services over lightly laid secondary routes. An example is Portugal whose machines range from 117 tonne Co-Cos rated at nearly 3,000 hp to modest 64 tonne Bo-Bos producing about 1,300 hp.

● **HYDRAULIC TRANSMISSION**

The Deutsche Bundesbahn, now German Federal Railways (DBAG), favoured, for its large diesels, hydraulic transmission made by Voith, of Heindenheim, Brenz. This works like automatic gearboxes in cars. Between 1968–79, four classes of Bo-Bo machines were built, culminating in Class 217. Of this, there are two types. One is fitted with the Pielstick 16 PA 4V 200 engine producing 3,000 hp and a 140 kph top speed. Their weight in working order is 78.5 tonnes, compared with the Class 234's 123 tonnes.

Austrian Federal Railways (ÖBB) also favours Voith transmission in its relatively small 1,475 hp machines whose work is decreasing as lines are electrified.

● **ABOVE**
German Federal Railways (DBAG) Class 218 is the last in a long line of locomotives of similar appearance, 500 being built in 1968–79. The most powerful of these Bo-Bo diesel-hydraulics is rated at 2,061 kW, about 3,000 hp. Nos. 218.905 and 908, rebuilds from Class 210, are pictured at Brunswick, Lower Saxony, in 1991.

● **RIGHT**
The unmistakable French lineage of this Portuguese Railways Class 2601 stands out in 1996 as a diesel-electric Bo-Bo built by Alsthom passes Santa Clara, in Beira Litoral Province, south-west of Coimbra, Portugal's former capital.

European Main-line Electrics

World War II left mainland Europe's railways heavily damaged. Many administrations could see that electrification was the way forward but a neutral country, Switzerland, led the way.

● SWITZERLAND TURNS TO HYDRO-ELECTRIC POWER

Switzerland has no natural resources for power apart from abundant water. In the war, coal for steam-engines was practically unobtainable, so engineers turned to the source already harnessed, hydroelectric power (HEP). The country had used electric locomotives and railcars for many years but there was now a need for powerful, relatively fast mixed-traffic machines with a high power weight ratio and good adhesion. This pointed to providing motors on all axles.

In 1944 it was the Bern-Loetschberg-Simplon (BLS) railway that set the trend. It did so with a small class of eight Bo-Bo locomotives weighing only 80 tonnes, having four, fully suspended, single-phase motors driving all four axles. Current at 15 kV, 16⅔ Hz from overhead-line equipment enabled the locomotive to operate at an hourly rating of 3,238 kW.

● UNIFIED GERMAN SYSTEM

West Germany's large, efficient fleet of steam locomotives operated into the 1970s on main-line duties but here, too, Bo-Bo locomotives of similar dimensions to the BLS machine were introduced, Class 110 in 1956 for mixed-traffic work and Class 140 in 1957 mainly for freight

● ABOVE
SNCF Class BB2600 dual-voltage "Sybic" 26053 heads an express-train.

● TOP RIGHT
A Deutsche Bundesbahn Class 120 is waiting to leave Munich Main Railway Station, Bavaria, in 1989 at the head of a train of Netherlands Railways double-deck coaches then on trial. A prototype batch of five of these advanced-design locomotives with three-phase motors entered revenue service in 1979. The production batch did not come on stream until 1987. These 60 machines have a one-hour rating of 6,300 kW, about 8,445 hp, and a maximum service speed of 200 kph.

● RIGHT
In 1995, a direct descendant of the trend-setting Bern-Loetschberg-Simplon (BLS) railway Bo-Bo of 1944 stands at Interlaken West Station at the head of the Thunersee from Berlin. It is one of a class of 35. With an hourly rating of 4,990 kW, about 6,690 hp, it has a maximum service speed of 140 kph.

● LEFT
Deutsche Bundesbahn (DB) 11 081-6 heads north out of historic Boppard, in the Rhine Valley south of Koblenz. This class of 227 locomotives is an improved version of the prolific Class 110.

but often seen on passenger-trains. Several hundred of these and variants are working in western Germany. In eastern Germany, a class was developed using thyristor control. This went into batch-production in 1982, proving so successful that it is widely used across the unified German system – the DBAG – as Class 143. The locos weigh 82 tonnes and have a one-hour rating of 3,720 kW.

● FRANCE USES DUAL VOLTAGE

In France, development after the war was different, not least because the various constituents of the system that had finally embraced all the main railways in 1938, the Société Nationale des Chemins de Fer Français (SNCF), had, where electrification had been tried, used noncompatible traction current. No classes of locomotive had been made in large numbers although several small batches established a development line, which might be said to lead to the impressive BB26000 Class, the Sybic, an acronym for "Systeme Bi-courant". These dual-voltage machines operate either on 1500 V d.c. or 25 kV single-phase a.c. They went into service in 1988 and gradually proved themselves. They are so successful that their numbers are increasing rapidly towards a projected target of more than 300 units. They weigh 91 tonnes, have a rating of 6,400 kW and are authorized to travel at 200 kph.

France's Trains Grande Vitesse (TGVs) – high-speed multiple unit trains – reach high speeds. The SNCF holds an official electric-traction record for on 28 March 1955 Co-Co, 1,500 V d.c. locomotive CC 7107 achieved 330.9 kph (205.6 mph) with a 100-tonne load. Next day, this record was equalled by Bo-Bo 9004 with an 81-tonne train.

● RIGHT
Until 1988, the French National Railways (SNCF) CC 6500 Class of 1500 V d.c. locomotive was its most powerful along with dual-voltage subclass CC 21000. They are fitted with mono-motor-bogies, enabling the gear ratio to be changed easily. At high-speed setting, maximum speed is 200 kph. They are rated at 5,900 kW, just more than 7,900 hp. CC 6563, in low-gear mode is pictured near the large marshalling yards at Villeneuve-St-Georges, Paris, in 1996.

● **LEFT**
The need to produce a modern main-line electric locomotive to cope not only with express-traffic on level ground but also with heavy gradients in Austria's mountainous regions, led Austrian Federal Railways (ÖBB) to buy a batch of ten thyristor-controlled locomotives of the Swedish Railways Class Rc2 in 1971. Class 1044 was quickly developed by the railway authorities and introduced into service in 1974. No. 1044-092, pictured at Jenbach, in Tirol, east of Innsbruck, is one of the batch with a 160-kph service speed and a one-hour rating of 5,300 kW, just more than 7,100 hp. A later version has a 200 kph service maximum. One machine is approved for 220 kph.

● AUSTRIAN AND HUNGARIAN DESIGNS

Austria, so often challenging in steam design with the Gölsdorf locomotives and the Giesl ejector, has a most successful Bo-Bo Class 1044 that owes something to an earlier maid of all work, Class 1042, but also to the Swedish Rc2.

Hungary, too, has the numerous Class V43. This leans on German technology, in that the first small batch was built by Krupp, of Essen, Germany. Ganz, a world-renowned locomotive works, in which Hunslet of Britain has a financial interest, is keeping pace with modern locomotive technology.

● **RIGHT**
The Netherlands, a relatively small country, has an extensive railway network, part of which is in the European international system. Class 1600 and the almost identical Class 1700 are built by Alsthom, France, based on the French National Railways (SNCF) Class BB 7200. The Class 1600s entered service in 1981, the 1700s in 1990. Capable of 200 kph, they are restricted to 160 kph. Here, in 1989, No. 1643 has just brought an express-train into the border town of Maastricht in Limburg Province.

● SWITZERLAND'S LOK LEADS FIELD

Switzerland, however, is again leading the field with a very "hi-tech" design developed by the Swiss Locomotive and Machine Works (SLM) of Winterthur. Known as Lok 2000, the technological advances are so many that a small book would be needed to do it justice. A notable feature is its quietness when running. Swiss Federal Railways Schweizerische Bundesbahnen (SBB/CFF/FFS) know it as Class Re 460. The BLS has a variant – and the most powerful version – Class 465. A broad-gauge variant is in service on Finland's railway system. Examples have run trials in other countries.

The machines entered service on the federal railways in 1991, generally performing well. Teething troubles, however, slowed the progress of their introduction into general service. With problems solved, the class of 119 locomotives is operating widely throughout the country.

LOK 2000	
Date	1992
Builders	Mechanical: Swiss Locomotive & Machine Works (SLM), Winterthur, Switzerland Electrical: ABB Transportation Systems, Baden, Zurich, Switzerland
Client	Swiss Federal Railways
Gauge	1,435 mm
Class	Re460
Axle arrangement	Bo-Bo
Catenary voltage	15 kV
Length over buffers	18,500 mm
Weight in working order	84 tonnes
Number of traction motors	Four
Rating	1,100 kw (8180 hp)
Maximum service speed	230 kph

● RIGHT
Lok 2000 No. 460 015-1 of Swiss Federal Railways waits at Lausanne in Vaud Canton in 1993 after bringing in an express-train from Basel.

● LEFT
Belgium has a dense network of lines and demands a powerful mixed-traffic locomotive able to handle anything from light "push-and-pull" trains, through freights to expresses. The Class 21, introduced in 1984, comprises 60 machines rated at 3,310 kW, about 4,437 hp, with a 160-kph maximum service speed. They were built in Belgium by La Brugeoise et Nivelles SA and are almost identical to the chopper-controlled more powerful Class 27. No. 2157 is pictured in 1992 leaving Ghent Sint Pieters Station in the East Flanders provincial capital of Ghent on its way to the depot at Dendermonde, East Flanders.

● RIGHT
Italy has long produced striking and seemingly unconventional designs of locomotives. In the Class 656 Bo-Bo-Bo with its articulated body, F.S. Italia has one of the most successful designs of recent years. It is based on well-tried technology for it derives from the 636 Class dating back to 1940. Provided speeds above 150 kph are not required, these locomotives handle expresses almost anywhere in Italy. They first entered service in 1975. By 1989, 608 had been built. Here, No. E 656-469 waits to take over a train at Domodossola, in Novara Province of the Piedmont Compartimento, in 1996.

European Local Passenger – Locomotive-hauled

Until the late 1960s, it was possible to enjoy the sights and sounds of steam-hauled local passenger-trains soon to be displaced by electric and diesel traction. Because of the increased use of multiple units (MUs) with their favourable weight-per-person ratio and flexibility, many local services lost the familiar locomotive at the train's head.

The locomotive remains in use on such services for two main reasons. Firstly, and more obvious, certain lines have a mixture of relatively light passenger- and freight-traffic so that both functions can be fulfilled by a locomotive.

● "PUSH-AND-PULL" TRAINS

Second, in heavy passenger-traffic areas, displacement of locomotives by MUs, which often hauled trains of obsolescent coaches, meant that relatively modern machines would either have to be scrapped or sold at bargain prices. One solution was to select a class of

● ABOVE
Extensive improvements are being made to the line as German Railways (DBAG) Class 143 228-5 runs into Belzig-bei-Potsdam, south-west of Berlin, with a rake of double-deck coaches in 1992.

SWISS FEDERAL RAILWAYS CLASS 450

Date	1989
Builders	Mechanical: Swiss Locomotive & Machine Works (SLM), Switzerland Electrical: ASEA Brown Boveri
Client	Swiss Federal Railways
Gauge	1,435 mm
Class	450
Axle arrangement	Bo-Bo
Catenary voltage	a.c. 15 kV, 16.7 Hz
Weight in working order	78 tonnes (locomotive only)
Rating	One hour, 3,200 kW (about 4,290 hp)
Maximum service speed	130 kph

● LEFT
Swiss Federal Railways (SBB) No. 450 067-4 on S-Bahn service at Zurich Main Station in 1994.

● LEFT
The striking S-Bahn livery suits this German Federal Railways (DBAG) Class 218 as it sits beneath the impressive roof of Cologne Main Station in North-Rhine Westphalia in 1986.

locomotives with adequate power and good acceleration, refurbish them, fit remote-control equipment so they could be driven from a driving-trailer and match them to a set of high-capacity refurbished coaches. After receiving a colour scheme that matched with or blended into the livery of the MU fleet, the "new" sets were in business. Because they are driven by one person and from either end without uncoupling the locomotive, they can take their place in intensive local services.

Both diesel and electric locomotives are fitted for "push-and-pull" working. Indeed, this is now a feature of express services, too. Another advantage is that replacement is simple, if the locomotive requires maintenance.

A good example of such working can be found in Germany's industrial Ruhr and around Cologne in North-Rhine Westphalia. However, the reason the local "push-and-pull" working was adopted in other areas and countries was not because a use had to be found for displaced locomotives. It was common practice on the former Deutche Reichsbahn to use electric locomotives where appropriate, and diesels elsewhere, coupled to rakes of double-deck coaches.

● MODERN SWISS DESIGNS

In Switzerland, in 1989, purpose-built locomotive Class Re450 was matched to three double-deck coaches, one of which was a driving-trailer. Initially, they operated in the environs of the Switzerland's largest city, Zurich. As the S-Bahn network is extended, however, they can be found far from the city. Multiple-unit working is common, and it is not unusual to see three sets coupled together. The locomotives were the first in a new era of rail technology in electrical, mechanical and body design. They were built by the Swiss Locomotive and Machine Works (SLM) and operate on 15 kV $16\frac{2}{3}$ Hz supply. Four, three-phase, nose-suspended motors produce nearly 4,300 hp for a weight of only 78 tonnes.

● ABOVE
Diesel-electric Co-Co No. 5105 of Belgian National Railways (SNCB) rolls into Sint Pieters Station, Ghent, East Flanders, with a commuter train in 1992.

● ABOVE
French-built steeple-cab Bo-Bo electric No. 3618 of Luxembourg Railways, the Société Nationale des Chemins de Fer Luxembourgeois (CFL), runs into Esch/Alzette, Luxembourg's second city, in the south of the country, in 1995.

European Light Rail and Metro

Mainland Europe had few truly light-rail systems in the early 1950s, apart from street tramways. As for electrified metros, the most famous must surely be the Paris *chemin de fer métropolitain*. The Métro, opened in 1900 – although one of the oldest in the world in Budapest, Hungary, was opened on 23 May 1896. Probably the most ornate in the world is the one in Moscow, opened in 1933. Similar rolling stock to that in Moscow can be seen in Budapest.

● **LIGHT RAIL**

There were many tramway systems in Europe after World War II, some of them of an interurban nature. In the combatant countries, most were

THE "EUROTRAM" IN STRASBOURG

Date (year into service)	1994
Builder	ABB Transportation, York, England
Client	Compagnei des Transports, Strasbourgeois, Strasbourg
Gauge	1,436 mm
Class	Eurotram
Axle arrangement	Variable
Catenary voltage	750 volt d.c. Power is fed to traction-inverters in the car
Maximum rating	38 kW (50 hp) per motor
Speed	21 kph

● **LEFT**
In complete contrast to the Strasbourg tram, delightful reminders of a past, more ornate period can be found in small trams still tackling the narrow streets and hills of the old city in Lisbon, the Portuguese capital.

● **LEFT**
This tram is operating on an entirely new system in Strasbourg, France, the first 12.65 km (8 miles) of double-track having been officially opened on 26 November 1994. It runs on reserved track, in-tunnel or, as in this 1996 picture, in pedestrianized streets.

● LEFT
One of Europe's most extensive tram systems is in Budapest, Hungary. A modest underground heavy metro and a web of tram routes, some with reserved track, combine to provide an efficient, cheap means of getting around the city. Moskva tét in Buda is a focus of many tram routes. Car 4158 with its sister tram is pictured in 1993, about to start its Route 61 run.

damaged, some badly. Trams were put back on the streets as quickly as possible because they were and are one of the most efficient means of moving many people fast, especially in heavily populated areas.

Numerous old vehicles survived for many years until recovering manufacturing industries were able to supply the demand for new and more efficient vehicles. Smaller towns tended to replace trams with buses, particularly in France. Others turned to trolley-buses and various experimental schemes were tried, including guided buses and even Mag-lev. In Germany, the Langen-type suspended railway between Barmen and Elberfeld in Wuppertal, an industrial city in North-Rhine Westphalia, not only survived but continues to operate with comfortable modern double-cars.

Probably two tram builders made the most impact on the postwar scene, Duewag of Germany and CKD, of Prague (Praha), Czech Republic, with Tatra cars. Both produced robust reliable vehicles, which are widely used in many countries.

More recently, demand for easier access to public-transport vehicles has led to the development of sophisticated low-floor cars, some incorporating elegant and advanced bogie designs allowing low floors throughout the vehicle. General advances in control equipment used on heavy rail have readily found use on tramways.

● LEFT
Vienna is served by an expanding underground railway system. However, one of the best ways to get a feel for the city is to take the frequent trams. Routes 1 and 2 operate in opposite directions around the Ringstrasse. Standard Series E2 No. 4311, on Route 65, is pictured in 1987 standing at Karlsplatz, near the interchange with the underground.

● LEFT
Some systems fall between light-rail and heavy-metro categories. One is that in Utrecht, a bustling city and major rail junction in the Netherlands' eponymous smallest province. This unit, one of 27 built between 1981–3 by SIG of Neuhausen, Switzerland, although called a tram, operates more like a true heavy metro and has an 80-kph service speed. Here, it is pictured near Utrecht's main railway station in 1989.

● LEFT
Austria's private railways have for many years taken advantage of the availability of good secondhand equipment. The rolling stock waiting to leave the terminus of the Salzburger Stadtwerke Verkehrsbetriebe (SVB) near the main station in Salzburg in 1986 originated on Germany's Cologne-Bonn private railway (KBE). Today, the SVB terminus is in an underground complex, and services are operated by a fleet of light Bo-2-Bo units.

The impression of 20 years ago that the tram was noisy, rough riding and uncomfortable has changed to such an extent that suitable devices have had to be devised to warn pedestrians of their quiet approach, especially in areas restricted to public transport. Where track is well laid and maintained, the ride can be as good and often better than on heavy rail.

An ideal arrangement to take advantage of the relatively high-speed capability of the modern tram is the use of reserved track and, in some instances, redundant heavy-rail formations for part of the route. In others, light-rail vehicles are used for urban and suburban services over tracks carrying normal main-line trains such as the Swiss Federal Railway line from Geneva to La Plaine.

● ABOVE
The use of light-rail type vehicles on main-line tracks is spreading. Switzerland's section of line between Geneva and La Plaine is electrified at 1,500 volt d.c. for through-working to Geneva by standard French locomotives. Swiss Federal Railways have introduced these lightweight EMUs to replace time-expired main-line stock.

● BELOW
An EMU train on suburban service in Paris.

● RIGHT
The popularity of lightweight, low-floor units to replace the main-line type of construction is leading to their widening use on metre-gauge railways in Switzerland, especially where the route is substantially in an urban-style environment with frequent stops. Unit Be4/8 33 is pictured at the outer terminus of the Wynental und Suhrentalbahn line, at Menziken, south of Aarau, in 1996, about to leave for Aarau, an important station, in Aargau Canton, on the federal railways' main line from Zurich to Bern.

● BELOW
Another German interurban line is the Wuppertal Schwebebahn running 13.3 km (8 miles) from Oberbarmen to Vohwinkel. Its articulated cars were built from 1972–4 by MAN. They are suspended from massive girderwork dating back to the turn of the century. The route is over a river for a considerable way and elsewhere follows the course of roads.

● METRO SYSTEMS

Such systems are generally used in large cities or densely populated conurbations, usually to provide a high-frequency, high-capacity service. In some instances, the routes are wholly or substantially in-tunnel. In other cases, tramway or heavy-rail routes have been linked or diverted to run partly in tunnel. In many instances, the term has been used on reorganized and refurbished heavy-rail routes to provide the ensuing improved services with a "brand name", a growing practice.

● PARIS MÉTRO

For overall utility and its mixture of retained antiquity coupled with modern technology, the Paris Métro is hard to beat. Under the streets of Paris, it has wide tunnels built by cut-and-cover method, incorporating closely spaced stations with many interchanges with other Métro lines whose tentacles spread deep into the suburbs.

Where lines emerge into daylight, they may be on viaducts or bridges spanning the River Seine, some giving fine views. The narrow multiple-unit sets in places grind around sharp curves or have to tackle steep gradients. The opportunity should not be missed to ride on one of the lines, which uses pneumatic-tyred wheels for traction and guidance, with conventional flanged wheels on rail as a fail-safe.

Using the Métro and the modern, quick RER system, which goes deep into the surrounding countryside, is the finest way to get around Paris, a remark true for all cities and conurbations that have increasingly adopted the Métro concept as a transport system for the future.

● ABOVE
Germany's Oberrheinische Eisenbahn-Gesellschaft (OEG) is an example of an interurban system. It operates through four states – Bavaria, Rhineland-Palatinate, Baden-Württemberg and Hesse. It has 61 km (38 miles) of metre-gauge routes from the spa town of Dürkheim, through the commercial and manufacturing cities of Ludwigshafen am Rhein and Mannheim to Heidelberg. Trains run in or alongside roads, in pedestrianized areas and on the reserved tracks. Unit 109, built by Duewag of Düsseldorf and Uerdingen in 1974, stands in the station at Viernheim, a suburb of Mannheim, in 1986.

International European Services

● BELOW
The latest Pendolino development is the ETR 470 Cisalpino. These dual-voltage trains are operated by an Italian-Swiss consortium. Services began in September 1996 from Milan to Basle and from Milan to Geneva. A train from Geneva to Milan is pictured snaking into Lausanne in 1996.

Initially, electrically powered international services were little different from the days of steam. Locomotives hauled their rakes of, usually, the best stock the originating country could provide, to the border-station where one locomotive was removed and another from the next country was added. This was not always easy. For example, at Venlo in Limburg Province of the Netherlands, the electrical system differs radically from that in Germany and the international platforms are provided with special wiring that can be switched to either power-supply. It was found convenient to use a diesel-shunter to attach and detach the main-line locomotive.

● Germany, Austria, Hungary and Switzerland

In Germany, Austria, Hungary and Switzerland there was and is little difficulty in through-working because the electrical supply is common at 15 kV a.c., 16.7 Hz. These countries share the German language, to a greater or lesser degree, so the main constraint is that of differing signal aspects and operating regulations, which can be overcome by training.

The French already had much experience because the railways, electrified from early days, used 1,500 volt d.c. and 25 kV single-phase a.c. In 1964, they plunged into the multicurrent field with a class of locomotives designed to cope with most situations. These had the capacity to work on 1,500 volt–3,000 volt d.c., 15 kV single-phase and 25 kV three-phase a.c. They were thus able to cross all their rail frontiers, although in practice they worked mainly Paris-Brussels-Amsterdam.

However, the complete unit, incorporating power-cars, came to the fore. Austrian Class 4010 six-car sets, introduced in 1965, working in multiple, operated an express-service from Zurich to Vienna, although they have been supplanted by locomotive-hauled stock because of inadequate passenger-capacity. Such units still work to Munich, Bavaria.

● ABOVE
Germany's DBAG multicurrent Inter City Express (ICE) uses conventional technology to achieve speeds of up to 330 kph. The "Thunersee" from Interlaken is pictured leaving Olten railway junction in Switzerland, for Berlin in 1996.

● France develops TGVs, Germany ICEs

More recent developments are the French Trains Grande Vitesse (TGVs) – "high-speed trains" that have become multicurrent, running into neighbouring Belgium and Switzerland. From these have developed the Thalys, that is, TGVs running the Paris-Brussels-Amsterdam services. These in turn have given rise to an experimental unit, still under trial in 1996, specifically for Thalys but capable of much wider use.

Germany has produced the Class 401 Inter City Express (ICE) units in large quantity. Broadly, these match the TGV in performance and, like them, use proven technology. Most Swiss standard-gauge railways' common electrical system

● **BELOW**
Conventional technology and new high-grade track brought success for France's Train Grande Vitesse (TGV). Journey-times were revolutionized with a 300-kph top speed, as this image of a TGV Atlantique at speed shows.

● **ABOVE LEFT**
The quadricurrent development of the TGV for the Thalys services (Paris-Brussels-Amsterdam) was still under trial when this picture was taken at Paris, Gare du Nord, in June 1996. TGVs painted in Thalys red livery were still operating revenue services in November 1996.

● **BELOW RIGHT**
The ETR 450 can be regarded as the first commercially successful tilting train. "Pendolino" is an accepted nickname for the type.

enables them to run lucrative international services such as the Thunersee from Berlin to Interlaken.

Franco-British co-operation in constructing and operating cross-Channel international expresses involves yet another electrical complication on the British side – 750 volt d.c. supplied from a third rail.

● **ITALY DEVELOPS PENDOLINO**

Italy has developed the tilting train to the extent that the concept, with which several countries have experimented for some years, has become acceptable for public service. The Pendolino, as it is called, draws heavily on pioneering work by British Railways with its Advanced Passenger Train (APT). The aim is to be able to use existing infrastructure for higher speeds by relieving passengers of gravitational forces in curves. Other technological developments have enabled speeds and ride-quality to be improved even more.

THE PENDOLINO (ETR 450)

Date	1987
Builders	Fiat/Marelli/Ansaldo
Gauge	1,435 mm
Class	ETR 450 (Elletro Treni Rapidi 450)
Axle arrangement	1-A-A-1
Catenary voltage	d.c. 3,000 volt
Weight in working order	400 tonnes
Rating	4,700 kW (about 6,300 hp)
Maximum service speed	250 kph

The Preservation of European Trains

At the turn of the century, enlightened railways and historians realized the importance of preserving equipment that had helped to make railways one of the most important developments the world has seen. Equipment was put either into a museum or on to a plinth, in the latter case often being damaged beyond repair. Mainland Europe has several fine museums, those at Nuremberg in Germany, Mulhouse in France, Vienna in Austria and Lucerne in Switzerland among them.

● RIGHT
No. 298.51 pushing a snowplough reaches Grünberg in Oberösterreich (Austria) from Garsten on the 760 mm gauge line to Klaus.

● Preservation – Working Railway Museums

Static exhibits though informative are lifeless. Private individuals' efforts were largely responsible for restoring locomotives and rolling stock to working condition. Funds were raised, often slowly, to obtain unwanted and sometimes derelict items. On these, teams, usually of volunteers, laboured for months or years to achieve their aims. These were often either to run locomotives and carriages on sections of line bought after abandonment by original owners, or to persuade main-line or other companies to allow the stock to be run from time to time over their rails. For the latter, high standards had to be met and maintained. It is a great credit to the army of volunteers that all over Europe a pool of stock is available. However, from the 1970s onward, national railways and private companies began to realize the commercial and advertising potential of possessing and running their own nostalgic services. Locomotives emerged from static display to be restored by the companies and operated frequently in connection with line or station anniversaries.

● **RIGHT**
All three types of motive power, visible at Gmünd depot, Austria, in 1987.

● **BELOW RIGHT**
Preservation volunteers' skills are shown in this beautifully restored electric-railcar of the metre-gauge Martigny Châtelard Railway built in 1909 in Switzerland.

AUSTRIAN FEDERAL RAILWAYS – ÖSTERREICHSCHE BUNDESBAHNEN (ÖBB) CLASS 16

Date	1911
Designer	Dr Karl Gölsdorf
Builder	Maschin Fabrik der Österreichisch-Ungarischen Staats-Eisenbahn Ges, Vienna
Client	Kaiserlich - Königlich - Österreichische Straatsbahrien (KKSTB)
Gauge	1,435 mm
Class	BBÖ 310 ÖBb 16
Axle (wheel) arrangement	1C2 (2-6-4)
Capacity	2 cylinders (390 x 720 mm) and 2 (630 x 720 mm). Compound
Wheel diameter	2,100 mm
Weight in working order	86 tonnes
Maximum service speed	100 kph

● **OPPOSITE**
Gölsdorf-designed No. 310.23 is pictured being cleaned before taking part in Austrian Railways' 150th anniversary.

● **RIGHT**
In Switzerland, a double-headed train snakes into Filisur in 1988.

● LEFT
A Belgian streamlined 2B1 4-4-2 built by Cockerill of Liege in 1939 and a Deutsche Bundesbahn No. 23.023 at Utrecht, in the Netherlands, in 1989.

● TOURIST RAILWAYS

Tourist railways take several forms. They range from narrow-gauge lines in pleasure-parks such as Vienna's Prater – an imperial park since the 16th century but now a public place, through lines specifically built to support tourism – to main lines and branches built for trade but which attract tourists.

Lines built with the tourist in mind are often in mountainous areas and take skiers, climbers and walkers to suitable points to start their activities as well as many passengers who ride the trains just to enjoy the view. Examples are too many

● ABOVE
In Hungary, on the Children's Railways in the hills above Budapest, a Mk 45-2002 arrives in Szenchenyi from Huvosvolgy.

● LEFT
The Flying Hamburger part-preserved unit was displayed at the Nuremberg 150th anniversary exhibition in Germany in May 1985.

● OPPOSITE
The beauty of the preservation of modern steam is epitomized by this then Czechoslovakian Railways Class 241 4-8-2 No. 498-022.

to mention in Switzerland; Austria's Achensee, Schafberg and Schneeberg; and in Germany the Drachenfels, at 320 m (1,053 ft) one of the Siebengebirge of the Westerwald, on the eastern bank of the Rhine where, according to legend, Siegfried slayed the dragon.

A group of Swiss lines illustrates railways fulfilling a general commercial need but attracting tourists. These are the metre-gauge systems of the Brig-Visp-Zermatt in Valais Canton, Furka-Oberalp in Uri Kanton and the extensive Rhaetischebahn in Graubünden Kanton, which together cover the Glacier Express route.

Finally, there are lines, usually narrow gauge, which have lost the bulk of their original passenger and freight traffic to the roads but still maintain limited services. Examples are the railways of the Harz Mountains in central Germany, Gmünd to Gross Gerungs in Austria's Neider-Österreich Province, and the "Little Yellow Train" in the Cerdagne, France.

● **ABOVE**
In Italy, beneath France's 4,807 m (15,781 ft) high Mont Blanc, the highest mountain in the Alps, a lightweight 1C (2-6-0) with inside-cylinders and outside-valve chests, built in 1910–22, waits at Pré Saint Didier to return to Aosta, the town at the junction of the Great and Little St Bernard Passes, in Aosta Province of Piedmont Compartimento.

Commonwealth of Independent States (CIS)

In 1991, the former Soviet republics of the Union of Soviet Socialist Republics (USSR), the Soviet Union, formed a loose organization called the Commonwealth of Independent States (CIS). The CIS inherited more than 151,000 km of railways (94,000 route-miles) of 5 ft and more than 2,400 km of narrow-gauge railway. The narrow gauge is mostly 2 ft 6 in, with a small amount of metre- and 2-ft gauge. In addition, there are 61,000 km (38,000 miles) of light industrial railways within the former Soviet Union.

The industrial, mineral, agricultural and forestry lines were not subject to state railway motive-power policy and stayed with steam rather longer, especially where waste from sawmills afforded a ready supply of fuel. TO-4, TO-6A and TO7 diesels have taken over where this cheap supply of fuel is not available.

• LEFT
A Class CS4T electro-locomotive stands on shed awaiting repair.

CLASS P36 4-8-4

Date	1954
Builder	Kolomna Locomotive Works, Russia
Client	Russian State Railways
Driving wheels	6 ft $0^3/_4$ in
Capacity	Cylinders 22–$22^5/_8$ x 31 in
Boiler pressure	213 lb per sq in

• World Records

Freight traffic dominates rail operations with the 2,000,000 ton-miles produced annually being more than the rest of the world's rail traffic put together. The L Class 2-10-0 built after World War II has been an outstandingly successful goods-engine. More than 5,000 have been built. The L Class 2-10-0s followed the successful E series 0-10-0s, some 14,000 of which were produced in slightly

• LEFT
S2D 4-8-4 P36 No. 0250 train No. 1 Russia in Skovorodino (formerly Rukhlovo), a town in the Amur Oblast (administrative division) of Soviet Russia, on the Trans-Siberian Railway for which it is a junction. It connects with the Amur River, 56 km (35 miles) south, on the Sino-Soviet frontier.

● LEFT
A Russian EA Class 2-10-0 locomotive stands at Manzhouli, in the Inner Mongolian Autonomous Region, just inside China's border with Russia, across from the Russian railhead, a terminus of the Trans-Siberian Railway (TSR), at Zabaikalsk. Manzhouli is about 1,000 km (700 miles) north of Beijing, China's capital. It was on the former Chinese Eastern Railway (CER) in what was then known as northern Manchuria and, until China's Communist Party set up the People's Republic in 1949, was part of Heilungkiang Province. A Mongol trading town, in 1905 it was declared a foreign treaty-port town. When part of Japan's puppet-state of Manchukuo (1932–45), it was called Lupin.

varying forms, making them the most numerous steam-class in world history.

The express-passenger streamline P36 Class 4-8-4 was the last main-line express-type built in the USSR, the first example appearing in 1950. This was a successful locomotive with many modern features and graceful lines. About 250 were built by Kolomna Locomotive Works, between 1954-56.

The S Class 2-6-2 standard express-locomotives, of which more than 4,000 were built, is the most numerous passenger-class in the world. It was introduced in 1910, and building continued until 1951.

● PARTY CONGRESS PHASES OUT SYSTEM

In February 1956 the Communist Party Congress declared that steam should be phased out. That year, all steam construction ceased.

Today, nearly a fifth of the standard gauge has been electrified. The basic freight-hauler on a.c. lines is the eight-twin-unit type VL80. The d.c. system uses VL10 Bo-Bo twin units – also made in a four-unit version.

Passenger electrics are supplied by the Skoda company from its works in the Czech Republic. The most numerous is the CS4T Bo–Bo for a.c. lines.

Diesel-powered freights are hauled by TE3 and 21762 12-axle twin-unit locomotives. To cope with ever-longer trains, three-and four-unit sets have been built – the 3TEIOM, 4TEIOS and 4TE130S Series.

Diesel passenger trains use the Skoda-made TEP60 in one- or twin-unit sets. A TEP70 series of Co-Cos developing 4,000 hp per unit and weighing 129 tonnes has been introduced for longer, 25- to 30-car passenger-trains. These units have a maximum speed of more than 178 kph (110 mph).

● BELOW
A Class VL80S electric-locomotive stands on shed awaiting its turn of duty.

● BELOW
This 2-10-0 Ty4 109 former Deutsche Reichsbahn Class 44 was a German Army engine in World War II and formerly S160 Tr203 229 of the United States Army Transport Corps (USATC). It is pictured at Malbork, Poland, in 1974. The city, a railway junction, was assigned to Poland in 1945. Formerly part of East Prussia, it had been known as Marienburg.

THE MIDDLE EAST

The former Hejaz Pilgrim Route to Mecca forms an important part of the railway networks of Syria and Jordan. The route, built to the 3 ft 5¼ in gauge, still sees steam operation in both countries. Syria also has a standard-gauge network, which originated with the Baghdad Railway. This passed through Aleppo, north-west Syria. The former Prussian G8 0-8-0s and British War Department 2-10-0s used on these lines all disappeared in 1976. The system has been diesel-operated ever since.

Jordan Railways operates between Der'a in Syria on the border with Jordan, southwards towards Saudi Arabia. The Pilgrim Route originally went as far south as Medina, but the northern reaches in Saudi Arabia have long since been abandoned. Mecca, the ultimate destination, was never reached. In 1975, Jordan Railways opened a branch to Aqaba on the Gulf of Arabia extension of the Red Sea. Jordan's last steam locomotives were a batch of Japanese Pacifics. Its steam survives as Mikado 2-8-2s.

IRAQI STATE RAILWAYS METRE-GAUGE Z CLASS 2-8-2

Date	1955–6
Builder	Esslingen, Baden-Württemberg, West Germany
Client	Iraqi State Railways
Gauge	Metre
Driving wheels	4 ft
Capacity	Cylinders 18 x 24 in
Total weight	68 tons

• ABOVE
One of the Moguls built by Borsig of Berlin in 1911 for the Baghdad Railway rolls on to the pier at Hisarönü on the Black Sea coast of Turkey in Asia.

• OPPOSITE ABOVE LEFT
A scene on Syria's Hejaz Railway between Damascus and Der'a in Syria, on the border with Jordan. The engine is No. 91, a Hartmann 2-8-0 built to the Hejaz 1.05 metre gauge.

• BELOW LEFT
A quartet of modern diesels standing outside Haifa depot, Israel.

• BELOW RIGHT
A 2-8-0 engine built by Borsig of Berlin in 1914, pictured at Der'a from which it worked the twice-weekly mixed-traffic train branch to Busra in southern Syria.

● **JORDANIAN PHOSPHATES**

Another railway organization in Jordan is the Aqaba Railway Corporation (ARC). This began operations in 1979, to carry phosphates from mines at Al Hassa and later from Wadi el Abyad to Aqaba. General Electric 100-ton 2,000-hp Co-Co diesel-electrics are used and are powerful units for the Middle Eastern gauge.

Abdul Aziz ibn Saud (1880–1953), the first King of Saudi Arabia (1932–53), was keen on railways. He promoted a standard-gauge line about 600 km (370 miles) long to connect Ryadh – the joint capital with Mecca – with Ad Dammãm, the town on the Gulf opposite Bahrain, and the related oilfield at Damman. Diesel-electric Bo-Bos and Co-Cos were used from the outset. In the 1970s, a consortium worked on plans to re-open the Jejaz southwards from Jordan. Many field-surveys were made, but work did not proceed.

● **ACCESS TO MEDITERRANEAN SEA**

Iraq's railways comprise a mixture of metre- and standard-gauge systems. Iraq has an outstandingly keen will to develop its railways, by modernizing and by building new lines. One such is westwards from Baghdad through Syria, to provide access to the Mediterranean Sea. Investment in powerful diesel-locomotives has been made for standard-gauge lines, using 3,600 hp engines. Iraqi Railways has about 450 diesel-electrics in service, mainly on standard gauge. It retains 75 steam locomotives on its books for metre-gauge use in the south.

Iran phased out steam in the 1950s in favour of General Motors (GM) diesel-electrics.

Israel's 900 km (560 mile) railway system is also fully diesel-operated.

● **ABOVE RIGHT**
A Jordanian Railways Hejaz 2-8-2 engine built by Jung in 1955 at the shed in Amman, the Jordanian capital, in 1979.

● **RIGHT**
A brace of Syrian 1.05 metre-gauge 2-6-0 tanks built by SLM of Switzerland in 1894 raise steam at Sergayah on the Syrian-Lebanese border before returning to Damascus, the Syrian capital, with excursion-trains.

INDIAN STEAM TRAINS

India's final steam-development phase was irretrievably influenced by American designs, which flooded into the country in World War II. The American engines' simple, robust construction, free steaming and accessibility to moving parts suited Indian conditions. When new standard designs were required for the broad gauge, to replace the ageing British X Series, India turned to American practice.

CLASS WT 2-8-4T

Date	1959
Builder	Chittaranjan Locomotive Works, Chittaranjan, West Bengal
Client	Indian Railways
Gauge	5 ft 6 in
Driving wheels	Diameter 5 ft 7 in
Capacity	Cylinders 20 x 28 in
Total weight in full working order	123 tons

● WP EXPRESS-PASSENGER ENGINE

After talks with Baldwin in the mid-1940s and before independence in 1947, the WP express-passenger engine was conceived specifically for Indian conditions. The first batch was delivered in 1947. They proved successful, well-balanced, free steaming and – because of their 18-ton axleload – capable of rolling heavy trains at 60 mph. Building continued over a 20-year period and the class totalled 755 engines.

A heavyfreight version was introduced in 1950, classified WG. These had the same boiler, motion and other parts standard with the WP but smaller driving wheels and larger cylinders. Again, they were a complete success, and the class had reached 2,450 examples when building ended in 1970.

As the years passed, WGs often worked turnabout with WPs on express-passenger duties for increasing numbers of diesel engines, and electric engines were used on India's heaviest freight-trains. It is a tribute to the American engines' design that there was little tangible difference between them.

The suitability of American engines after World War II resulted from changing conditions in India. Maintenance, track condition and general standards of workmanship not being

● LEFT
Indian Railways operated 30 of these massive 2-8-4 tanks, designed in India for heavy suburban services. Their coupled wheels and cylinders were the same dimensions as the WP Pacifics, but the boiler was smaller. This example, taking water at Rajahmundry, did cross-country traffic work around the Godavari Delta, Andhra Pradesh State.

● **OPPOSITE**
WPs were standard express-passenger power across India over the last 30 years of steam but no two were ever exactly alike. Many had delightful ornamentation and decoration.

what they once were. A lighter Pacific was needed for the more restricted routes in the North West and 104 examples of the WL Class went into service. These engines, built in 1955–68, have a 17-ton axleload.

● END OF STEAM

A similar locomotive standardization applied on India's huge network of metre-gauge lines with the introduction of the YP Pacific and related YG 2-8-2 in the early 1950s. The metre-gauge YL 2-6 2s with an axleload of eight tons – appeared in 1952 to complete a trio of standard designs.

As dieselization and electrification advanced, India, popularly regarded as the world's last great steam country, began to lose its steam heritage. Steam ended on the broad-gauge main lines in 1995. By the end of 1996, the metre gauge was but a shadow of its former self. On the erstwhile narrow gauge, diesels and closures had taken their toll, almost decimating a fascinating, extremely diversified group of veterans.

● **TOP**
Each year, Indian Railways held a locomotive beauty competition. Each regional railway was invited to submit an ornately embellished WP for the grand judging in Delhi, India's capital. Here, engine No. 7247, the Eastern Railway's exhibit, leaves the depot at Asansol, West Bengal, before proceeding to Delhi.

● **ABOVE**
This depot scene on the 5 ft 6 in gauge lines shows a WP Pacific (left) and a WG Class 2-8-2 (right). These post-World War II Indian Standards totalled more than 3,000 locomotives.

● **LEFT**
Northern India's sugar-plantation lines have many vintage locomotives running on 2 ft gauge systems. Most locomotives are of British or Continental European origin, augmented by a batch of Baldwin 4-6-0s built for military service in Europe in World War I and pensioned off to India for further use. A veteran takes water on the Katauli system.

INDIA GOES ELECTRIC

India's first electric-trains were operating before the famous X Series standard steam locomotives entered service in the late 1920s. By the 1930s, extensive electrification was operating over the two main lines from Bombay on the Great Indian Peninsular Railway (GIPR). This was encouraged by the long climb to the Deccan Plateau through the Ghats. Two routes, one to Calcutta, one to Madras, involved a 600 m (2,000 ft) climb on 2.5 per cent grades. The locomotives were from Metropolitan Vickers 2-Co-1s for passenger operation and a C-C with coupling-rod drive for freight. Operations were on 1.5kV d.c.

● LEFT
An Indian Government Railways WAM4 Co-Co freight-train.

INDIAN RAILWAYS (IR) ELECTRIC LOCOMOTIVE CLASS WAM4

Date	1971
Builders	Chittaranjan Locomotive Works, Chittaranjan, Damodar Valley, West Bengal OR Bihar State, India
Client	Indian Railways
Gauge	5 ft 6 in
Line voltage	25 k V a.c.
Wheel arrangement	Co-Co
Weight	113 tons

● THE DISAPPEARANCE OF STEAM

India had a long transition period from steam to diesel and electric. It was to be another 65 years before main-line steam disappeared. One of the 4-6-0 passenger designs from the BESA Series early in the century was still being built in 1951.

By the mid-1950s the aim of Indian Railways was to advance electrification and diesel as a general policy. Electrification was the preferred mode, the country having an abundance of coal and, at that time, no indigenous oil industry. Electrification of main long-distance lines was sound investment in a country with so vast a population and a railway system that was the lifeline of a surging economy. By 1961, 718 km (446 miles) of broad-gauge line were electrified. This rose to 3,540 km (2,200 miles) over the following decade.

Electrification of suburban services in Calcutta, both Howrah and Sealdah, used the 25 kV a.c. system, which was to become an Indian standard. The standard diesel-electric locomotive WDM1 from America was followed by many standard WDM4s, which were Alco-designed and built at the diesel-locomotive works at Varanasi, Uttar Pradesh State. Later, electric-locomotives adopted many features of these six-motor workhorses.

● INDIAN-BUILT ELECTRIC-LOCOMOTIVES

In 1962 the first Indian-built electric-locomotive appeared from Chittaranjan Locomotive Works near Asansol in West Bengal. The WCM-type, 3,600 hp engine

● RIGHT
In June 1994, Air Foyle/Antonov transported the world's first "flying" train – a 109 tonne diesel locomotive from Canada to Ireland.

● **RIGHT**
A brand-new Class WAG 6C Co-Co 25 kV a.c., resplendent in blue-and-white livery.

● **BELOW LEFT**
One of 1,200 electric multiple units owned by India's Northern Railway pictured on the line between New Delhi and Palwal, a place of great antiquity important to Aryan traditions, in Haryana State, south-east of Delhi.

● **BELOW RIGHT**
A Class WAP 1-25 passenger Co-Co of India's Northern Railway about to depart.

was for the Central Railways d.c. line. In 1964, India's first a.c. electric-locomotive was the WHE1 Bo-Bo, designed by a European consortium.

By the 1970s, Indian Railways operated 600 electric-locomotives and more than 1,100 diesels, 700 of which were standard WDM2 2,500 hp Co-Cos. A year later, Chittaranjan built its last steam locomotive, a YG Class 2-8-2 for the metre gauge. India's first key route to be electrified was the main line between Delhi and Calcutta. Next came Delhi-Madras, Delhi-Bombay, Calcutta-Madras-Bombay. By 1987, about 8,000 km (5,000 miles) had been electrified.

● **SELF-SUFFICIENCY**

The days when India imported vast packages of locomotives and rolling stock, mainly from Britain, are history. The country is self-sufficient in all aspects of railway production, with hi-tech plants and skilled production. The locomotive industry developed in India since the 1960s has enabled steam to be phased out on the broad gauge. Metre-gauge systems with YP and YG Pacifics and Mikados remaining in certain areas, especially the Western and North-East Frontier Railways, were expected to be phased out in 1997.

● **LEFT**
This locomotive built by Alco waits for the right of way.

Chinese Locomotives

The Steam Age has been in decline across the world since the 1950s. By 1970 steam had disappeared from large areas, notably North America, Britain and most of Europe. In the mid-1970s, the fact that China was still building steam-locomotives at the rate of more than one a day was worldwide news reported extensively by the media.

● **DATONG AND TANGSHAN**

China's main building centre was at Datong, west of Beijing, in Shanxi Province, close to the border with the Inner Mongolian Autonomous Region. The area is noted for hot summers and bitterly cold winters when temperatures drop to minus-20 degrees Celsius.

Datong, opened in 1959, built steam-engines based on a 1950s design from the Soviet Union. It produced two standard classes: the Qianjin (Forward) Class, QJ 2-10-2, freight, first produced in 1965, and the JS 2-8-2 for general purposes. Some of these engines were being sent to new lines as railway building continued apace in China.

Shortly after activity at Datong was discovered by the West, news came of another works, producing locomotives for industrial use. It was located in Tangshan, a coalmining and industrial centre about 260 km (160 miles) east of Beijing, in Hebei Province. Tangshan had produced the Shangyang (Aiming at the Sun) or SY Class locomotive, but had been largely destroyed by an earthquake in 1976. The quake was unparalleled in modern history, with a 242,000 death-toll from a population of 1.06 million. The city was rapidly rebuilt and steam-locomotive production continued. Tangshan has built about 1,700 SY Mikados.

Datong finished building steam in the late 1980s. In summer 1996, however, continued building at Tangshan was confirmed, albeit on a reduced scale.

● **ABOVE**
A QJ Class 2-10-2 locomotive is assembled in the erecting shop.

● **LEFT**
A brace of QJs resides amid the smoky gloom of the steam-testing shed at Datong works. Both locomotives have spent the day running trials on the specially constructed test-track.

• STEAM BUILDING

Other works built steam locomotives for China's 762 mm gauge forestry lines. These are standard 28-ton 0-8-0 engines. Isolated building of these may have continued.

To witness steam-building is unforgettable. A vast shop contained 20 or more boilers in varying stages of construction. Inner and outer fireboxes contrasted with boiler shells. All was illuminated and silhouetted in ghostly patterns by the welders' blinding flashes and set to a deafening cacophony of heavy drilling. The memories flooded back – Crewe, Derby, Doncaster, Swindon it mattered not, as if by time-machine the witness was back among the living vitality of the Steam Age, and something for many years suspected was confirmed: the Steam Age was every bit as fabulous as remembered.

(QJ) CLASS 2-10-2

Date	1957
Builder	Datong & Dalian
Client	China Railways
Gauge	4 ft 8½ in
Driving wheels	1,500 mm
Capacity	2 cylinders 650 x 800 mm

• TOP LEFT
Welding an inner-firebox at the Datong Locomotive Works, Datong, Shanxi Province, China.

• TOP RIGHT
Welding-operations on cylinders and smokebox saddle for a QJ Class 2-10-2 engine.

• ABOVE
Measuring tolerances of machining on a QJ Class 2-10-2's driving-axle.

• LEFT
QJ Class 2-10-2 driving wheels in the foreground. The locomotive behind is waiting to leave the erecting shop for steaming trials.

CHINA'S WORKING STEAM

● **BELOW**
An industrial SY Class 2-8-2, built at Tangshan, tips molten slag down the slag bank at Anshan Iron and Steel Works. Anshan, in Liaoning Province, is China's steel capital.

Steam's rapid decline in India in the 1990s has left China by far the biggest user. In 1996, China had about 6,500 steam-locomotives at work. This is far more than the rest of the world put together. When India had 6,500 active locomotives, they comprised more than 150 different types. China's centralized planning has meant there have been just five types – only three main-liners, one industrial and one narrow-gauge type predominate.

● MAIN-LINERS

Of the main-liners, most are QJ class 2-10-2s of which about 3,000 are active. These are followed by the JS Class 2-8-2 with about 1,300 examples, backed up by a mere 25 survivors of the once-numerous JF Class 2-8-2. The SY Class 2-8-2 industrial accounts for another 1,700 engines. On 762 mm gauge lines about 500 standard 0-8-0s bring the total to some 6,500 locomotives. In contrast with the ubiquitous QJs are the JF Mikados, now rapidly disappearing from main-line service. These were the forerunners of the JS Class and once numbered more than 2,000 locomotives. The earliest ones date back to 1918.

Most of China's rail-connected heavy industries use SY Class 2-8-2s. Many are

● **LEFT**
The daily workmen's passenger-train heads across the 700 mm gauge rails of the Anxiang in north-eastern China.

● **OPPOSITE**
A trio of QJ Class 2-10-2s bask amid the sooty magic of the steam-locomotive sheds at Shenyang, Liaoning Province, north-eastern China.

SY CLASS INDUSTRIAL 2-8-2 (PICTURE NUMBER 2)

Date	1969
Builder	Tangshan Locomotive Works, Hebei Province, China
Client	Industrial users across China
Gauge	Standard
Driving wheels	1,370 mm
Capacity	2 cylinders 530 x 710 mm
Total weight in full working order	143 tons

relatively new engines but are, in essence, typical light-American Mikados, the type of engine common on many American roads before World War I.

The odd main-line rarity does occur in industrial locations. In November 1996, it was confirmed that at least one KD6 Class 2-8-0 remained active. This engine is one of the famous United States Army Transportation Corps (USATC) S160s, more than 2,000 of which were built in America to the British loading gauge for World War II operations around the world.

● UNIQUE 2,000-TON TRAINS

China is also the only country in which steam locomotives can be seen out on main lines heading 2,000-ton trains. The mighty QJ Class often run in pairs and are put through their paces over the steep gradients presented on many main lines.

● QJS WORKING NEW LINES

The concept of China as a steam paradise was heightened on 1 December 1995 when a new 950 km (590 mile) long railway opened across the Inner Mongolian Autonomous Region. It is completely QJ-worked, has six locomotive-sheds and is semaphore-signalled over much of its distance. The line runs between Tongliao, a town in the region's far east, and Jining, east of the region's capital Hohhot. The Jingpeng Pass sees double-headed QJs working up a 50 km (31 mile) bank through six tunnels, around horse-shoe curves and over a 90-degree curved viaduct.

● ABOVE LEFT
The pride of the Harbin shed was Zhoude, the QJ Class locomotive named in honour of Chinese Communist revolutionary hero Marshal Zhu De (1886–1976) who became Commander-in-Chief of the People's Liberation Army (PLA) and second in the Communist Party's hierarchy only to Mao Tse-tung. Zhoude is commemorated on the smokebox-doors' brass bust.

● ABOVE RIGHT
An industrial SY Class 2-8-2 resides in silhouette among the smoky gloom of the engine-shed at Anshan Iron and Steel Works.

MODERN CHINA

Since the establishment of the People's Republic of China in 1949, China's national system has more than doubled its track route mileage and increased its passenger and freight traffic by ten and 20 times respectively.

● LEFT
Mainland China has only three cities with tramway systems – Changchun, Anshan and Dalian. This scene at the run-down depot in Changchun shows the decline that has set in and caused many parts of this once prolific network to be abandoned.

● CONTINUED GROWTH

From 2001 to the end of 2005 more was spent on railways and other fixed assets than in the previous 50 years. This level of investment is due to continue with the development of high-speed links. Steam will remain for some years: coal is cheap and plentiful, whereas oil is not, and the annual intake of new electric- and diesel-powered locomotives is insufficient to keep up with the expanding traffic, so that steam is being replaced only slowly.

Both standard- and narrow-gauge steam locomotives are still being made although in small numbers. By the 1980s, Chinese railway building had reached unprecedented levels. Getting at the coal had become China's most pressing transport need. Shanxi Province has a third of China's coal reserves and millions of tons were lying on the ground awaiting conveyance. At present, coal accounts for well over 50 per cent of freight on China's four major rail trunk lines. These are:

- Beijing – Guangzhou.
- Shenyang – Lanzhou – Lianun Gang.
- Beijing – Shanghai.
- Harbin – Dalian.

Lanzhou (Lanchow) is in Gansu (Kansu) Province. Llanyun Gang (Lienyun Harbour) is in Jiangsu (Kiangsu) Province. Harbin is in Heilongjiang (Heilungkiang) Province. Dalian (Talian) is in Liaoning Province.

Many diesels have been built since the late 1950s and by the 1980s 20 per cent of China's railway traffic was diesel-

● ABOVE LEFT
In Liaoning Province, the shape of things to come on the main line between Shenyang and Dalian, which until the late 1980s was one of China's most famous steam-operated main lines. A freight-train heads away from Shenyang and passes beneath the Fushun line at the Hunhe River. Fushun, north-east of Shenyang, works China's largest opencast coalmine.

● LEFT
A China Railways Co-Co diesel hydraulic locomotive, Class DFH3, heads a passenger-train between the cities of Jilin and Changchun, in Jilin Province, north-eastern China. Changchun was developed by the Japanese as capital of their puppet-state of Manchukuo (1932–45).

● **RIGHT**
A brace of China Railway's DF4 class diesel-electric locomotives head a freight-train past Zoujia on the Changchun to Jilin line in January 1994.

CHINESE RAILWAYS CLASS DF4 DIESEL ELECTRIC

Date	1969
Builder	Dalian Locomotive Works, Liaoning Province, China
Client	Chinese Railways
Gauge	4 ft 8½ in
Wheel arrangement	Co-Co
Weight	138 tonnes
Maximum speed	100 kph

hauled. A large fleet of locally built 3300 Dong Feng (East Wind) 4 freight Co-Cos is expected to reach more than 4,000 units by the end of the century. In the early 1980s, General Electric (GE) supplied more than 200 Type C36-7 4,000 hp Co-Co diesel electrics for freight-haulage. A repeat order for 200 locomotives three years later was placed with the same company.

● **DEMAND EXCEEDS SUPPLY**

A 5,000 hp Dong Feng Co-Co is the standard passenger diesel locomotive. Expansion of diesel and electric traction is inadequate to keep up with demand, so Class QJ 2-10-2s and Class JS 2-8-2 continue to be used.

Priority in the early 1990s was to electrify the double-track coal-line from the railhead in Shanxi Province to the port of Qinhuangdao, Hebei Province, as well as the 322 km (200 mile) coal route from Datong, Inner Mongolia, south to Taiyuan, capital of Shanxi Province.

The building of new lines and further electrification is to increase the coal-carrying capacity, because China's domestic needs are 70 per cent met by coal. Coal is also a top foreign revenue-earner with millions of tonnes being exported yearly. To serve the newly electrified lines, Chinese builders have supplied 138-tonne Shaoshan SS3-type electric-locomotives. Demand is so great, however, that 80 microprocessor-equipped, thyristor controlled, 138 tonne, 4,800 kV Co-Cos have been bought from Japan, as well as 100 electric-locomotives from Russia.

● **LEFT**
Harbin, the capital of Heilongjiang Province in north east China, once had a tramway network. By the late 1980s, this was down to one line. This picture was taken at Harbin tram depot in the final year of operation.

JAPANESE FREIGHT

Japanese railways were largely built to the 3 ft 6 in narrow gauge, to save money crossing often mountainous terrain. Gauge and terrain meant slow services. Then, road services started to compete. New motorways, often built along shorter, more direct routes, allowed shorter journey-times. The railways had to respond and the solution devised for the passenger service was the Shinkansen.

● EFFICIENT MOVEMENT OF LARGE TONNAGES

The solution for freight-traffic was not so positive but followed the practice in most other countries of focusing on what railborne traffic could do best, the efficient movement of large tonnages over a limited number of routes. This can be either block-loads of bulk commodities such as stone or ore, or containerized-traffic where handling-costs can be minimized. Despite this concentration on particular types of

● **BELOW**
JR Freight locomotives on-shed at Shin Kawasaki depot. Right, EF 66 29, a 1968-built mixed-traffic locomotive. Several locomotive classes have the same body style, being built to work under different catenary voltages. Left, EF 200 8, an early 1990s design. As the legend on the side indicates, this uses inverter technology.

● OPPOSITE
Chichibu Railway electric locomotive No. 103 on a freight-working at Chichibu, Honshu, in 1995. The freight-services run all week and are also fairly frequent on Saturdays.

traffic, freight is still loss-making. Traffic fell from 68.6 million tonnes in 1985 to 58.4 million tonnes in 1991. The number of marshalling yards has been cut, from 110 to 40 in 1986. Freight-train-kilometres were cut by 25 per cent in 1985 alone.

● BREAK-UP OF JAPANESE RAILWAYS

As part of the break-up of Japanese railways, which started in 1987, JR Freight was formed to operate all freight services. The company owns its own locomotives (1,069 in 1994), wagons and terminals, paying passenger-companies for the use of their tracks.

Only a couple of the private railway companies operate freight-trains. The Chichibu Railway, serving Chichibu, 50 km (30 miles) north-west of Tokyo, runs more freight than any other private company, linking a limestone quarry and a cement works to the JR network.

● ABOVE
JR diesel DE10 1521, a shunting and trip-working locomotive. These 1966-built diesel-hydraulic locomotives have the unusual wheel arrangement AAA-B. They work at many of the few stations that still have a freight-terminal. The engine is pictured at Fuji, Honshu, in 1994, which is below the 3,775 m (12,388 ft) high sacred mountain, Japan's highest peak, known as Fuji-no-Yama, 113 km (70 miles) south-west of Tokyo. Its volcano last erupted in 1649.

● BELOW
Electric locomotive EF 65 22 on a container-train at Odawara on the original Tokaido line, in 1994. This locomotive class was introduced in 1964. It shares body design with other classes, as well as with exported designs, notably locomotives built under licence in Spain. Odawara is a town in Kanagawa Prefecture, south-eastern Honshu, the largest of Japan's four chief islands and considered as Japan's mainland. Odawara is 80 km (50 miles) south-west of Tokyo (ancient Edo or Yedo). Tokaido is the great coastal road along the Pacific Ocean between Tokyo and Kyoto, Japan's capital until 1869 and a great manufacturing centre, along the Kanto Plain beneath the Kanto Mountains. Tokaido means "Eastern Sea Route".

CLASS EF 66 ELECTRIC LOCOMOTIVE

Year into service	1968
Builders	Mechanical: Kawasaki Heavy Industries, Japan Electrical: Tokyo Shibaura Electric Co., Tokyo, Japan
Gauge	1,067 mm
Catenary voltage	1,500 kV d.c.
Wheel arrangement	B-B-B
Rated output	3,900 kW
Weight in working order	100 tonnes
Maximum service speed	120 kph

JAPAN'S "BULLET TRAIN"

Japan's "Bullet Train", called Shinkansen – Japanese for New Super Express – was developed to provide fast, regular and reliable passenger-services between main conurbations.

All the routes were to be newly built and segregated from the rest of the network. This allowed them to be constructed to standard gauge rather than to the narrow 3 ft 6 in (1,067 mm) gauge of the national railway system. The lines were to be designed for high speed, the initial expectation being to operate eventually at 250 kph.

● ABOVE
A 100-Series Shinkansen arriving at Tokyo Station in 1994.

● TOKAIDO LINE

The first route, the Tokaido line on Honshu, opened in 1964 in time for the Olympic Games that year. It ran between Tokyo and, about 400 km (250 miles) away, Osaka, Japan's second city in size and the industrial metropolis of the Orient, via Nagoya and Kyoto. Three further routes subsequently opened on Honshu:

- The Sanyo line running south across the country from Osaka.
- The Joetsu line crossing the country from Tokyo to Niigata to the north.
- The Tohoku line running north from Tokyo to Morioka.

A branch has been built off the Tohoku line, to Yamagata, a silk-industry centre. However, this route is an upgrading and regauging of an existing line, not the full high-speed line of the other routes.

● BELOW
An E-2 Series "Max" Shinkansen E153 102 at Utsunomiya, Honshu, in 1994. These double-deck super expresses were built to increase capacity on commuter and holiday services on lines north of Tokyo.

● FIVE SERIES OF TRAINS

The Shinkansen has five series of trains. The 0-Series are the original sets, which now run the stopping-services on the Tokaido and Sanyo lines. The 100-Series run the semi-fasts and the 300-Series the fast – Nozomi – trains, both on the Tokaido/Sanyo lines. The 200-Series run the Joetsu and Tohoku services and are distinguished by a green rather than a blue stripe along their sides. The 400-Series are short, narrow sets, which look distinctly different from the others and run the Yamagata service. The E-2 Series are double-deck sets for use on the Joetsu and Tohoku routes and have been christened "Max".

The Shinkansen are fitted with an in-cab signalling system. This can be

SHINKANSEN 0-SERIES TRAIN	
Date	1964
Builders	Mechanical: Niigata Tekko; Hitachi Mfg Co; Kawasaki Heavy Industries, Japan Electrical: Hitachi Mfg. Co.; Tokyo Shibaura Electric Co., Mitsubishi Electric Co., Japan
Gauge	1,435 mm
Catenary voltage	a.c. 25 kV, 60 Hz
Powered axles per unit	All axles driven
Rated output per unit	11,840 kW
Maximum service speed	220 kph

seen in a driving-simulator unit at Tokyo Transport Museum. The original lines operated at 220 kph, increased to 240 kph on the northern routes. Nozomi trains run at 270 kph. It is planned to run the next generation of stock at an increased speed of 320 kph, experimental sets having run much faster.

There is a dense service pattern. For example, ten trains leave Tokyo on the Tokaido line between 08.00-09.00 hrs, six terminating at Osaka, one continuing to Okayama seaport, two to Hiroshima and one service going through to Hakata. The fastest service covers the 515 km (320 miles) to Osaka in 2 hours 32 minutes, with two intermediate stops, and overtakes four trains *en route*.

● ABOVE
A 200-Series Shinkansen 222-18 at Utsunomiya, 97 km (60 miles) north of Tokyo, in 1994. The gentleman in white is a train crew-member. This station is the terminus of the JR branch line to Nikko, one of Japan's main centres for temples and shrines, a city and mountain resort at 609 m (2,000 ft) in the Nikko Mountains of central Honshu Island.

● BELOW
A 0-Series Shinkansen at Shin Fuji in 1994, one of many stations, which allow fast trains to overtake the stopping-services. The much-photographed section of route, with Mount Fuji as a backdrop, is just north of this station.

Japanese Multiple Units

Japanese Railways (JR) have a long history of electrification. By 1991, 11,700 km (7,300 miles), 58 per cent of the total JR network, were electrified. Intensive operation of many lines has led to significant use of multiple unit trains. Although only 58 per cent of the lines are electrified, electric multiple units (EMUs) outnumbered diesel multiple units (DMUs) by a far greater proportion. In 1991, there were 3,189 diesel-powered passenger-coaches (13 per cent) and 20,548 electric-coaches (87 per cent).

Multiple Units exist in each segment of Japan's railways – both private and JR, suburban, outer-suburban and long-distance (and high-speed if Shinkansen are included), as well as in the luxury-train market. The EMU's variants and history are vast.

● LEFT
JR suburban EMU No. 22-23 at Akihabara, Tokyo, in 1994. This is a variation on the standard design suburban EMU. On suburban networks, each line's trains are painted a different colour, the same colour as used on network diagrams. The crowd waits on a Saturday morning when the service operates every ten minutes.

The two most common EMU designs, of which there are many variants, are the suburban set and the outer-suburban set. The Odakyu EMU represents the many small builds of specialist EMUs. The Class 165 EMU described in the technical box represents about 20 classes of trains built during 1959–71 for the railway's different electrical systems and with small changes in detail. This example runs in three-coach sets. Other variants run in sets of up to ten coaches.

● RIGHT
Shonan monorail EMU 505 approaching Ofuna, south of Yokohama, Honshu, in 1994. This line, built in 1970, connects JR's Tokaido line with Enoshima resort area. It has steep gradients and two tunnels. It is a means of transport, not a tourist or showground operation.

● DISTINCTIVE DESIGNS

Private railways run a variety of EMUs. Some have a JR pedigree, either secondhand or to similar designs. Many railway companies, however, have developed their own often distinctive designs.

Because electrification focused on busier routes, most lines around the main conurbations are operated by electric traction. DMUs, being limited to through-services from lesser-used routes, are seldom seen in such built-up areas. Diesel-powered services tend to increase the farther you travel from Tokyo. They are concentrated on the northern and south-western ends of the main island, Honshu, and on the two islands of Hokkaido and Kyushu, respectively Japan's second- and third-largest islands.

JAPANESE RAILWAY (JR) CLASS 165 ELECTRIC MULTIPLE UNIT (EMU)

Date	1962
Builders	Mechanical: Nippon Sharyo Seizo Ltd, Kinki Nihon Sharyo and Hitachi Mfg Co., Japan Electrical: Hitachi Mfg Co., Mitsubishi Electric Co., Tokyo Shibaura Electric Co., Japan
Gauge	1,067 mm
Catenary voltage	d.c. 1,500 kV
Configuration	Two power-cars per three-car unit
Wheel arrangement	Four powered axles per power-car
Rated output	480 kW per power-car
Weight in working order	108 tonnes per three-car set
Maximum service speed	110 kph

● ABOVE
An express-EMU of Odakyu Railway (OER) approaching Shinjuku Station, inner Tokyo, in 1994. The OER, like many private railways, has several express EMUs, in addition to its large fleet of suburban trains. It serves a resort area south-west of Tokyo. Shinjuku Station is the world's busiest station, being served by JR, two private railways and several underground lines.

● ABOVE
JR outer-suburban EMU No. 401-76 at Ishioka, 64 km (40 miles) north-east of Tokyo, in 1995. This is representative of a widely used design, the 1960 multivoltage (1,500 volt d.c. and 20 kV, 50 Hz) version of the Class 165. The livery represents a group of routes, similarly to suburban trains. Background: DMUs of the Kashima Railway, Honshu.

● BELOW
Electric-railcars Nos. 109 and 108 of the Hakone Tozan Railway near Gora, Honshu. This 15 km (9 mile) line climbs 450m (1,477 ft) by means of three dead-end reverses and up gradients of up to 8 per cent. These trains, from 1927, were operating in 1994. Hakone is a mountain resort with hot springs and wonderful views of Mount Fuji, 32 km (20 miles) to the north-east.

● THE KASHIMA COASTAL RAILWAY ON HONSHU

All train categories exist as DMUs, ranging from two-axle railbuses, through rural all-station stopping-trains, to luxury-express units. Vehicle design has tended to follow that of EMUs, with small modifications to allow for engines.

Many of Japan's private railway companies are commuter operations which were electrified many years ago and operate large fleets of EMUs. However, some of these companies also operate DMUs, not only for rural stopping-train services but for other services as well. An example is the Kashima Coastal Railway (KRT) on Honshu. It runs DMUs on an 80 km route east of Tokyo, built in 1985, using both a high-capacity design and a streamlined version for its express services.

Japanese Long-Distance Passenger Services

● LEFT
JR Blue Train sleeping-cars passing Yarakucho, Tokyo, in 1994. The streamlined body style was very modern when these were introduced.

● LEFT
JR EMU No. 189 508 passing Oji, near Tokyo, in 1994.

● BELOW LEFT
Japan Railways (JR) electric-locomotive EF 66 44 passing Yarakucho, Tokyo, towards the end of its overnight haul of a Blue Train in 1994. Note the headboard with the train's name.

Japan's narrow-gauge railways and often mountainous terrain have prevented its railways competing successfully with the increasing competition of motorways and airways. The main response for passenger-services was the Shinkansen. However, long-distance passenger services still exist, although far fewer than 40 years ago. This is often the result of the opening of high-speed lines, which cause inter-city services to be remodelled to feed into the Shinkansen. Where new lines are unlikely, there are moves to increase speeds from the usual 120-kph maximum to 160 kph.

Long-distance services are in two categories: the usually EMU-operated day services and the locomotive-hauled overnight services.

The day services tend to be of limited frequency. They require compulsory seat-reservations and payment of a supplementary fare. A variety of EMUs, and some DMUs, are used on these services. Some feature passive tilt, to take curves faster. Double-deck stock, with its extra carrying capacity, features increasingly in new designs.

● BLUE TRAINS

The overnight trains, usually "Limited Expresses", are largely operated by a fleet of Blue Trains. These consist of coaching stock, predominantly sleepers, introduced since 1958. The sleeping-cars come in several forms. The difference between A- and B-sleepers is the bunk width. Some trains include dining-cars. Only a few include the addition of seated accommodation. These trains can be hauled by any locomotive. Those painted red with a shooting star on the side are reserved for sleeper services. "Ordinary Express" overnight trains, sometimes

● RIGHT
JR EMU No. 185 107 passing Hamametsucho, Tokyo, in 1994. Note the train's name display.

JAPAN RAILWAYS (JR) CLASS 185 ELECTRICAL MULTIPLE UNIT (EMU)

Date	1980
Builders	Mechanical: Niigata Tekko, Kawasaki Heavy Industries, Japan Electrical: Hitachi Mfg Co., Tokyo Shibaura Electric Co., Mitsubishi Electric Co., Japan
Gauge	1,067 mm
Catenary voltage	1,500 volt d.c.
Cars per unit	Four
Powered axles per unit	Eight
Rated output per unit	960 kW
Maximum service speed	110 kph

● LEFT
An accompanied car-carrying train of JR being loaded at Hamametsucho, Tokyo, in 1994. Note the unusual side-loading method. Car-drivers join the train at the same location.

with sleeping accommodation, are an endangered species.

Certain overnight trains also include wagons for accompanied cars. These are unusual for their method of loading – sideways on a pallet by fork-lift truck.

Private railways operate express stock, often with compulsory seat-reservations and supplements, but distances involved do not compare with JR's services.

● RIGHT
On Honshu Island, JR EMU No. 250-04 operating near Kogetsuenmae, between the Tokyo manufacturing suburb of Kawasaki and Japan's chief port, Yokohama, in 1994. These trains include seats from which passengers can see forward above the driver. This EMU is on the Tokaido line where it runs parallel with the Keihin railway, providing a fine train-watching location.

Japanese Light Rail and Metro

● BELOW
The Keihan interurban company runs a light-rail service out of Kyoto, Honshu. Nos. 89 and 90 made by Kinki Sharyo of Japan in 1967 are equipped with folding steps for stops on the street section. They are pictured passing a true high-floor interurban.

Japan is a paradise for students of electric mass transit. It is well serviced with light railways and metros to carry its vast population from place to place. More than 100 tramways, metros and interurbans exist, most linked with one of the extensive privately owned electrified railway networks. Definition is difficult, because interurbans can run down the street like tramways; metros can carry interurban trains; and railways, which started off as interurbans, today provide a dense network of express, limited-stop and stopping-trains to carry people into Japan's crowded towns and cities. In terms of transit interest, some say Japan has everything Switzerland can offer and more. With most of the 120 million population crammed into 25 per cent of the land area, efficient rail transit is of the utmost importance. The biggest cities have underground or elevated metro systems.

● BELOW
Kochi, on Shikoku, Japan's fourth-largest island, is a seaport city but the outer end of its tramway displays a rural village aspect. It is single-track with passing loops. The Hitachi Co. built Tram 201 in 1950.

● METROS AND TRAMWAYS

Tokyo's extensive metro has been developed partly with private capital. The result is two separate networks, three different gauges, with overhead and third-rail current-collection. Patronage is heavy, with ten-car trains and, at peak periods, pushers employed at some points to ensure train-doors close on the crush of passengers. In addition, some private railways running into Tokyo operate underground in the city. Through-operation of private railways on to urban metros can be found in Kobe and Osaka on Honshu and with JR trains at Fukuoka, the seaport on Hakata Bay, Kyushu Island. Sapporo's Metro on Hokkaido Island features rubber-tyred trains and elevated tracks, which are covered over as protection from heavy winter snow. Sapporo was laid out in 1869 by the Japanese government as a colonizing centre for Hokkaido Island and replaced Hakodate as the island's capital.

● **BELOW**
Car 7513 is pictured on the Arakawa tramway of Tokyo Metropolitan Transport Bureau, a 12 km (8 mile) long survivor of the citywide 1,372 mm-gauge system. All stops have high platforms. The tram was built in 1962 by Niigata Engineering.

Tramways have been in decline for some years. Those in larger cities were replaced by metros. Buses replaced trams in other places. There was little development elsewhere. Hiroshima, on Honshu, is the only city that has modernized an extensive network. The city was rebuilt after receiving the world's first atomic bomb on 6 August 1945, which ended World War II. It includes an interurban line with through-operation on to the city tramways.

However, in the 1990s there are signs of an upturn in tramway fortunes. Hakodate, the seaport city of Hokkaido Island, on the Tsurgaru Strait, and Kitakushu, across the Strait of Shimonoseki opposite Honshu, have retrenched but other systems have bought new rolling stock or rebodied older cars, segregation and traffic-management are making operation more efficient and further closures seem unlikely.

● **BELOW**
The town of Gifu in central Honshu, north-west of Nagoya, shows the interaction of trams and interurbans on street and segregated track. Articulated tram Nos. 875 and 876, which formerly worked in Sapporo, runs on the urban section of the Mino line where through-operation on to the interurban requires dual-voltage cars. Mino is 20km (12 miles) north of Gifu.

● **ABOVE**
The 1,067 mm gauge tramway of Toyohashi city, on Honshu, south-east of Nagoya, has three lines totalling 23 km (14 miles). Tram 3105 pictured approaching the railway-station terminus is secondhand from the tramways of Nagoya. It was built in 1943.

● **BELOW**
Japan's most northerly city, Sapporo on Hokkaido Island, has kept one tram-route to feed the metro. Car 255 was built in 1958 by the local railway workshops for the 1067 mm gauge system.

● **TRAMWAYS**

On Honshu, Tokyo's tramway is a single, largely segregated line in the southern suburbs, the survivor of a citywide system. There is also a privately operated outer suburban tramway on a private right of way. The system at Gifu, central Honshu, is a fascinating mixture of street operation and rural interurban (at different voltages) provided by a private company. Kochi, the seaport city on Shikoku Island, has a reputation for acquiring individual, secondhand trams from European systems. These are rebuilt to run as a tourist attraction within the regular service. On Honshu, Osaka's city trams were abandoned in 1969, but a suburban tramway, subsidiary of a private railway, continued operating. Other tramways have been continuously upgraded over the years and, although still legally tramways, they can be difficult to distinguish from interurban railways. One such tramway is at Enoshima, one of Honshu's popular seaside resorts.

HIROSHIMA ARTICULATED-TRAM

Builder	Alna Koki/Hiroshima
Gauge	1,435 mm
Power supply	600 volt d.c.
Bogie arrangement	B-2-2-B with two 120 kW motors
Overall length	26.3 metres
Unladen weight	38.4 tons
Maximum speed	80 kph

● **HOME OF THE MONORAIL**

Japan is also known as the home of the monorail. These offer proper urban-transit facilities in Chiba, a prosperous commercial town on the eastern shore of Tokyo Bay, and Kitakyushu. There is also the original line between Tokyo and

● **LEFT**
Japan's most modern city-tramway serves Hiroshima, Honshu, completely rebuilt since World War II. Car 3702 is one of an increasing number of modern articulated-trams. It was built in 1987 by Alna Koki.

● LEFT
The Hankai tramway in south Osaka, Honshu, comprises two standard-gauge lines totalling 18.7 km (12 miles). Car 169, pictured here at Ebisucho terminus, is one of many veterans from 1928 still in everyday service.

Haneda domestic airport, and a link between Ofuna, south-west of Yokohama, and Enoshima. More recently, several guideway systems have been built, usually featuring rubber-tyred cars and automatic train operation on elevated shuttle lines to new development. Examples on Honshu are the Portliner in Kobe, Newtram in Osaka, NTS in Hiroshima and VONA in Nagoya.

Japan, with its huge home market for electric-rail vehicles, supports many rolling-stock producers. Electrical equipment features the latest in power electronics. Among large orders for railways and metros, the producers are happy to process small but quite frequent orders from tramway undertakings. There has also been secondhand dealing within the country.

● LEFT BEHIND

Most systems operate single-bogie trams but a few articulated-cars can be found in Gifu, Hiroshima, Kagoshima, the seaport on the south of Kyushu Island, and Kitakyushu. A sign that Japan accepts it has been left behind in tramcar development and that new ideas can come from overseas is the recent announcement by Kumamoto, a city on Kyushu Island, that it has negotiated a local-assembly package for a German design of a low-floor tram of the type developed by AEG before it became part of ADtranz.

● BELOW LEFT
Rubber-tyred guideway systems are appearing in many Japanese cities. An example is the Astram line, built in Hiroshima in 1994.

● BELOW RIGHT
The tramways of Hakodate on Hokkaido Island and of Tokyo on Honshu Island have in common the 1,372 mm gauge. Hakodate has received secondhand trams from the capital, but Car 3003 is a 1995-built tram constructed by Alna Koki for use on Hakodate's two-route system.

The Pacific Rim

Some of the smaller countries that surround the Pacific Ocean have relatively limited railway networks.

● LEFT
Singapore Mass Rapid Transit Corporation (SMRT) metro sets Nos. 3126 and 3111 at Yishun in 1990. Yishun is the terminus of the north-south line.

● LEFT
Standard-gauge 800 hp, diesel-electric locomotive No. 38-150 of Vietnam Railways shunting at Luu Xa in 1989. Note the mixed-gauge track.

● REPUBLIC OF KOREA

The Korean National Railroad (KNR) of South Korea has just more than 3,000 km (1,860 miles) of track, built to standard gauge, of which more than 400 km (250 miles) had been electrified by 1987. The country's major route is between the capital Seoul and the major port of Pusan. KNR is unusual in that both freight- and passenger-traffic have been growing, although this has not been enough to ensure continued profitability. New lines and extensions continue to be built as the economy expands. Electrification is being gradually extended but most services remain diesel-hauled, except Seoul's suburban services. These are interconnected with the metro, thus requiring electric multiple units (EMUs) that can operate at both 25 kV a.c. and 1,500 v d.c.

Increasing competition from coach and air services led to acceleration of the Seoul-Pusan service, with the introduction of 150-kph diesel-sets. Improvements are continually being made to several routes by the introduction of centralized train control (CTC), which enables more efficient and consistent control of a route, thus allowing an improved, faster service.

● BELOW
KNR express diesel multiple unit (DMU) No. 132 at Yongsan in 1995. These units, introduced in 1987, run with two power-cars and five intermediate trailers. Yongsan, a southern district of Seoul, is a good location at which to observe the railways. The suburban service goes underground between here and the main station.

● MALAYSIA AND SINGAPORE

Singapore does not have its own national railway system. The sole main-line railway is a line over the Johore Strait Causeway that joins the island with Malaysia, terminating at Singapore Station, and a freight-only branch to the docks. A through-service operates from Singapore to Kuala Lumpur (KL), the Malaysian capital. A luxury-tourist service also operates from Singapore via KL to Butterworth, opposite George Town, Pinang Island, Malaysia.

Singapore has a significant mass transit network. The first section of the standard-gauge, third-rail electrified metro opened in 1987. The metro has tunnelled sections in the city centre

● **RIGHT**
Vietnam Railways metre-gauge 2-6-2T steam-locomotive No. 131 444 at Haiphong in 1989. French influence can be seen in the locomotive, Chinese in the rear coach.

and elevated structures through the suburbs.

Malaysia has a metre-gauge network totalling more than 1,600 km (1000 miles). Its main route runs from Singapore via KL to Butterworth. Electrified suburban services were introduced in KL in December 1995. The 18 three-coach EMUs were based on a British design, built in Hungary with Dutch electrical systems and fitted out in Austria.

Passenger-loads have been rising, but there was a steady fall in freight tonnage in the 1980s.

KOREAN NATIONAL RAILWAYS (KNR) 8000 CLASS ELECTRIC LOCOMOTIVES

Date	1972
Builders	Mechanical: Alsthom Electrical: AEG and ACEC
Gauge	1,435 mm
Catenary voltage	25 kV, 60 Hz
Wheel arrangement	Bo-Bo-Bo
Rated outputs	5,300 hp
Weight in working order	132 tons
Maximum service speed	85 kph

● **LEFT**
An Indonesian State Railways PJKA F10 Class engine, No. F1012, at Blitar, Java, in 1971. Between 1912–20, Java and Sumatra took delivery of 28 of these mighty 2-12-2Ts. This engine was built by Hanoang in 1914.

● VIETNAM

Vietnam's small railway network covers fewer than 3,000 km (1,860 miles). It is mainly metre gauge but does have a couple of standard-gauge routes, including the regauged line between Hanoi, the capital, and Haiphong, the port and industrial centre. The railways were devastated by the Indo-Chinese Wars (1940–75) and continued investment levels are still limited. Despite these problems, a completely new line between Hanoi and Ha Dong was opened in 1986.

● **RIGHT**
Korean National Railways (KNR) electric-locomotive No. 8001 at Chongnyangnii Station, Seoul, in 1995, just arrived with a long-distance passenger train. The French pedigree of these locomotives is obvious.

Hong Kong Systems

The territory of Hong Kong boasts three tramways, two on Hong Kong Island and one in the New Territories (NT). On the island, the funicular-railway Peak Tram between Garden Road and Victoria Gap, 397 m (1,303 ft) above sea level, with 1:2 gradients, celebrated its centenary in 1988. It has since been modernized. The north-shore tramway on the island was opened in 1904 and runs double-deck cars. The Hong Kong Tramways line, built to 1,067 mm gauge, runs for just under 17 km (11 miles) along the northern side of the island, through the Central District business, administrative and shopping areas of the capital, Victoria. All trams are two-axle cars operating off a 500 volt d.c. power supply. They were all rebuilt in the tramway's own workshops in the past ten years and now carry new bodies on old trucks. The 163 trams comprise the only all-double-deck fleet in the world. There was a fear that the Victoria tram line would close when the parallel Mass Transit Railway (MTR) metro line was opened. However, while there was a distinct drop in tram traffic, the tram's advantage for short journeys and as a metro-feeder has kept it in business. This is shown by the service pattern. Broadly, the tramway is a single-line of route but there are, typically, six separate routes operated between different turning-circles. Only a small proportion of trams operate over the full route.

● ABOVE RIGHT
A 12-coach commuter-train of the Kowloon-Canton Railway (KCR) near Fanling, NT in 1996 is externally similar to MTR units. Internally, however, it is far more comfortable, with higher seating capacity on transverse seats.

● RIGHT
In Hong Kong's New Territories (NT) Light-Rail Transit (LRT) Car 1022 is pictured at Yau Oi on route 720 to Tin Shui Wai in 1996. Note the 910 mm high platforms provided where there is street running.

TUEN MUN LIGHT-RAIL TRANSIT (LRT) CAR

Date	1988
Builders	Mechanical: Cars 1001–70 Comeng, Australia. Cars 1071–90 Kawaski Heavy Industrial, Japan. Cars 1201–10 Duewag, Germany (bogies) Electrical: Thyristor Control, Siemens, Propulsion, AEG, Germany
Operator	Kowloon Canton Railway Company
Gauge	1,435 mm
Catenary voltage	d.c. 750 volt
Overall length	19.4 m (63 ft 8 in)
Weight in working order	27.444 tonnes
Rating	390 kW (523 hp)
Maximum service speed	80 kph

● RIGHT
A double-headed train of cattle-vans filled with livestock pictured in 1996 heading for Kowloon, squeezed between the frequent electric multiple units (EMUs) on the Kowloom-Canton Railway (KCR).

The fleet has two special vehicles, Nos. 28 and 128, used for tourist services such as the daily Dim Sum tours. These also have new bodies, albeit designed, by the addition of brass fittings, to look old-fashioned. All service-cars carry advertising livery. It provides more than 10 per cent of the company's total revenue.

Apart from the double-deck cars tramway, there are three public rail systems in the territory.

● KOWLOON – CANTON RAILWAY

The Kowloon-Canton Railway (KCR) links the territory with Canton, the capital of Canton Province of China.

Construction of the 34 km (21 mile) long British section between Tsimshatsui at the tip of Kowloon and Lo Wu on the Sino-British border in the NT began in 1905. The line was opened on 1 October 1910. The whole 179 km (111 miles) was opened on 5 August 1911.

From 14 October 1949 to 4 April 1979 there were no through-passenger services except for infrequent, secret visits by Chinese leaders. Services terminated either side of the border. In the British sector, diesels replaced steam for all traffic, but electrification and modernization, completed on 15 July 1983, saw the introduction of electric multiply units (EMUs) for passenger work.

● MASS TRANSIT RAILWAY (MTR)

The first section of the Mass Transit Railway (MTR) linking the island and Kowloon by a submerged-tube tunnel opened in 1979. It is 15 km (9.3 miles) long and largely underground. A 10.8 km (6.7 mile) branch goes to the NT industrial town of Tsuen Wan. The units were supplied by Metro-Cammell of Britain. They operate on an overhead-line current of 1,500 d.c. and are designed for maximum loading, their seating being lengthwise down the sides only. A four-car set can carry 3,000 people of whom only 400 can be seated.

● LEFT
In 1996, a Mass Transit Railway (MTR) train speeds along one of the few open sections. This is on the Tsuen-Wan line serving this industrial centre in the New Territories (NT).

● TUEN MUN LIGHT-RAIL TRANSIT (LRT)

The territory's population explosion transformed the rural NT. New towns have been built and modern public transport is essential. The history is complex but the result is the Tuen Mun Light-Rail Transit (LRT), a 31.75 km (19.7 mile) network operated by single-ended cars sometimes paired in multiple. The 1201 Series are called "drones", because they are powered but do not have full driving capability. The first phase – 23 km (14 miles) between Tuen Mun in Castle Peak Valley and Yuen Long – was opened on 18 August 1988. The system is run by the Kowloon-Canton Railway Corporation (KCRC).

● LEFT
Hong Kong Tramways tram No. 90 en route in 1991. Such sections of street running have much delayed trams in frequently congested traffic.

AUSTRALASIA

● ABOVE
Tasmania, with a sudden rise in load sizes, had to obtain more powerful locomotives. The Z Class at 1,850 hp doubled the power of existing main-liners. These four Co-Co units entered traffic in 1972 and were a development of the Western Australian Railways (WAR) R Class. They were built locally under licence to English Electric and were followed by even more powerful units. The example's yellow colour scheme was intended to give better visibility at level crossings.

● ABOVE RIGHT
J & A Brown's 2-8-0 locomotive No. 23 was built at the Great Central Railway's Gorton Works in 1918. It is pictured hauling coal out of Sockrington en route to Port Waratah.

With the coming of the 1950s, the writing was on the wall for those fiery steeds that had served railways for more than a century: growling tin boxes on wheels were on the horizon. Steam locomotives were still built for Australian Railways for a few more years, however. Class BB13 1/4, No. 1089 was the last for Queensland in 1958. These final steamers, still needed by the community to overcome the problems created by the years of World War II, had very short lives.

● **DIESEL-ELECTRICS**

With the arrival of diesel-electrics, much individuality disappeared from the railway systems as they began to buy what were basically standard overseas designs, just like those in the automotive trade. These designs were modified to suit local gauge, track and climatic conditions, but between systems they varied by little more than colour schemes. A few steam-builders tried to enter the field. Beyer Peacock with Metropolitan Vickers of Manchester produced 48 2-Do-2 locomotives for Western Australia Railways (WAR) in 1954, this arrangement giving a lightweight distribution over the track. With a few exceptions, the market soon rationalized itself to four main brands, mostly built under local licence – English Electric, Alco, General Motors-EMD (EMD) and General Motors of America (GM).

● **FIRST MAIN-LINE DIESEL ELECTRICS**

The first main-line diesel-electrics to go into service in Australia were 32 V Class Bo-Bos supplied by English Electric in Britain to the tiny island-state of Tasmania, which had joined the Australian Commonwealth in 1901. These were hood units with a cab at one end. With major water problems on the long desert run over the Nullabor Plain in South and Western Australia, Commonwealth Railways (CR) soon followed with 11 A1A-A1A GM units built under licence by the then-local firm of Clyde Engineering in 1951. These were single-ended, full-width units with a streamlined cab. At the same time, New South Wales (NSW) Railways imported

● BELOW
An Australian heavy-hauled diesel-electric locomotive.

● RIGHT
New South Wales (NSW) Railways, to try to revive ever-decreasing country-passenger traffic, took the British high-speed train (HST) design and modified it for local conditions. The Paxman engines were retained but stainless-steel construction was used for the trains. The 19 Bo-Bo units of 2,000 hp were geared for 160 kph running. Here, a northbound XPT crosses Boanbee Creek Bridge on the north coast in 1990, about nine years after the first XPT train entered service.

40 A1A-A1A hood units, the 40 Class, from Alco in Canada. Overseas use of Bo-Bo units was common but Australia systems chose six-wheel bogies because of load limitations on the lighter track. From then on, the replacement of steam was rapid. NSW continued to favour Alco units, built locally, until the collapse of Alco in America in the late-1970s.

● STATES SELECT BUILDERS

Victoria soon became a GM state. Tasmania chose English Electric; South Australia, a mix of Alco and English Electric; Commonwealth Railways, GM; Western Australia GM and Queensland a mix of English Electric and GM. Because American designs eventually outnumbered the others and English Electric units were incompatible with the American, the building of EE locomotives in Australia ceased in 1976.

One local builder made an impact on the market, producing Bo-Bo diesel-hydraulic locomotives – Walkers Ltd of Maryborough, near Brisbane, Queensland: Emu Bay Railway bought four main-line units in 1963 and another seven in 1970; Queensland Railways (QR) bought 73 for shunting in 1968; the NSW Railways 50 in 1970 and WAR five in 1971. With the railways abandoning anything but block-loads, these shunters had a very short life as such. However, still being serviceable, most were sold off, and many were eventually converted to 2 ft gauge and put into service on the extensive Queensland sugar cane networks.

● RIGHT
Commonwealth Railways (CR) followed the WAR lead with its traffic increasing, in breaking the then 2,000-hp barrier. It ordered 17 3,000 hp CL Class locomotives in 1970. Following earlier policy, CR stayed with GM-EMD products. CR, unlike WAR, ordered a full-width streamlined body. Here, CL31 leads a mix of other classes on a heavy ore-train at Cockburn, south-west of Broken Hill, South Australia, in 1988. By then, CR had become Australia's National and swallowed the railways of South Australia and Tasmania.

● LEFT
A State Railways standard Class 2-8-2T engine, No. 26, pictured on the South Maitland Railway. Made by Beyer Peacock, these engines were nick-named "Bobtails".

● BELOW
An advertisement by the Vulcan Foundry, showing one of the 60 J Class 2-8-0s supplied to Victorian Government Railways.

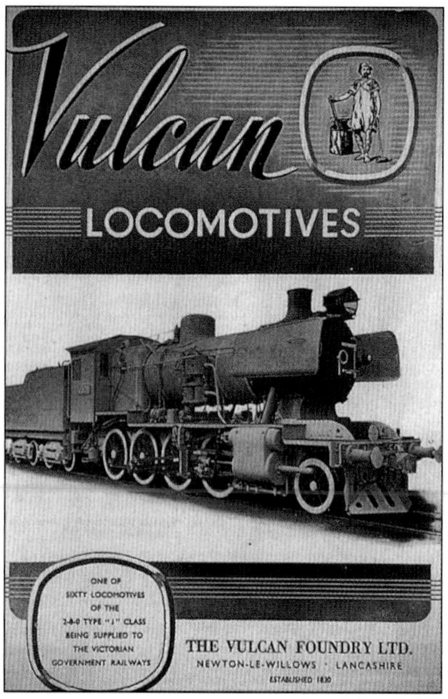

As to the trackwork in various states, not until 1987 did governmental lines consider anything more powerful than 2,000 hp. That year, WAR ventured into more power with 25 L Class Co-Co GM hood units, probably influenced by the private iron-ore lines in Western Australia, where superpower and record loads were seen as early as 1965. Since then, 4,000 hp has been reached on governmental lines with NSW obtaining 31 Co-Co units from GM-EMD in Canada, the 90 Class. The iron-ore lines are still ahead, with 29 GE Dash 438-hp locomotives having been imported from the Erie Railroad, USA.

Electrification did not advance far in most states. Queensland, however, with its tremendous mineral traffic, went into it in a big way. Since 1986 about 186 locomotives of the Bo-Bo-Bo wheel arrangement have entered traffic. This arrangement is unusual for Australia. These are all of 3,890 hp. Many have Locotrol transmitters, allowing trains to be run with several locomotives leading and several in the middle of loads. Loads often exceed 10,000 tonnes.

● NEW ZEALAND'S EXPERIENCE

New Zealand has passed through a similar period. It started with three English Electric classes from 1952. These included one of the unusual wheel arrangement of 2-Co-Co-2, the Df Class, again a matter of distributing weight. However, GM gained the upper hand here also, in 1955, with the introduction

● LEFT
Coal is one of the main commodities handled by New South Wales (NSW) Railways. Two 4-8-4+4-8-4 (AD) 60 Class Garratts roar through Cockle Creek with a bulkload in 1970.

● **RIGHT**
This S Class GM20 A1A-A1A Co-Co unit is pictured in typical South Australian countryside, south-east of Lake Eyre on the Marree line.

of 146 Da Class A1A-A1A units. Most locomotives being imported, New Zealand shopped around. In 1968, Mitsubishi, Japan, supplied 64 Bo-Bo-Bo diesel-electrics to dieselize South Island.

With more power needed on North Island, 1972 saw the introduction of 49 Dx Class Co-Co units from GE. At 2,600 hp, three were large units for the 3 ft 6 in gauge. In 1993 work started on upgrading these units to 3,200 hp as the Dxr Class. New Zealand Railways has now been privatized, and sold to America's Wisconsin Central Railway (WCR), which has turned it into a progressive, profitable enterprise.

● **PRIVATIZATION**

The announcement of the intended sale of the National Rail (NR) freight system left an uncertain future for 120 NR Class, 4,000 hp Co-Cos recently ordered from GM and for their builders Goninan & Co, which delivered the first of these powerful locomotives.

STATE RAILWAY AUTHORITY, NEW SOUTH WALES (NSW) CLASS 48

Date	1959
Builders	Alco/Goodwin/GE/AEI
Client	NSW State Railway
Driving wheels	Co-Co
Total weight	75 tonnes
Rated power	708 kW
Maximum speed	120 kph

● **LEFT**
In South Australia a 48 Class Alco locomotive, No. 872, works a goods-train at Minnipa on the isolated narrow-gauge Port Lincoln Division, Eyre Peninsula.

Australian Light Rail and Metro

Australia is one of the most urbanized countries in the world, with 70 per cent of its population living in towns and cities. The cites are concentrated in the coastal regions in the east and south. This is where the major cities – Sydney (New South Wales), Melbourne (Victoria), Brisbane (Queensland) and Adelaide (South Australia) – have developed. An exception is on the other side of the continent, Perth (Western Australia).

● **RIGHT**
Adelaide Tram No. 376 dates from 1929. It is pictured on the street track through the shopping centre at Glenelg seaside suburb. The pantograph is part of recent modernization.

● TRAMWAYS NOT METROS

None of Australia's major cities has a dedicated metro system, although the electrified urban-rail networks in both Melbourne and Sydney fulfil a similar role to some extent, with city-centre underground loops linked to suburban lines.

Tramways appeared in 13 Australian towns and cities in the late 19th and early 20th centuries. After World War II, uneconomic tramways in smaller towns were replaced by buses. In the 1950s and 1960s, all major cities apart from Melbourne followed the British trend to wholesale tramway abandonment. In Adelaide, one tram route has survived, the reserved track linking the city centre with Glenelg seaside suburb. This is operated by light modernized trams of 1929 vintage. Proposals for a new light-rail line in Adelaide were superseded by the project for the O-Bahn guided busway, opened in 1983. Debate continues about new rolling stock for the Glenelg line and its extension across the city centre to northern Adelaide.

● SOUTHERN HEMISPHERE'S LARGEST TRAMWAY

Melbourne's 238km (148 mile) tramway is the largest in the Southern Hemisphere. It has seen significant expansion in recent years as well as new rolling stock to replace most of the

MELBOURNE CLASS Z TRAM

Date	1974–7
Builders	Comeng/ASEA
Client	Melbourne Tram
Gauge	1,435 mm
Power supply	600 volt d.c.
Bogie arrangement	Bo-Bo with four 52 kW motors
Maximum speed	70 kph

● **LEFT**
Melbourne's Z Class trams were the first modern cars to enter service in quantity. Tram No. 110 is seen on the recent extension to Latrobe University.

● **RIGHT**
A prototype double-deck train for Victorian Railways, destined to operate on Melbourne's suburban system, runs into Heatherdale Station in the eastern suburbs.

● **BELOW**
Bourke Street in Melbourne shows articulated-trams on light-rail service operating through a pedestrianized area.

● **BOTTOM**
"Toast-rack" Tram No. 17 returns to the depot after private-hire duty on this heritage tramway running through the streets of Bendigo (formerly Sandhurst) in Victoria State. Bendigo was a Gold Rush town, founded in 1851.

traditional centre-entrance bogie trams. However, some of these are being refurbished for further use, including those on the City Circle line, which offers free travel around the central area. Changes from trolley-pole to pantograph current-collection and to one-man operation across the system are nearing completion. Most routes use modern bogie-trams and articulated-cars. The latest extensions and the recent conversion of rail lines to the St Kilda and Port Melbourne districts are built to light-rail standards.

In Sydney, a new tramline has been constructed to link the central railway station with the Darling Harbour redevelopment district. This was partly privately financed and is worked by Australia's first low-floor trams, the articulated Variotram design from ADtranz. Darling Harbour is also the site of a privately owned monorail offering a tourist link to the city centre's edge.

● **MUSEUM MOVEMENT**

The tramway-museum movement is well established in Australia. The operations in Adelaide (St Kilda), Ballarat in south-central Victoria and Sydney (Loftus) include alignments in or beside the public highway. In Bendigo, central Victoria, the tramway museum runs a daily heritage service carrying passengers between tourist attractions using street track through the town centre.

SOUTHERN AFRICA

Steam-locomotive deliveries to the Republic of South Africa (Union of South Africa, 1910–61) continued until the late 1960s.

● SOUTH AFRICA'S KAROO DESERT

The most dramatic post-World War II design was the 90 Class 25 condensing 4-8-4s of 1953. These were based on the 15F Class 4-8-2s, with large boilers, cast-steel integrated bed-frames and roller bearings throughout. Also built were 50 condensing engines classified 25NC.

The condensers, used for services on the main line through the arid Karoo desert of Cape Province, could save up to 85 per cent of their water consumption, a far cry from the early days when water had to be taken into the desert by train. The condensers had no conventional exhaust beat, only the whine of turbine-driven fans, which exhausted hot gases from the smokebox. The long banks of condensing elements in the engine's tender made the locomotives 33 m (108 ft) long.

● LAST GREAT GARRATTS

The next year, 25 GO Class 4-8-2+4-8-4 Garratts were delivered from Henschel of Germany as a lighter variation on the GMA type. The Republic's last Garratts were for the 2 ft gauge lines delivered in 1967–68, built by Hunslet Taylor, of Alberton, SA. These were the last Garratt

● ABOVE
In Cape Province, an SAR Class 24 2-8-4 Berkshire heads along the scenic branch line between residential George and Knysna, skirting the Indian Ocean. This is one of South Africa's most scenic lines. The Class 24s, with light axleloading, are ideal for such routes. These engines were introduced in 1948 to replace the multitude of ever-ageing 6th, 7th and 8th classes.

● BELOW LEFT
An SAR 25 NC Class Condensing 4-8-4 locomotive heads a freight-train through the Karoo. These engines were introduced for services throughout the Cape Province's waterless desert, especially between Touws River-Beaufort West and Beaufort West-De Aar. Exhaust-steam from cylinders is not blown into the atmosphere but conveyed to the tender, where it is condensed in an air-cooling system and recycled into the boiler.

SAR CONDENSER 25 NC CLASS 4-8-4

Date	1953
Builder	Henschel, Germany; North British, Glasgow, Scotland
Client	South African Railways (SAR)
Gauge	3 ft 6 in
Driving wheels	5 ft
Capacity	Cylinders 24 x 28 in
Total weight in full working order	234 tons

● ABOVE
South Africa's Red Devil 4-8-4 represented an attempt to improve steam-locomotive potential in the face of the avowed policy to eliminate steam-traction.

● LEFT
Painted in Imperial Brown, to match the coaching stock, Locomotive No. A371 glints in the sun at Figtree, south-west of Bulawayo, Zimbabwe (formerly Rhodesia), in 1993.

locomotives built. In contrast with the foregoing designs, a batch of 100 heavy-duty 0-8-0 shunting-locomotives was delivered from Krupp in 1952–53.

● RAPID MODERNIZATION

Motive-power modernization occurred as rapidly in South Africa as it had in so many other countries. The Republic was the preferred location for steam operations throughout the 1970s and most of the 1980s, attracting huge numbers of enthusiasts to see big steam locomotives in glorious landscape with idyllic weather conditions.

It had been hoped that the 25 NC 4-8-4s would be retained in Cape Province on the main line between De Aar, an important railway junction of main lines from Cape Town, Port Elizabeth and Kimberley, the world's diamond centre. The engines were relatively new and performing excellently. This was not to be and the changeover from steam has coincided with a partial rundown of the railway itself. On a happier note, South Africa retains enough steam operations to entice the visitor. These include some of the world's last Pacific 4-6-2s, active in industrial service on the goldfields.

● BELOW
A Landau Colliery Class 12A 4-8-2 heads a loaded train from the colliery to the connection with the South African Railway (SAR) main line. Landau, in common with many Transvaal collieries, used locomotives of main-line proportions. The 12As hauled 900 ton-trains over the steeply graded route.

● ABOVE
A former EAR Governor Class Garratt 4-8-2+2-8-4, with an 11-ton axleloading, plies across the frail line between Voi, the Kenyan railway junction on the Mombasa-Nairobi line, and Moshi, the Tanganyikan town on the slopes of Mount Kilimanjaro. This engine, No. 6024, is the Sir James Hayes-Sadler. The Governors, named after British colonial governors, comprised a class of 29 locomotives, all built in 1954, of which 12 were made under licence from Beyer Peacock, by Franco-Belge in Paris.

● SOUTH AFRICA AND NAMIBIA

South Africa has abundant cheap coal but no oil, so electrification was the preferred form of motive power. An early candidate was predictably the suburban service around Johannesburg, in Transvaal, Africa's largest city south of Cairo, and in the Witwatersrand, the world's richest goldfields, and Cape Town, South Africa's legislative capital and the first white settlement in southern Africa (1652). The lines of Namibia (formerly South West Africa) were the first to be dieselized, as early as the late 1950s, because of the waterless terrain. Prevalent among South Africa's diesel fleet are the D34.400 Class/35.200 Class of diesel-electric Co-Cos. Among electric locomotives are Class 6E1 Bo-Bos. Unlike the previous steam fleet, the nation's diesels and electrics are being built mainly in South Africa.

Vast tonnages are being conveyed compared with loads in steam days. The main freight line in Cape Province is the 865 km (537 mile) route from the Iron and Steel Corporation's mine at Sishen in Griqualand West to Saldanha on the coast north of Cape Town. This section is electrified on a 50 kV, single-phase a.c. system, and 9E Class Co-Co locomotives with an output of 5,070 hp haul trains up to 2.4 km (1½ miles) long. A motorcycle is carried on the leading locomotive for use when inspection of the train is needed.

● ABOVE
In Tanzania, an EAR Class 31 Tribal 2-8-2 heads away from Tabora, a modern town founded in 1820 by Arabs. These engines have an 11-ton axleloading for the lightly graded lines of East Africa and were built by the Vulcan Foundry, Lancashire, England, in the mid-1950s. The class is named after East African tribes. This engine is No. 3129, Kakwa.

● BELOW
A Zambian freight-train arriving at the Victoria Falls on the Zambezi River at the Zimbabwe-Zambia border.

● PROGRESS IN ZIMBABWE

In neighbouring Zimbabwe, steam-traction continued until the late 1950s when the last of the huge 20th Class 4-8-2+2-8-4 Garratts was delivered. Since then, steady progress towards diesel-electrics of both Bo-Bo and Co-Co types has been made. These mixed with the steam fleet through the 1980s. It was thought this situation would continue. By 1996, however, all but a handful of the steamers had been withdrawn. Almost all of Zimbabwe's steam fleet over its last 20 years of operation were of the Garratt type.

● DRAMATIC END IN EAST AFRICA

A similar situation occurred over the territories covered by the former East African Railway Corporation (EARC). Steam ended dramatically with the 34

MOUNTAIN CLASS GARRATT

Date	1955
Builder	Beyer Peacock, Manchester, England
Client	East African Railways (EAR)
Gauge	Metre
Driving wheels	4 ft 6 in
Capacity	4 cylinders 20½ x 28 in
Total weight in full working order	222 tons
Tractive effort	83,350 lb

● LEFT
A mighty Class 59 4-8-2+2-8-4 Garratt climbs the steep coastal escarpment above Mombasa on the Indian Ocean at the start of its 535 km (332 mile) journey to Nairobi, the Kenyan capital. During this steeply graded journey, the Mountain Class engines take 1,200 ton trains and climb almost one mile in altitude, Nairobi being on a plateau 1,500 m (5,000 ft) above sea level. The engine shown is No. 5933, Mount Suswa.

Mountain Class 4-8-2+2-8-4 Garratts of 1955. These 252 oilfired giants with a 21-ton axleloading worked from the Mombasa-Nairobi line. They were 32 m (104 ft) long and had a boiler of 7 ft 6 in diameter, more than twice the width of the tack gauge, and an 83,350 lb tractive effort. Incredible though this is for metre-gauge operation, a 372-ton 4-8-4+4-8-4 locomotive was proposed with a 25-ton axle loading but the attraction of diesel-electrics prevented these Garratts from being built. Delivery of Tribal 2-8-2/2-8-4 Types continued until the mid-1950s when all-out dieselization began across the then British-controlled territories of Kenya, Uganda and Tanganyika.

● STEP TOWARDS PAN-AFRICAN NETWORK

One of the most dramatic events in Africa was the Tanzania-Zambia Railway – known as TAZARA and TANZAM – built in the 1960s to a 1,067 mm gauge. With a 1,860 km (1,155 mile) route length the line runs from Dar es Salaam to Kapiri Mposhi in the Zambian Copperbelt, north of the Zambian capital Lusaka. China provided the finance, technical support and Bo-Bo diesel-hydraulics. This route serves export and import traffic between the Indian Ocean and Botswana, Malawi, Zaire, Zambia and Zimbabwe. The vision's potential has not been reached because of endemic economic and political problems but the railway is a tangible step towards the Pan-African railway network the continent so desperately needs.

● BELOW
In 1953–4, Beyer Peacock, of Manchester, England, delivered very British-looking locomotives to the then Southern Rhodesia (at that time part of the central African Federation with Northern Rhodesia and Nyasaland). One of them, a Rhodesian Railways 14A Class 2-6-2+2-6-2 Beyer Garratt, pauses in Matabeleland for refreshment at Balla Balla on its way from West Nicholson to Bulawayo.

Northern Africa

● ABOVE
Trams at Helwân, the town and baths on the Nile in Lower Egypt, opposite the ruins of Memphis.

Desert condition in Algeria made dieselization inevitable, and steam disappeared in favour of American diesels in the 1950s. Electrification had begun in 1932 on iron-ore lines with about 40 electric-locomotives active.

● NORTH AFRICA – ELECTRIFICATION AND DIESELIZATION

In Morocco (El Maghreb el Aqua, the "Far West"), electrification began as early as 1927. Today, 50 per cent of the nation's railways are electrified. The system is modern, having overhead 3 kV d.c. Non-electrified sections are all diesel-operated.

Tunisia operates an intensive suburban service from Tunis, the capital, on standard and metre gauges. The country has a long-term statutory commitment to reopen lines and build new lines of metre and standard gauge.

Egyptian railways have been dieselized during the past 20 years. Freight has declined but passenger traffic is healthy. Investment in double-tracking, reopening of abandoned lines and the building of new lines is all taking place. About 350 diesel-locomotives are on the books of Egyptian State Railways (ESR).

The 42 oilfired Class 500 4-8-2s supplied to Sudan by North British works, Glasgow, Scotland, were that builder's last big steam order and also the last placed by Sudan Railways.

Dieselization of main-line trains began in 1959 with a class of English Electric Co-Cos, which bear a striking resemblance to British Rail's Peaks. No sections are electrified. Sudan Railways is mainly diesel-operated but does use steam for some line work, particularly in the south with Class 500s and lightly axleloaded Pacifics and Mikados.

● RIGHT
A Class 500 4-8-2 of Sudan Railways, one of 42 engines built in the 1950s by North British of Glasgow, Scotland. Although 3 ft 6 in gauge, they have a 35,940 lb tractive effort, almost identical with that of an LMS Stanier 8F 2-8-0. The engine is pictured heading across the line between Kosti, in the Blue Nile Province, south of Khartoum, and Khana.

● BELOW
The Location Locomotive Works of Ghana Railways displays a contrast of diesel-electrics.

● RIGHT
An Algerian National Railways (SNCFA) 3 kV d.c. Co-Co electric-locomotive. These operate over a 256 km (159 mile) route between Tèbessa, near the Algerian-Tunisian border, and ‘Annaba on the Mediterranean Sea.

● BOTTOM LEFT
An industrial diesel working in Ghana, West Africa. Before independence in 1957, the territory was known as Gold Coast.

● BOTTOM RIGHT
A Co-Co English Electric diesel of Sudan Railways waits to leave Khartoum with the 15.50 hrs freight-train to Sennar Junction between the White Nile and the Blue Nile in 1981.

ALGERIAN RAILWAYS CO-CO ELECTRIC

Date	1972
Builders	Mechanical: LEW Electrical: Skoda
Client	Algerian National Railways (Société Nationale des Chemins de Fers Algériens) (SNCFA)
Gauge	Standard
Line current	3 kV d.c.
Rated output	2,700 hp
Length	18,640 mm
Weight	130 tons

● WEST AFRICA – OBLIVION AND WILLPOWER

Sierra Leone is the largest, most-populated country to have lost its railways altogether. The system comprised 515 km (320 route miles). As recently as 1955, 4-8-2+2-8-4 Garratt locomotives were supplied by Beyer Peacock of Manchester, England. In later years, the system also received diesel-hydraulics. After Sierra Leone's independence from Britain in 1961, the railway fell rapidly into oblivion.

The same could have happened in Ghana but a national will to retain the railway against massive economic and operational odds prevailed and the system is fighting back from the brink of ruin. All the once-elegant steam locomotives have vanished, to feed Ghana's large steel plant at the seaport town of Tema. Diesel locomotives operate all services. Some Ghana Railways engineers feel that the simplicity of steam locomotives was better-suited to Ghanaian conditions than more complex diesel-electrics. This sentiment is often expressed in developing countries.

West Africa's largest railway network was in Nigeria. The plenitude of oil, however, meant massive competition from road transport. This greatly eroded the railway's premier place. In the 1980s, the system was down to only 50 operable main-line diesels. As in Ghana, the railway is making a comeback with foreign aid.

WORLD STEAM SURVIVORS

It could have been little realized by Richard Trevithick in 1804 that the pristine machine crawling out of the Pen-y-Darren Ironworks in South Wales would have such enormous an effect worldwide or that steam locomotives would still be active 200 years later.

● PRESERVATION AND CONSERVATION – CHINA'S ROLE

So significant was the steam locomotive to the development of world transport, industry and commerce, that railways were laid almost everywhere. From the 1850s, when railways became widely established, until 1950, the steam locomotive was largely unchallenged as the dominant form of transportation. The very depth of the heritage means there are far more locomotives still in existence than is popularly believed.

Over the past few decades, many countries have come to realize the attraction of steam-railways and now run their own tourist-trains. These, combined with the enormous preservation effort, particularly in Britain, America, Europe and Australasia, ensure that steam is kept alive.

● LEFT
The Hawaii Philippine Co.'s 3 ft gauge locomotives on the Philippine island of Negros are known as "Dragons". Dragon No. 6, a Baldwin 0-6-0 of 1920, is pictured trundling a rake of sugar-cane empties back into the fields.

● ABOVE
Locomotive No. 8 is a 0-8-0 tender-tank of 1927 built by Orenstein & Koppel. This veteran works at the Meritjan sugar mill, Kediri, Java, Indonesia, and burns bagasse, that is the pulp remaining after extraction of juice from sugar cane or similar plants.

● BELOW
An oilburning 5 ft 6 in gauge, inside-cylinder 0-6-0 of Pakistan Railways heads a special passenger-train in Punjab.

● INDIA AND PAKISTAN

In January 1997, an expedition to India found an incredible list of types including former Great Indian Peninsular Railway (GIPR) Ghat bankers, both 2-8-4Ts and 0-8-4Ts; British-built XE 2-8-2s of 1928 and a Kitson Pacific – all of 5 ft 6 in gauge. On the metre gauge, there were two F Class 0-6-0s, a type dating back to 1874, and two Sharp, Stewart 2-4-0s of 1873, contrasted with more recent metre-gauge classics like the last of the MacArthur 2-8-2s of World War II. On the 2 ft gauge, a Bagnall 0-4-0ST was operating at a brickworks on a system, which could have existed in rural Wales at the dawn of the Industrial Revolution.

● SOUTHERN AFRICA AND SOUTH-EAST ASIA

Even great steam countries of yesteryear like South Africa and Rhodesia (now Zimbabwe) still offer many lingering survivors, especially in industrial environments. It is still possible to make rewarding visits to these and other African countries including Mozambique and Sudan.

In south-east Asia, Java's sugar plantations offer a fabulous variety of battered, multi-hued veterans of continental European, British and American origin. The American engines on the Philippine island of Negros remain active albeit in dwindling numbers. Main-line steam continues in Vietnam and North Korea.

● EASTERN EUROPE, THE CIS AND LATIN AMERICA

Industrial engines survive in Eastern Europe and in the former Yugoslavia. There are also many discoveries to be made in Russia where engines are known to exist as stationary boilers, carriage-

● **RIGHT**
A Rhodesian Railways 14A Class 2-6-2+2-6-2 Garratt with a freight-train romps along the main line north of Bulawayo, Zimbabwe's main industrial centre, in Matabeleland. These light Garratts were for secondary-route operation and have an axleload of only 13¾ tons. The type was delivered from Beyer Peacock, of Manchester, England, in 1953–4.

RHODESIAN RAILWAYS A CLASS 14A GARRATT

Date	1953
Builder	Beyer Peacock, Manchester, England
Client	Rhodesian Railways
Gauge	3 ft 6 in
Driving wheels	4 ft
Capacity	4 cylinders 16 x 24 in
Total weight in full working order	132 tons

heaters, shunters or in the industrial environment with some isolated main-line working, too.

As indicated in preceding sections, pockets of steam survive throughout Latin America. Cuba is the last bastion of classic American locomotives, few of which are more recent than the 1920s. The island has become one of the world's great steam attractions – a working museum to be admired and enjoyed.

Genuine working-steam has disappeared from Western Europe, North America, Australia, New Zealand, Japan and most of the Middle East but there is still much to see, research and enjoy. It will be many more years before the last fires will be dropped and man's most animated and influential creation passes into extinction.

● **LEFT**
The United States Army Transportation Corps (USATC) 0-6-0Ts of World War II were one of the most famous military designs of the 20th century and served in many countries. All came from three American builders – H. K. Porter, Vulcan Works and Davenport Works. Here, one of the examples that passed to Greece is pictured shunting at Salonika, the Macedonian port.

● **ABOVE**
The last Uruguayan B Class 2-6-0 tank, attached to a six-wheeled, outside-framed tender. She was built by Beyer Peacock, of Manchester, England, in 1889.

● **BELOW**
A Pakistan Railways 5 ft 6 in gauge AWD Mikado, one of the most important locomotive classes on the Indian subcontinent in post-World War II years.

GLOSSARY

Articulation
The connection of two or more parts of the otherwise rigid frame using pivots, to increase flexibility and allow the locomotive to take sharper curves.

Axleloading
The weight imposed on the track by the locomotive's heaviest pair of wheels.

Bar-frame
A structure of girders, instead of steel plates, on which the wheels and boiler are mounted.

Big three
Baldwin, Alco and Lima, the three principal builders of locomotives in America.

Bogie
A truck with a short wheelbase at the front of the locomotive, pivoted from the main frame.

Brick arch
An arch of firebricks in the firebox, which deflects the hot gases and distributes them evenly among the flue tubes.

Caprotti valve-gear
A locomotive valve-gear for regulating the intake and emission of steam. It uses two pairs of valves operated by cams whose angle can be varied to adjust the cut-off.

Class
A category of locomotives built to a specific design.

Compound locomotive
A locomotive in which the expansion of the steam is carried out in two stages, first in a high-pressure and then in a low-pressure cylinder, arranged in series.

Condensing locomotive
A type of locomotive used in areas where water is not easily available, in which exhaust steam is condensed and recycled as feedwater for the boiler.

Conjugated valve-gear
An arrangement in three-cylinder locomotives by which the valve-gear of the inside cylinder is worked by a system of levers connected to those of the outside cylinders.

Coupled wheels
The driving wheels together with the wheels joined to them by the coupling-rod. This arrangement enables the power to be spread over several wheels, thereby reducing wheel-slip.

Cowcatcher
A semi-vertical plate or grid above the rails at the front of the locomotive designed to push obstructions off the tracks in order to prevent derailments. Called a "pilot" in America.

Cross-stretcher
A girder or plate joining the main plates of the frame to give rigidity.

Cut-off
The point in the piston stroke at which the admission of steam is stopped.

Cylinder
One of two, three or four chambers in the locomotive, each containing a piston, which is forced backwards and forwards by the admission of high-pressure steam alternately on each side of it through steam ports controlled by valves.

Diagram
The work schedule of the locomotive.

Double-header
A train pulled by two locomotives.

Firebox
The part of the boiler that contains the fire, with a grate at the bottom; the sides and top are surrounded by water spaces.

Fireless locomotive
A locomotive with a boiler charged with steam from a separate source.

Footplate
The floor of the cab on which the crew stands, or the running-plate.

Frame
The structure of plates or girders that supports the boiler and wheels.

Franco-Crosti boiler
A boiler with a pre-heater drum to heat the feedwater, by means of exhaust steam and hot gases piped from the smokebox.

Gauge
The size of the track, measured between the insides of the rails.

Grate area
The interior size of the firebox at grate level, used as a measure of steam-raising capability.

Heating surface
The total surface area of the firebox, flue tubes and superheater elements.

Outside-frame
A locomotive class in which the frame is outside the coupled wheels.

Outside valve-gear
A locomotive class in which the mechanism for opening and closing the steam admission valves lies outside the frame.

Piston valve
A valve for controlling steam admission and exhaust in the form of two short pistons, attached to a valve rod, which operate over steam ports with a cylindrical profile.

Plate frame
The main frame of the locomotive consists of two thick steel plates, slotted to accommodate the axleboxes of the driving and coupled wheels.

Route availability
The tracks available to any class of locomotive, determined by its weight and other dimensions.

Running-plate
The footway that runs around the sides and front of the boiler.

Saddle-tank
A saddle-tank or saddleback locomotive has a tank that straddles the boiler.

Side tank
A tank locomotive with its tanks on the main frame at each side of the locomotive.

Slide valve
A valve for controlling steam admission and exhaust shaped like a rectangular lid.

Smokebox
The front section of the boiler, through which hot gases from the fire escape through the chimney and exhaust steam is expelled through the blastpipe below. The door at the front allows cinders to be cleared out.

Superheater
Superheater elements subject the steam to an extra heating on its way to the cylinders, so that even though its temperature drops in the cylinders it will remain sufficiently hot not to condense.

Tank locomotive
A locomotive that carries its fuel and water in bunkers and tanks attached to the main frame, not in a separate tender.

Tracking
A term describing the locomotive's ability to negotiate curved or irregular track.

Tractive effort (TE)
The force that the wheel treads of a locomotive exert against the rails: a measure of pulling-power.

Type
A category of locomotives conforming in function and basic layout, including wheel arrangement.

Valve-gear
The linkage connecting the valves of the locomotive to the crankshaft.

Vertical cylinder
A locomotive in which the cylinders are mounted in a vertical position.

Walschaert's valve-gear
A valve gear co-operated by a link, which is rocked to and fro by a return crank connected to the piston rod and a combination lever connecting the crosshead and the radius rod.

Wheel arrangements
The various combinations of leading, coupled and trailing axles are described by a three-figure formula known as the Whyte notation. The first figure refers to the leading wheels, the second to the coupled wheels and the final figure to the supporting wheels.

INDEX

This edition published by Lorenz Books, an imprint of Anness Publishing Limited
info@anness.com www.lorenzbooks.com
www.annesspublishing.com

A CIP catalogue record for this book is available from the British Library

Publisher Joanna Lorenz
Editorial Director Helen Sudell
Designer Michael Morey
Production Controller Ben Worley

This book has been written and picture researched by the Milepost Publishing Production Team: Milepost also conserves and markets collections of railway transparencies and negatives.

Milepost 92½, Newton Harcourt, Leicestershire LE8 9FH, UK

Publisher's Notes

Although the advice and information in this book are believed to be accurate and true at the time of going to press, neither the authors nor the publisher can accept any legal responsibility or liability for any errors or omissions that may have been made.

For historical reasons, the measurements in this book are not always given with their equivalent metric or imperial measurements. See right for a conversion chart.

Printed and bound in China

The Publishers would like to thank the following for their kind permission to reproduce photographs in this book:

A. E. Durrant: pages 36 (bl), 38 (br), 233 (m), 236 (m), 238 (tl), 243 (t,m). **Howard Ande**: page 4. **Barnaby's Picture Library**: pages 176, 177 (tl,b). **British Waterways Archive**: page 8 (t). **Ian D. C. Button**: page 207 (b). **H. H. Cartwright**: 140 (t). **Colour Rail**: page 64 (b). **Roger Crombleholme**: page 15 (t,b), 16, 17 (b), 18 (t,b), 19 (b). **Richard Gruber**: pages 75 (t), 76 (b). **Alex Grunbach**: pages 48, 49 (t,b), 118, 119, 236 (t), 237, 238 (b), 239, 240, 241. **John P. Hankey**: pages 22 (t,m), 23 (t), 26 (t), 27 (m), 28 (top), 30 (b), 32 (t), 33 (b), 72 (b), 73 (t), 74 (t), 75 (m), 77 (m), 83 (t), 85 (t). **Ken Harris**: page 201 (tl).**Maurice Harvey**: page 244 (br). **Michael Hinckley**: page 15 (m). **Fred Hornby**: pages 102 (t), 103, 106 (t), 108 (br), 109 (t), 110, 111, 187 (m), 190 (t), 192 (t), 196 (b), 205 (b). **International Railway Journal**: pages 208 (bl), 212, 213 (t,m), 244 (br). **Frederick Kerr**: page 132 (b). **Locomotive Manufacturer's Association**: Page 67 (br). **Dennis Lovett**: page 14 (b). **Arthur Mace**: pages 10 (b), 13 (tr), 63 (t,b).**William D. Middleton Collection**: pages 44 (b), 45 (t,b). **Mitchel Library**: pages 29 (b), 33 (t,m), 39 (br), 44 (t), 45 (m), 47 (t), 49 (m), 50 (m), 52–3, 117 (t), 121 (m), 124 (b). **Alan Pike**: pages 37 (b), 50 (t), 98, 99 (b), 100 (b), 101 (b), 102 (b), 104, 105, 178, 179 (t,b), 180 (t,m), 181, 182, 183, 184, 185 (t,b), 186, 187 (t,b), 188 (t, bl, 189 (t), 190 (b), 191, 192 (b), 193, 194, 195, 197, 198, 199, 200, 202, 203, 204 (m,b), 205 (t), 209 (tr), 254 (r). **Graham Pike**: pages 107 (l), 179 (m), 180 (b), 185 (m), 189 (b), 234, 235 (t,m). **Popperfoto**: pages 23 (m), 29 (m), 32 (b), 35, 36 (br), 47 (b), 54 (t,b), 92 (m), 93 (m), 123 (tr). **William Sharman**: pages 58 (b), 59 (t), 68 (b) 69 (t), 146 (t,b), 147. **Brian Solomon**: pages 23 (b), 24 (t,b), 28 (m,b), 30 (t), 31 (m,b), 70, 71 (m,b), 72 (t), 73 (m), 74 (b), 76 (t), 80 (t), 84 (b), 85 (m,b), 87 (b), 150, 151, 152, 153, 154, 155, 156, 157, 158, 159 (t,b), 160, 161, 162, 163, 164, 165, 166 (b), 167, 168, 169, 170, 171 (b), 253 (br), 255 (b). **Richard J. Solomon**: pages 71 (t), 73 (b), 77 (b), 80 (b), 82, 83 (b), 84 (t), 86 (t, br), 87 (t,m), 88, 89 (t,m), 90 (top), 91, 92 (t,b), 93 (t,b), 159 (m), 166 (t), 171 (t). **Gordon Stemp**: pages 58 (t), 61 (b), 64 (b), 81 (t), 132 (t), 133 (t), 138 (b), 256. **Michael Taplin**: pages 144, 228, 229, 230, 231. **J. M. Tolson**: pages 106 (b), 232 (m), 233 (t), 246 (t), 247 (br). **Verkehrsmuseums Nürnberg**: pages 36 (t), 37 (t). **Max Wade-Matthews**: page 8 (b). **Neil Wheelwright**: pages 108 (bl), 220, 221, 222, 223, 224, 225, 226, 227, 232 (t,b), 233 (b), 235 (b).**Ron Ziel**: Jacket and pages 26 (t), 77 (t), 81 (b), 90 (b), 117 (br), 127 (b), 206 (b).

All other pictures courtesy of **Milepost 92½**.

t=top b=bottom l=left r=right m=middle tr-top right tl=top left ml=middle left mr=middle right bl=bottom left br=bottom right lm=left middle

Conversion Chart

To convert:	*Multiply by:*
Inches to centimetres	2.540
Centimetres to inches	0.3937
Millimetres to inches	0.03937
Feet to metres	0.3048
Metres to feet	3.281
Miles to kilometres	1.609
Kilometres to miles	0.6214
Tons to tonnes	1.016
Tonnes to tons	0.9842

82